COMPETITION IN EUROPE

HENK DE JONG

Photograph by Werry Crone, Photo Trouw.
With kind permission of Perscombinatie Amsterdam.

Competition in Europe

Essays in Honour of Henk W. de Jong

edited by

Peter de Wolf

Erasmus University,
Rotterdam, The Netherlands

KLUWER ACADEMIC PUBLISHERS
DORDRECHT / BOSTON / LONDON

Library of Congress Cataloging-in-Publication Data

Competition in Europe : essays in honour of Henk de Jong / edited by
Peter de Wolf.
p. cm. -- (Studies in industrial organization ; v. 14)
Includes bibliographical references.
ISBN 0-7923-1050-0 (alk. paper)
1. Industrial concentration--Europe. 2. Industrial organization--Europe. 3. Competition--Europe. I. Jong, H. W. de. II. Wolf, Peter de. III. Series.
HD2844.C66 1990
338.6'048'094--dc20 90-20543

ISBN 0-7923-1050-0

Published by Kluwer Academic Publishers,
P.O. Box 17, 3300 AA Dordrecht, The Netherlands.

Kluwer Academic Publishers incorporates
the publishing programmes of
D. Reidel, Martinus Nijhoff, Dr W. Junk and MTP Press.

Sold and distributed in the U.S.A. and Canada
by Kluwer Academic Publishers,
101 Philip Drive, Norwell, MA 02061, U.S.A.

In all other countries, sold and distributed
by Kluwer Academic Publishers Group,
P.O. Box 322, 3300 AH Dordrecht, The Netherlands.

Printed on acid-free paper

Printed in the Netherlands

CONTENTS

PREFACE

Competition in Europe, which has been chosen as the title for the Essays in Honour of Henk W. de Jong, contains two key concepts, that characterize his scientific contribution to Industrial Organisation. Professor H.W. de Jong is in the first place an economist who is highly inspired by the dynamics of markets in general and the dynamics and conditions of competition in particular.

In the second place, H.W. de Jong is a real *European* economist, not in the sense that his theoretical insights are limited to Europe, but in the sense that his ideas and policy suggestions - especially those concerning competition policy - reflect his sincere involvement in the European integration process and the economic conditions and perspectives of a Common Market for the European Community. In his many illustrations of the evolution of markets and the performance of enterprises in different business environments, H.W. de Jong also demonstrates his knowledge of historical and political aspects of different economies in Europe, often in comparison with the United States and Japan.

I would like to express my gratitude to the authors, who all reacted spontaneously when the idea for this book was raised. They made this present for H.W. de Jong possible. Their contributions show a variety of aspects of competition or absence of competition, running from the theoretical foundations of dynamic market theories to the description of estimated effects of the latest forms of harmonized regulations with regard to competition in the European Community. Besides being interesting reading, these essays will also indicate the authors' evaluation of the scientific contribution of H.W. de Jong to Industrial Organization.

Special thanks also goes out to Emeritus Professor H.W. Lambers, H.W. de Jong's promotor, for his personal introductory contribution.

Because we realised that the proper place of H.W. de Jong is among his distinguished international academic friends, we asked him to be so kind as to write down his valedictory address, so that it could be included in *Competition in Europe.*

We appreciate the joint decision of Mrs. Marie Stratta of Kluwer Academic Publishers and Professor W.G. Shepherd to include this volume in the *Series of Industrial Organization*, of which H.W. de Jong is one of the initiators.

I would also like to thank the Organising Committee of the Economic Faculty, especially professor J.G. Lambooy (Dean at that time) and dr. R.E.M. van den Brink, Paul Holle and Taco van Someren, for their confidence by asking me as editor for this book, dedicated to H.W. de Jong, who was my promotor at the University of Amsterdam in 1987. Paul and Taco have done a lot of work, including inviting most of the authors.

Finally we express our great admiration and gratitude to Mrs. Wil Sommeling of the Erasmus University in Rotterdam, who is responsible for the lay-out and the preparation of the total manuscript.

Peter de Wolf
Rotterdam, October 1990

1 *INTRODUCTION* GROWTH WITHOUT BENDING

HENK W. LAMBERS

Professor Hendrik Wouter de Jong, of the University of Amsterdam, is a pioneer in the dynamic theory of industrial organisation, or "market theory" as it is now mostly called in Continental Europe.[1] That approach to micro-ecnomics focuses on the central institution of our economic order: the market. It opens a wide field of research. Adherents to market theory form a very loose union based on their common tendency to regard competition among firms as the core, and the relations in the triad: "structure-conduct-performance" as the analytical framework.[2] More loosely expressed, the common aim is to get a deeper insight into the currents and cross-currents that shape real markets.

In the words of De Jong: "I will try to establish that dynamic industrial organisation theory may provide a solution to these apparent contradictions by focusing on the heart of the matter: the competitive market process".[3]

De Jong has, indeed, contributed much to our knowledge and understanding of the dynamics of markets. In the first place by a series of original research projects which combine acumen and precision. In the second place by numerous publications based on critical and consistent theoretical analysis as well as a wide knowledge of international literature. In the third place as editor - or co-editor with Professor A.P. Jacquemin and Professor W.G. Shepherd - of a series of publications - monographs or well-programmed compilations of original essays - which have made a major impact on the international co-operation in this branch of economics.

To single out one example: the two volumes of Mainstreams in Industrial Organisation (1986)[4] have, by the intelligent distribution of themes among authors of different nationalities, set an example for a new kind of text-book in a field which is becoming increasingly transnational as the development towards a mondial corporate economy proceeds.

De Jong is a sturdy man, in body as well as in mind. His retirement in 1990 from the chair of theory of external organisation at the University of

Amsterdam is, luckily, due only to regulations on the professorial retiring age.

There was spontaneous consensus among friends and colleagues of many nationalities that this was the opportune moment to show De Jong their deep appreciation of his steadfast efforts. The outcome of that consensus is this set of essays in his honour. They circle around the theme "Competition in Europe", one of the first - and lasting - fields of investigation of De Jong.

The list of contributors in itself suffices to show that De Jong is an outstanding international economist. That is why there is a book, and why, to really honour De Jong, it had to be about dynamic market theory and its potential for the understanding of European market developments.

At the same time, De Jong has remained a genuine Dutchman with a Dutchman's deep interest in the working and steering of the Dutch economy, especially its markets, both on the corporate and on the government side. His independency of mind is well known, as is his expertise.[5] His opinions are sought after and listened to. In economics that does not mean, of course, that they are always immediately accepted and acted upon. If not, De Jong re-enters the fray.[6] In the Netherlands he has vitalised the dynamic approach to markets in theoretical economics. Therefore, the rest of this introduction will be an attempt to draw some lines from his deep roots in Dutch culture and Dutch academic economics to the autonomous body of thought he has built.

H.W. de Jong was born (1925) and raised in Rotterdam. In 1944 he took his matriculation; he had to wait until the liberation of the Netherlands in May 1945 for the reopening of the Universities, when he enrolled as a student of the Nederlandse Economische Hogeschool at Rotterdam. As he took his academic degrees, including his doctorate, at that institution, some lines on its conduct and performance, and its possible influence, may be functional.

The Netherlands, a nation dependent on international trade, has always had a deep respect for knowledge, integrated information. Not only to know how but at least as much to know why. In 1859 an entrepreneurial banker in Rotterdam stimulated his co-citizens to found an international library with the admonition: "Trade without knowledge means fortune by coincidence".[7] A few decades later, in this same Rotterdam some young businessmen decided that the complexities of modern international business called for the theoretical education of merchants. In 1913 they founded the "Nederlandsche Handels-Hoogeschool", mostly known abroad as the "Rotterdam School of Economics".[8] It was the first institution of higher learning in the Netherlands specifically directed at the study of economics.

Professor F. de Vries (1913-1945) was the first professor of general - that is, theoretical - economics. He set his analytic and learned mark on the curriculum. When Rotterdam had proved a success, Amsterdam followed in 1921 by adding a faculty of economics to its University (growth-cycle theory, no irony intended). Its architect was Professor Th. Limperg, a highly intelligent chartered accountant and a very dominating personality. Economics for him started with the internal organisation of the firm; that finished, one turned outward to its environment: "the theory of external organisation".

The undergraduate curriculum at Rotterdam had as compulsory subjects economics, business economics, economic history, economic geography and law. De Jong is one of the very few of the thousands of students who successfully passed through this curriculum who in his work has woven together all those themes into one balanced pattern. But, thanks to academic tradition, he still teaches "the theory of external organisation".

Pride and prejudice exist in the groves of Academy. The pride of Rotterdam was that it was not prejudiced. The first advice was to observe and have an open mind. As a consequence there were centres of common interest but no "Schools" in Rotterdam. There was however a general style in the approach to economics. Shepherd's remarks on soft analysis as focusing on core ideas that are valid and testable[9] would have been welcomed. "Plausibility" and "Relevance" were household words.

When De Jong concludes his pioneering article "European Industrial Organization" with the remark: "It is a dubious gain to acquire greater scientific precision at the cost of relevancy"[10], one smiles at seeing a style kept alive.

To this School, then, De Jong found his way in 1945. He must have been a very attentive student. He recollected, in 1981, how Lambers - micro-economics - had told his students that supply and demand, of course, were zones.[11] Owing to their slopes they had to intersect somewhere; he called the meeting place the tolerance plane. "Tolerance" because within its limits three dynamic forces: competition, combination and concentration, had some freedom to struggle for influence on the price level. There were limits to the plane due to general economic tendencies (shadows of Marshall and the Austrians); if these limits seemed too wide socially, there was government regulation. That last statement was at any rate clear to students living under post-war rationing.

Lambers did not know then that the exploration and solution of the theoretical implications hidden in these near-factual observations would entail the forging of new tools to build a consistent theory. De Jong did the forging under his own sail, with the structure-conduct-performance paradigm as his port of departure.

First, however, he had to finish his studies (1951) and enter into his first long-term employment: research economist with a highly specialised Dutch multinational (1952). In a sense pioneering began there: research economist in business was a young occupation, a spin-off from econometrics. There he acquired his inside knowledge of business aims and business wishes, easily recognisable to anyone who has himself been part of it. In that period (1952-1965) the demand for targeted research may have hammered out his direct style of writing. Sensible combining of facts, figures and literature, close reasoning, and clear conclusions; no ambiguities, no redundancy. "In plain Dutch" as he likes to put it. A succinct sentence like: "Synergy has to be organised by the management"[12] is a joy to anyone who had to sit through business meetings listening to rosy prose on synergy as if it were a gift from heaven.

At the same time the sentence is a character witness. His research took him at an early period to the European Economic Community. His deep interest in dynamics - that is, a sense of history - and the urge to do theoretical work made the transfer to the Europa Institute at Leyden a logical step in development.

That he belonged to the circle of experts became visible in the next few years when he was invited to join a European delegation as a witness on concentration before a US Senate Committee.[13]

This rounded off the phase of development (not that of research!). There followed, after a very short introduction phase, his first academic appointment in 1969, his first book in 1971. From that moment onwards the paradox of a one-man firm showing simultaneously constant maturity and continuous expansion and differentiation was to hold during two decades.

So much for the sketch of roots and early growth. The full work of twenty years in a tireless man's life cannot be reviewed in a mere introduction. I will conclude, therefore, with a personal view of De Jong's main business, his convictions and his many-sided relevance.

It takes courage to grapple with the flow of market shapes in time. A flashback suggests itself to a heroine of old, before chaos theory made its entry: Alice, in Wonderland, the personification of disturbance wrought by growth, and her complaint: "Things flow about here so".

De Jong might agree on one aspect. He rejects finalism and determinacy; there is no makeable economy. Then, certainly, he would begin to educate: if one cannot order markets to behave, one can at least analyse their behaviour orderly.

He began to prove so in his first book: "Ondernemingsconcentratie" (1971), as much a *tour de force* as a *tour d'horizon*. He laid the material foundation in separate chapters on concentration problems in the then six EEC countries, with the USA and Japan added for good measure. The framework of his theoretical concepts had now been made visible; the full construction followed quickly in "Dynamische concentratietheorie" (1972). De Jong has had the privilege, and the stamina, to write the synthesis of his theoretical work himself. He did so in the, well revised, fourth edition of his 1972 book, now entitled "Dynamische markttheorie" (1989). The changed title makes clear that the scope had widened from concentration to markets. Concentration has become one of three normal co-ordinating principles in markets: competition, combination, concentration. These are inherently unstable. To elucidate their mutually changing influence such as they work out in the interactions between structure and process is the main business of dynamic market theory. De Jong's analytical tool is the growth cycle or product-life cycle in its consecutive phases: development, introduction, expansion, maturity, stagnation. To indicate its function in analysis, De Jong uses a fine old Dutch word: "leidraad", that is, the thread a gardener uses to train the branches of young fruit trees along a wall, so that there will be more fruit and easier pickings.[14] The lines fixed, harvesting begins. Down they come: competition, cartels, integration, diversification, mergers and joint ventures. Everything in its proper place, no loose ends. While harvesting, De Jong comments on various other gardeners and some weak sections in their tools. The structure is stable, the conduct gentlemanlike, the performance splendid. The more so as he keeps cool:

"The growth cycle explanation was less adequate for the conglomerate movement which developed later in the sixties".[15]

De Jong's interest in economics, and in markets in particular, rests on his unshakable allegiance to personal freedom and democracy. The decisive link is his conviction that a society based on those values needs a dynamic and competitive market system, probably to survive, certainly to thrive.

His investigations have convinced him that the cycle of competition will be continuous as long as entrepreneurs in search of value added are urged on by emulation and imitation.[16] As soon as, by public power or by private power, business corporations are exempt from emulation or imitation, loss of innovation and growth will set in. Active government policy on competition will then be needed. This has been impressively worded in the final chapter of Jacquemin-De Jong "European Industrial Organization", where they argue that an active competiton policy and democratisation of decision-making in the EEC will be necessary if the promised "new contours" are ever to be filled to satisfaction.[17]

De Jong is wary of the dominant firm. In this first, 1971, book he reasoned against the notion, made popular by business organisations, that bigger markets "naturally" called for bigger business units. Already then, he formulated a proposal for materially preventive merger control.[18] Consistently, in a recent study he urged the EEC to complement its active policy against combinations with measures restricting concentration.[19] With respect to public power he warned against the visible government finger on the invisible hand, carrying a sheaf of subsidies for mature industries,[20] and pressed for a more active policy towards competition, to start with cartels.[21] Nationalised industries are not, to him, instruments that favour innovation, as may be seen from his comment on a proposal to have the performance of public enterprise judged by the standard set by other public firms: "It does not help Renault very much if it performs better than British Leyland or Alfa Romeo, it should be able to stand up against the Japanese.[22] In brief, De Jong as a monitor thinks that the first duty of an intellectual is to use his intellect. Having done that, his moral duty is to be faithful to the conclusions reached by reasoning.

Three qualities, his independence of mind, his scholarship, and his sense of purpose, have together created the many-sided relevance of De Jong's work. He is scholar and a teacher. He is an author whose opinions I have heard quoted at Board meetings on mergers as well as in government councils on resale price maintenance. He is an editor in a wide international field and co-responsible for the, loose, institutionalisation of market theory. He is an adviser to government[23] and the EEC.[24] He is a monitor under his own flag.

By being all this, he has given relevance to micro-economics in the eyes of those who in the last resort decide on the fate of theoretical economics, the rising generation of professional economists.[25]

When the son of Odysseus set out into the world, Athena stood next to him in the guise of Mentor, an experienced man, to be trusted in word and deed. De Jong has proved to be a Mentor; may his curve run on, without bending, for many a year to come.[26]

Notes

1. H.W. de Jong and W.G. Shepherd (eds): *Mainstreams in Industrial Organisation*, vol. I p. V, Dordrecht, 1986.
2. W.G. Shepherd, *On the Core Concepts of Industrial Economics*, Mainstreams I, p. 24, Dordrecht, 1986.
3. H.W. de Jong: Free Versus Controlled Competition in B. Carlsson (ed.), *Industrial Dynamics*, p. 272, Dordrecht, 1989.
4. H.W. de Jong and W.G. Shepherd (eds.), *Mainstreams in Industrial Organisation*, Books I and II, Dordrecht, 1986.
5. W.J. de Ridder, Preface of H.W. de Jong, *Fusies en overnames*, SMO 88-2, The Hague, 1988.
6. H.W. de Jong, *De ontucht van economen*, ESB 1987, p. 755.
7. W.C. Mees, *Man van de daad*, p. 90, Rotterdam, 1946.
8. In 1973 the N.E.H. merged with the Medical School of Rotterdam to found Erasmus Unversiteit Rotterdam.
9. W.G. Shepherd, On the Core Concepts of Industrial Economics, *Mainstreams I*, p. 28.
10. H.W. de Jong: European Industrial Organization, *Mainstreams I*, p. 107.
11. H.W. de Jong: Marktorganisatie, mededinging en prijsvorming, *ESB*, 1981, p. 1268.
12. H.W. de Jong, *Dynamische concentratietheorie*, p. 245, Leyden, 1989.
13. H.W. de Jong, Concentration in the Common Market, Hearings on Economic Concentration, part 7, Washington 1968, pp. 3608-3636, cited in *Ondernemingsconcentratie*, p. 47, note 11.
14. H.W. de Jong, *Dynamische markttheorie*, p. 81, Leyden, 1989.
15. H.W. de Jong, Theory and Evidence concerning Mergers: an International Comparison, in A.P. Jacquemin and H.W. de Jong (eds.), *Markets, Corporate Behaviour and the State*, p. 122, The Hague, 1976.
16. H.W. de Jong, *Dynamische markttheorie*, p. 272-274, Leyden, 1989.

17. A.P. Jacquemin en H.W. de Jong, *European Industrial Organization*, pp. 253-254, London, 1977.
18. H.W. de Jong, *Ondernemingsconcentratie*, pp. 40-41, Leyden, 1971. In 1977 the Social-Economic Council of the Netherlands advised legislation on the preventive testing of mergers. In the preparation of that advice, De Jong had a vital part. It was not acted upon.
19. H.W. de Jong, *Fusies en overnames*, p. 58, SMO.88-2, The Hague, 1985.
20. H.W. de Jong, Het Nederlandse structuurbeleid: de zichtbare vinger aan de onzichtbare hand, in *WRR, Sectorstructuurbeleid: Mogelijkheden en beperkingen*, p. 58, The Hague, 1980.
21. H.W. de Jong, Nederland: het kartelparadijs van Europa? *ESB*, 1990, p. 244.
22. H.W. de Jong, The State as Entrepreneur, in H.St. Seidenfus (ed.), *Deregulierung - eine Herausforderung an die Wirtschafts- und Sozialpolitik in der Marktwirtschaft*, p. 188, Berlin, 1989.
23. H.W. de Jong, *De concentratie in het perswezen*, The Hague, 1989
24. H.W. de Jong, *Reports on the pharmaceutical industry, the food industry, the passenger car markets, the production and distribution of books, for the Netherlands*; Series "Evolution of Concentration and Competition", Commission of the European Community, 1974, 1975, 1981, 1982.
25. Since the mid-1980s the number of PhD-studies in the field has steadily increased, clearly owing to the stimulus of De Jong's dynamic market theory.
26. I should like to express my thanks to Drs. P.W. Holle, Drs. T.C.R. van Someren and Dr. P. de Wolf for their assistance in collecting basic material for this introduction.

2 SOME ASPECTS OF DYNAMIC ANALYSIS AND INDUSTRIAL CHANGE

WILLIAM G. SHEPHERD[1]

Among the many gifted European scholars of industrial organization, Henk de Jong has provided a special blend of creativity, analytical validity, and knowledge of actual markets. He has helped the European field of industrial economics to develop a growing richness of theory and empirical testing, while the American field of industrial organization was moving after 1970 toward pure abstraction and Chicago-UCLA-School optimism.

Throughout, he has firmly kept market power in focus as a threat to economic progress. His central concern with dynamics and innovation has avoided a narrow focus on static efficiency. He has continually tested his ideas against reality and applied them to a wide range of real policies. And he has done all this, and more, while remaining the consummate professional: energetic, collegial and supportive.

To appreciate the magnitude of de Jong's whole contribution, one must read the works themselves and learn deeply about western European industrial policies. Given the large scope of his research and policy activities, that is a challenging task. I will try here only to discuss several points of his theoretical contributions, as they relate to: (1) the field of industrial organization itself, and (2) actual industries and the soundness of public policies toward industries.

My main point is that de Jong's dynamic and realistic approach is well suited to complex real markets and policies, more than are the pure abstractions that have gained currency in the recent U.S. literature. Theories enriched with factual knowledge, and imbued with historical perspective, are the most reliable basis for the field's future development. They may lack the flash and certitudes of pure theory, with its single-concept, axiomatic approaches and sharp-edged answers. But they protect against naivete, imbalance and frequent absurdities.

In this essay I will first review the mainstream field as de Jong entered it in the 1960s, discuss his dynamic approach, and compare it with the recent trends in the field, in Section I. Next, in Section II, I will analyze a basic property of market structure and profits, showing how a "dynamic" process may make competition degenerate into market dominance. Finally, in Section III, I will note several lessons for actual markets in European markets.

1. De Jong and the Industrial Organization Field

For over a century, the field has been an intellectual battleground among proponents of conflicting methods, facts and interest groups.[2] Very roughly, the struggles are between free-market adherents who say that actual market structures are generally efficient and low in monopoly power - essentially that monopoly is benign - and others who regard tight structure as a source of frequently harmful market power. The main contest has been for the methodological center: for the right to say that certain concepts and research methods are superior to others.

The same basic struggle has continued to the present, and it surely will go on without end in the future. The technical terms and research techniques have evolved, but the struggle for the center is little changed.

1.1. Evolution of the Field

Beginnings

In the 1880s in the US, a group that may be called the Darwinians (including Willam Graham Sumner, Jeremiah Jencks, Arthur T. Hadley, and to some extent John Bates Clark) defended the emerging trusts as necessary reflections of "modern" large-scale technology. They were challenged by skeptics (such as Henry C. Adams, Richard T. Ely, and later Charles J. Bullock) who regarded the trusts mainly as embodying monopoly instead, with little proven efficiency justification. The Darwinians offered mainly a crude version of the theory of natural selection, applied to industrial affairs. The skeptics offered theoretical challenges and eventually an overwhelming array of practical evidence about real markets. The same issues recurred in the 1920s, 1950s and since 1970.

Europeans conducted a complex but similar debate with broadly parallel contending ideas (featuring Menger, Weiser, Levy, Schumpeter and on to Arndt and more recent scholars), which de Jong has well summarized.[3] Indeed some key participants (such as Marshall and Schumpeter), have been influential in the literatures on both sides of the Atlantic. And for that matter, the basic arguments are as old as markets themselves, as groups with power attempt to legitimize their power against skeptics and victims. Sometimes, in some industries, the defenders of leading firms are right; but those facts, and the underlying theories, need constantly to be subjected to skeptical testing.

The Mainstream Field, Through the 1960s

By 1925, virtually all important current concepts had been advanced and explored, some of them with great sophistication. By 1945, oligopoly theory was developing rapidly, and by 1960 potential entry and quantitative research were also making important advances. The 1960s brought extensive research on innovation and organizational behavior. By 1970, virtually all of the important conceptual elements of the field had been developed and tested in some degree, and the debates were often sophisticated.[4]

To summarize them briefly: markets were seen as complex and evolving, and the influences exerted by structure were seen as tendencies, not laws. Structure was seen as partly endogenous to behavior and performance, as various types of industries passed through various life-cycles from birth to maturity. Market imperfections were recognized to be significant in many cases, and strategic techniques of exploiting market power were explored.

Technological progress was regarded as important, as Schumpeter had stressed, probably more important than static efficiency. Free entry could be powerful, and some dominant firms had justly earned their positions by displaying superior performance in the past. Economies of scale were probably small in most industries. Pure competition was seen as merely a set of theoretical conditions, *not* as a practical goal for policy in any real industries.

In 1986 de Jong and I published a collective review of the field's mainstreams and other schools, trying to clarify the status of the contending points of methods and opinion.[5] The principal question then, as now, is whether the work of the recent pure theorists, Chicago-UCLAns, and "contestability" specialists have displaced the field's mainstream by offering sufficient research content. That survey indicated that the newer schools were modifying the mainstream, rather than displacing it, and matters have not changed by much since then.

De Jong's work has been firmly in that mainstream, helping the European field prosper while the US was developing increasingly narrow theoretical interests. His research has extended the mainstream literature, particularly in analyzing industry life-cycles and the innovative effects of entrepreneurs.[6]

Using the lenses of hindsight and self-interest, recent Chicago-UCLA analysts have belittled the field as it had developed by the 1960s. They assert that it was dominated by "naive structuralism, and because it "had no theory" it "lacked rigor and content." But this version is a biased caricature, with little relation to the actual field and its literature. There was a serious interest in structure, which has continued, but no blind structuralism among researchers. US antitrust and regulatory policies were mostly moderate, not extremist. European policies were even more moderate, on the whole.

New Schools

In contrast to de Jong, the three "new IO" schools in the US after 1970 moved away from this mainstream, by stressing pure theory and extreme cases:

1) Pure theorists dwelt on duopoly models, using Cournot/Bertrand/Nash assumptions. This school is now moving more deeply into pure game theory.[7]
2) Chicago-UCLA specialists advanced the "efficient structure" hypothesis, urging that causation flows from performance to structure, rather than the traditional view.[8]
   Only state-created monopoly is harmful, they said.
3) The "contestability" school claimed that perfectly free entry-and-exit conditions supersede internal structure in generating competitive results.[9] They also urged that the theory applies widely to real markets.

These extensions of mainstream research topics are interesting, and some useful implications have been developed. The main lessons of duopoly theorizing, for example, have been to reaffirm that concentration fosters collusion. But there are narrow limits and major weaknesses, which have been noted in many other writings.[10]

The duopoly modeling, in particular, almost always assumes that the firms' behavior is entirely noncooperative. Thus it rules out all direct collusion, which is actually the main problem to be studied when concentration is high! Accordingly, the many hundreds of articles using game theory have as yet provided few lessons for real markets, and most of the analytical elements are not amenable to empirical testing.

Chicago-UCLA theorists have provided little empirical support for their assertions, as I will note shortly. And "contestability" theory is (after eight years) even more bereft of research support.

Perhaps the two most constricting trends - common especially to the duopoly and "contestability" theorists - have been: (1) to frame the field's analysis strictly in static-efficiency terms, and (2) to focus on duopoly to the exclusion of single-firm market dominance.

On the first point, maximizing consumer (plus producer) surplus becomes the only test of good economic performance and of good policies. Innovation, equity and other more complex values are ignored. Virtually all of the "rigor" of the new theories comes from this exclusive focus on the maximization of static surplus. The approach in its pure form seems unbalanced, even absurd, but it has become widespread and unapologetic in the US.

The second point has led to the frequent assertion that collusion is the only form of market power. The mainstream field has shown for many decades that dominance is harmful when markets have imperfections. By assuming away the imperfections, in order to achieve "rigor," many "new IO" theorists are able to deduce that dominance is innocent while collusion is the only remaining "real" market power. Yet that idea is also absurd. Direct dominance inevitably exerts more market control than does collusion among separate firms.

Fortunately, much mainstream research has continued in the US, despite disparagements for "lacking rigor" and being "empty of theory." Yet many game-theoretic papers offer no more substance to justify their conclusions than an appeal to intuition and/or mainstream ideas. Naive theorizing remains a problem for the field in the US, not only because it is often sterile but also because it crowds out more substantial research. Moreover, officials guided by simple Chicago-UCLA and "contestability" ideas dominated the US policy agencies during the 1980s, sharply cutting back US antitrust and regulatory policies to minimal levels.

1.2 A Few of De Jong's Contributions

Important elements of de Jong's contribution are:

1) A stress on dynamics, treating competition as a process rather than a set of equilibrium conditions.[11] His theory relies on industry life-cycles in explaining changes in market structure.
2) A focus on technological progress as a (or the) main element of good economic performance. Also, de Jong emphasizes the role of the entrepreneur, as distinct from pure neoclassical competitive theory. Here de Jong reflects the best of the Schumpeterian and mainstream traditions.
3) An emphasis on market power (primarily embodied in dominance or tight oligopoly) as a source of economic harm. The harm to innovation and good management is important.
4) Deep reliance on real evidence and cases to develop sound theories. In de Jong's work, no rule is rigid, no model is simple, no policy is permanent. All need to change with the real conditions.

In lesser hands, there might result a series of ad hoc points about specific sectors. De Jong instead develops a battery of complementary and alternative ideas, which combine and interact to illumine real trends.

Dynamics

His dynamic theory especially reflects this sophistication. Industries are seen as evolving along common stages, following the familiar product-cycle ideas. There are four main stages:

1) As the industry begins, there are few suppliers, high risks and much creativity.
2) Then rapid growth occurs, as the products are standardized and innovations are diffused. During this rapid build-up of the industry, the rapid growth of demand outstrips supply. Therefore excess profits occur, and they draw in new suppliers. Concentration declines and competition is "free;" that is, effective.
3) Then saturation and maturity are reached. The capacity growth outpaces the dwindling growth rate of demand, and the resulting excess capacity leads to financial losses, failures by weaker firms, mergers,

and a rise of concentration. The remaining firms engage in "controlled competition," with collusion and vertical integration.

4) Finally, the industry recedes and firms restructure and diversify. Competition becomes severe again.

Of course, as always with de Jong, the time path and stages are not uniform, and yet they do explain the trends of many industries. Note that structure is partly endogenous to the process; and that it *is* a process. Game theorists tend instead to identify the conditions of duopoly at one point of time and then to model them, but the model is often just one slice of the ongoing complex reality. Though the short-run results are often interesting, they frequently tell little about the larger choices and changes which comprise the firms' main reality.

The endogeneity of structure is important, because "contestability" theorists recently have claimed that (1) no previous writers have treated structure as endogenous, and (2) that their static-efficiency theories do "explain" structure.[12] Instead, de Jong provides an important schema for explaining and predicting structure, without making structure seem to be merely a side-effect of other conditions. And the game-theoretic "explanations" of structure are in fact merely short-run and of little empirical validity.

De Jong's process posits an industry which evolves from high initial concentration to lower concentration and then back to higher concentration as it develops and matures. Actual cases need not fit this sequence exactly, and there are many exceptions. But the main lines of change are widespread, and de Jong's analysis gives a basis for prediction and for analyzing the exceptional cases.[13]

Moreover, de Jong applies the concepts fruitfully to whole economies and time-periods, particularly the European Community and the US. He notes that "the EC has shifted from free competition, prevalent during the 1950s and 1960s, toward guided or controlled competition during the 1970s and early 1980s. This has promoted labor market rigidity, concentration and rationalization in big business, subdued entrepreneurship, and contributed to rising unemployment."[14] The concepts lead to sophisticated general policy lessons, relevant to a wide range of economies and industries.

Entrepreneurship

The other main dynamic aspect of de Jong's work involves *entrepreneurs*, whose role goes beyond the common neoclassical analysis. The entrepreneurs' function is broadly "the creation of added value or surplus value," but their activities range from pioneering, organizing, and negotiating to include technical skills, financing, and so on. The needed activities often change as the firm develops through the industry life-cycle.

Commonly, entrepreneurship occurs through the creation of new firms and the appearance of new business leaders. But de Jong notes that much creative entrepreneurship occurs within existing firms, as they bring out new products and change their own structures. To de Jong, entrepreneurship is essentially innovation, wherever it occurs, and it creates extra value which becomes profit. Therefore de Jong's view is broader than that of Schumpeter, who focuses on the personal side (new people, new firms).

Supra-normal profit in standard equilibrium theory arises mainly from reduced cost, from random disequilibrium conditions, or from monopoly. The entrepreneur creates extra profit by organizing for innovation and/or by inspiring greater effort by employees. In simple equation form:

Profit = f (Costs, Monopoly, Innovation, Effort, Randomness)

Causation is simultaneous, though, because the firms' employees' degree of effort is influenced by excess profits: high profits encourage slackness and reduced effort.

Effort = f (Profits)

In any event, the entrepreneur is the creative force, which moves the economy out of existing technology and allocations. That is what adds to the economy's productivity. When competition is free, entrepreneurs function well to innovate and enhance productive value. Controls and restrictions inhibit the creative force of entrepreneurs.

De Jong's focus on change and time-processes does not fit well within game-theoretic, short-run models. Instead, one looks to longer-run analysis, covering the sequence of choices that is made over time. In athis spirit, the following analysis of the evolution of market dominance suggests how the interaction of market structure with performance might be analyzed further. It complements de Jong's dynamic analysis, which focuses on outside influences. I focus on the sequence of internal choices.

2. Analyzing the Process of Structural Change

A normative dilemma may arise in the competitive process, from a possible conflict between motive and effect. Firms seek to dominate their markets, so as to gain excess profits. Yet if one firm competes so successfully that it attains dominance (the standard definition of dominance is one firm with over half the market and no close rival), then competitive parity is lost and competition usually becomes ineffective.[15]

Hence the competitive process may be unstable, with a tendency to eliminate itself. Preserving the firms' motive for winning, without suffering the effects when a complete victory occurs, may seem to be impossible. And dominant firms will denounce any effort to restrain them as being harmful to incentives.

The dilemma would be sharper if dominance arises because of large economies of scale or superior efficiency, as Chicago-UCLA-school analysts say is common. Then policy steps to restore competition might be directly anti-efficient. If an efficiency-created dominant firm is restrained so as to restore competitive parity, then its (and other firms') incentives for high effort and superior efficiency will be reduced or eliminated.

Accordingly, market dominance might present the economy with a Faustian bargain: in order to motivate firms' competitive efforts to attain superior performance, it may be necessary to sacrifice effective competition itself.[16]

The seeming dilemma can be an important one, and the possibility has been used to challenge antitrust policies since their beginning. Yet like most supposed dilemmas, it is actually a matter of degree, rather than a pure binary either-or choice. It is a balancing among several elements in the process by which high market shares are acquired and maintained. It may be resolved by analyzing the sequence of choices made by firms.

Moreover, the dilemma is a false one, whenever firms obtain dominance from market imperfections rather than by superior performance.

And finally there is a further gap in the dilemma: the urge to perform well may be just as strong if the profit rewards are barely above competitive levels, rather than lavish. Unrestrained monopoly profits may be unnecessary; it may be both necessary and sufficient if the following condition holds:

$$\text{Monopoly profits} > \text{Actual profits} > \text{Competitive profits}$$

In fact, the nature and strength of the incentive function has been much asserted but never researched. Moderate profit expectations serve to provide powerful motivations throughout the mass of competitive industries. And high excess profits seem more likely to stifle later performance than to be necessary to stimulate it.

The dilemma disappears if dominant firms inherently obtain sufficient rewards - that is, profit rates at least as high as competitive levels - both while they rise to dominance and while their market shares recede. If the rewards are lessened and the periods of dominance are shortened, then the economic harms imposed by dominance can be minimized, while sufficient incentives for efficiency are still maintained. These lessons may not be easy to apply in practical antitrust policies, but the seeming dilemma can at least be set aside.

At any rate, one central relationship in the problem is the *structure of rewards* (i.e., the gradation of firms' profitability) as it relates to the *structure of the market* (embodied in firms' market shares). Also important is the rate at which high market shares decline over time.

Dominance may emerge from either or both: (1) some degrees of scale economies or superior efficiency, and/or (2) an unstable dynamic, cumulative process, in which the profit yields of market share in each period generate a sequence of rising profits and market shares. How that process may occur is a key topic.

Concepts: Market Structures and Reward Structures
The Market Share-Rate of Return Function.

The central relationship between market share and profit rate can be called the MS-RR function.[17] It is a partial relationship, because other conditions (including entry barriers) also influence profitability. Of course it is only a tendency, not a tight function:

Profits = f (Market share, ...)

The causation involving market power has been challenged. Chicago-UCLA analysts stress the opposite causation: good performance yields high profits and market shares, they say. Each case may blend these factors in varying ways. The MS-RR function persists, in any event, in a variety of econometric testing.

As confirmed by extensive research, MS-RR is a positively-sloped association. It reflects the common tendency for higher market shares to yield higher rates of return on investment, from monopoly effects.[18] The MS-RR function has a dual meaning, for both (1) static conditions and (2) the dynamics of the competitive process over time.

Consider *statics* first. The MS-RR function shows the set of attainable profit rates at any given time, over a range of possible market shares. The marginal yields (shown by A, the slope of the relationship) may be steeply or slightly gradated, depending on the particular conditions of the given market. MS-RR would not be level and cannot be down-sloping, if a dominant firm exists; all firms on a down-sloping curve would instead choose to be at smaller market shares and would therefore immediately subdivide themselves. In fact this virtually never occurs.

The MS-RR yields might be curvilinear, rather than the straight-line case illustrated here with constant A values. Also, the MS-RR boundary is usually a soft, blurred zone, rather than a sharp line; because of other influences and randomness, it may not be precisely determinate. In any event, the firm's location at any market share, at a given time, will influence its attainable profit-rate yield.

Next consider *dynamics*: the sequence of the competitive process. The MS-RR function shows the successive profit rates which a firm attaining dominance can obtain, as its market share rises. A rise along the MS-RR function can generate dominance, because the profits realized in each period enlarge the range of competitive strategies available to the firm in subsequent periods: higher profits permit more aggressive, expensive strategies. Each period's change in market share then reflects the previous period's profitability:

Change in Market Share, period 2 = f (Profits, period 1...)

A ratchet effect over time may therefore take hold. A firm obtaining rising market shares will gain successively higher financial resources, which it can then deploy in the next period against its increasingly outmatched rivals. Conversely, low profits reduce a firm's competitive weapons and range of action in the next period, and that may cause a downward spiral in market share.

Hence the MS-RR function can make the competitive process an unstable one, which degenerates into dominance or even pure monopoly. Under perfect-market conditions, this process may occur with immediate determinacy, as all conditions are known, anticipated and yield the final outcome without delay. But if there are imperfections in real markets, including in capital markets, then the effects require time to occur. The process is dynamic, in the context suggested by de Jong and others.

The strength of instability of competitive structure varies directly with the marginal profit yield of market share. A steeper MS-RR function is less stable and more prone to monopoly, because the successive profit advantages over firms with lesser market shares are larger. Dominance can result more rapidly, even if there are no underlying economies of scale or superior efficiency.

There may be a "pioneer effect" at the outset, or merely a random rise in market share. In either case, it sets the unstable process in motion toward dominance driven by the differential market-share yields and the linkage among time-periods. Hence the attainment of dominance may reflect this process, rather than superior performance by the firm.

During the process, the firm may sacrifice some current profits in order to obtain higher future market shares. But the sacrifices need not drive the realized profits below the competitive levels. The firm may eliminate rivals even while obtaining normal or excess profits: that is the advantage conferred by the profits from high market shares. At the end, the dominance may have been obtained without requiring any period of recoupment to offset earlier losses. In such cases the dominant firm "deserves" no period of excess profits as a reward. Its profits have been sufficient throughout.[19]

Imperfections in the market may accentuate the unstable process. Imperfections are of many sorts, including asymmetric control over information, strategic actions, consumer loyalties inculcated by advertising, the intimidation of small rivals, and access to capital and other inputs at favorable prices.[20] These conditions usually favor the firm with the larger market share, because it has larger resources for winning competitive episodes.

Counter-forces

The cumulative process toward dominance encounters three opposing forces. One is the *general process of decay* which competition imposes on high market shares, as rivals probe for weaknesses and exert maximum effort to raise their own shares. When small rivals are numerous and/or strong, they will explore many directions of attack on the larger firm, perhaps applying more creativity.

The resulting general process of erosion is common in markets, though its rate (call it E) may vary over a wide range from case to case. And some firms are able to avoid it altogether. Nevertheless the rate of decay (E) is likely to be positive.

A second counter-force is *diseconomies of scale.* In most markets, minimum efficient scale is reached at rather low market shares, such as 3 to 10 percent of the market.[21] At larger sizes there may be constant average costs, as the research literature suggests. Yet many industries involve significant diseconomies, which progressively offset the monopoly-based rising marginal profit yields of market share.

The third counter-force is the dominant firm's own tendency toward *X-inefficiency and a retardation of innovation*, as competitive pressure is reduced. That tendency will slow the rise in the firm's market share and reinforce the tendency toward erosion. The size of this effect will also vary from case to case.

In combination, these conditions leave each market structure in a state of tension among the opposing tendencies.[22] Higher marginal yields may offset diseconomies and the erosion process, inducing a higher level of dominance by one firm or several. Low yields will induce a lower level of dominance.

The net outcome will be a vector of these conditions. They can be brought together analytically by comparing the rates at which profits will cumulate, against the natural rate of erosion of high market shares. Each firm's preferred market share is a function of three factors:

$$\text{Optimum Market Share} = f\ (\ A,\ E,\ C\ )$$

where C reflects the slope of the average cost curve. The partial relationships cannot be defined precisely, but the signs can be predicted. A's sign will be positive, E's is negative, and C's is negative. The actual values are an important topic both for research and for guiding public policies. Note that the profit gains may induce dominance even in the range of significant (or even large) diseconomies of scale, if A is higher than C.

Empirical Evidence

There is growing evidence about the three elements, A, E and C. It may be worth some review of details.

Values of A (the profit yield)

The A slope varies among individual industries, reflecting varying technology, imperfections in information and possibilities for strategic action. Entry barriers may also have some influence.

The cross-industry patterns of general MS-RR functions have been studied in some detail.[23] The now-standard form for estimation is a multiple regression of profit rates on various structural variables, including market share. This has yielded repeated consistent estimates of the partial MS-RR relationship, as an indicator of the average relationship occurring in a wide variety of industries.[24]

If there is systematic bias in the estimates, it is probably toward underestimating A. That is because the profit-reducing effects of X-inefficiency are embedded in the observed MS-RR conditions. Because this depressing effect is stronger at higher market shares, the observed MS-RR function is probably rotated clockwise away from the underlying function. This bias may reduce the estimated A values by possibly one-fourth.

The estimated values lie mainly in the range 0.15 to 0.3, with an intercept at a competitive profit rate which approximates the opportunity cost of capital. Geroski arrives at a consensus estimate for A of about 0.2, after reviewing several other studies as well (Martin, 1983, Kwoka, 1979, Gale, 1972, and Ravenscraft, 1983). For consumer goods, A is generally higher, mainly in the 0.3 range, while A may range down toward 0.1 for producer goods markets, especially for standardized products like cement, oil, steel and meat. The A values are only moderately sensitive to the height of entry barriers.

Evidently, the observed A values are substantial. Of course, they provide strong inducements to gain dominance. In contrast, the A slopes implied by Chicago-UCLA analysis are low. The MS-RR function would rise toward monopoly rates of return only at very high market shares (above 80 percent).[25]

As for "contestability," it implies that the MS-RR functions are horizontal, because entry is the controlling factor. The horizontal MS-RR functions for individual industries would lie at different levels, each determined by the height of the entry barrier. For markets that are fully or nearly "contestable," the horizontal MS-RR functions would be at the competitive profit rate.

Instead, the observed MS-RR functions conflict with both of these predictions.

The E Value (the Rate of Erosion of High Market Shares)

The rate of erosion appears generally to be low.[26] In the US, Japanese and other economies, its average has ranged between 0.3 to 1 percentage point per year.[27] Antitrust actions have caused some of the erosion.

Weiss and Pascoe observed only a 7 point average decline during 1950-75 (only 0.3 points per year), in a panel of 23 large US firms with initial market shares above 40 percent.[28] During the 1970s the rate of decline may have risen, but it has fallen in the 1980s. A panel of 47 UK firms showed declines averaging 0.3 to 0.8 points per year (Shaw and Simpson, 1985).

In Japanese dominant-firm industries during 1952-1966, shares declined an average of 1.5 points per year. The conditions in these trade-exposed Japanese industries were probably more turbulent than in US and UK industries. Market shares in the range of 30-50 percent declined more slowly, at about 0.7 point per year. The function is apparently asymptotic, as Geroski also noted in 1987, tending to level off at market shares in the 10-20 percent range.

Geroski concludes that shares do decline, "but only at a glacial pace," possibly 0.3 point per year, whereas my estimates have been closer to 1 point per year. A consensus estimate for general purposes might be 0.5 point per year, subject to wide variations among individual cases. Retention of dominance for a decade or more is therefore normal, and further rises often occur (e.g., in 32 of the 108 firms surveyed by Geroski). On average, a 70 percent market share might usually take 20 years to decline to 60 percent; such a 60 percent share still involves dominance.

Moreover, Geroski concludes that declines occur primarily from "sleepiness" in dominant firms, not because they are overwhelmed by market forces. Dominance can usually be sustained, as long as the firm does not succumb to X-inefficiency and a retarding of innovation.

The C Value (Diseconomies of Scale)

Research on the diseconomies of scale has been sparse. Economies (in the range below Minimum Efficient Scale) have been studied in more than 40 industries, but the range to the right of MES has largely been ignored. The assumption has spread that costs are roughly constant above MES, and this hypothesis cannot be refuted with the evidence now available. Yet if pecuniary economies are significant, then filtering them out from observed horizontal cost surves would, by implication, leave up-sloping cost curves.

Combined Effects

Together, the high A values and low decay rates indicate that there are usually high and sustained profit rewards for the capture of dominance. Also, the incentives to defend dominance are high. Therefore many market structures are likely to be unstable, with a dynamic tendency toward cumulative, non-efficient dominance.

The key is the high A values and low E values: to put it briefly, monopoly usually pays and monopoly usually stays. If the reverse conditions existed, they would pose the incentive dilemma: the profit rewards to superior-efficiency dominant firms could be so low that any restraint would stifle incentives. Instead, dominance appears to yield high, sustained profits even if superiority is absent. Market imperfections and linkage can account for much of dominance, and they permit significant social costs to occur.

The normative dilemma therefore is imaginary rather than real, in the normal case. Dominance can be expected to evolve and persist because its private rewards are high, but it has little or no general claim for existence on normative grounds. The social optimum would be better approximated if profit yields were lower and erosion were faster. For example, values of A approaching zero and decay rates (E) of 2 to 5 points per year might be consistent with the social optimum. They are, after all, approximately the levels that Chicago-UCLA analysts have claimed to be the actual values.

3. Lessons for Actual Markets and Policies

From the discussion of dynamic processes, the policy lessons are reasonably clear. There is a need to reduce existing dominance in most cases, and to avoid new dominance. The recent game-theoretic modelling and Chicago-UCLA literatures do not reflect these conditions. And US antitrust policies in the 1980s were misled by these theories.

Western Europe

In de Jong's spirit, we can turn these suggestions toward actual European conditions. In western European countries, the main need is to avoid permitting new dominance by mergers, as EEC integration increases. As competition increases for many dominant firms, the incentives for horizontal mergers will rise. Also, proponents will define their markets as being EEC-wide and/or world-wide, to indicate that the mergers are harmless. Currently there is a stampede mentality and enormous commercial pressures, favoring quick permissive treatments of mergers.

Yet preventing the emergence of new dominance can be important. The "new" wider markets will often have distinct sub-parts, as national differences persist. Moreover, the competitive pressures from extra-European sources may not be strong, and so the strength of both actual and potential competition may be slight in many industries.

It would be wiser to prevent most significant horizontal mergers for at least the next several years, as the new wider markets are becoming established. Few genuine economies would be lost, while substantial competition would be protected. Later there will be ample opportunity to allow those mergers which genuinely provide efficiencies without reducing competition.

This lesson contradicts the current Chicago-UCLA permissive policy toward mergers, because the process-based analysis indicates the greater threat of dominance. US experience during the 1980s strongly reflects the harm that shallow laissez faire can inflict on competition, as occurred for example in the US airline industry during 1985-88.

Eastern Europe

In Eastern European economies, the problems offer a sharp contrast. Existing state enterprises typically are already monopolies. And their industries tend to be older, capital-intensive heavy industries, many of them in the more advanced stages of their life-cycles.

The task is to convert them into competitive markets, both by introducing some degree of private ownership and by assuring competitive structural conditions. Structure alone is not enough, of course. Competitive capital markets also need to be created, and there need to be protections against anti-competitive actions by the incumbent monopoly firms as they cling to their positions.

But the structural changes are important nonetheless, and reducing the monopolies' market shares is the main need. It can be done by several alternative methods:

1) restructuring the firms into several separate enterprises,
2) creating new competitors by direct investment,
3) allowing western European firms to build new firms or branches, and/or
4) allowing competition by imports from western or other eastern countries.

Probably a large amount of (1) direct restructuring is needed, if monopoly is really to be reduced. The least reliable method is, in contrast, simply to permit new entry and hope that it will occur. When monopolies are entrenched, as most eastern European ones are, they commonly can repel new entrants, especially when markets are just emerging. The problems are accentuated when, as de Jong notes, the industries are mature and tend toward even greater degrees of monopoly.

Above all, there is a need to resist the current stampede toward mergers and joint arrangements between western firms and the eastern state monopolies, or *kombinats*. Firms will attempt to do first the actions which give them the most monopoly power, with its excess profits and immediate capital gains. Such precipitate east-west mergers will simply entrench the state monopolies further, blocking the emrgence of effectively competitive markets.

This policy lesson is of utmost urgency, but current actions seem largely to be ignoring it. The rush to open up markets to private enterprise and competition is fostering hundreds of mergers and quasi-mergers that will take many years to undo or offset, if corrective action is possible at all.

For one example, there is the East German insurance monopoly, Deutsche Versicherungs. Allianz AG, Europe's largest insurance company, sought a controlling interest in Deutsch Versicherungs in June 1990, as reunification of the two Germanys neared. Other insurance firms made counteroffers, and "antitrust authorities in both countries" were said to be reviewing the merger.[29] But their powers to intervene may be limited, especially because Allianz' financial terms would exceed those of other proposals, with their lesser monopoly impact.

Similar links are in progress among the leading automobile firms, banks, electrical equipment makers, and machine tool companies, among many other manufacturing firms.[30] The rush into Hungary, Poland and other eastern European countries is more advanced. Moreover, US, Japanese and other firms are also joining the process, seeking to set up links with firms throughout Europe, so as to reduce competitive pressures.

As de Jong and other knowledgeable observers might expect, this process is occurring faster than policy officials can act to study and restrain it. Indeed, it is happening even before effective laws can be written and enacted. This is threatening the creation of competitive markets in Europe, accentuating the process by which dominant firms may emerge naturally. The resulting tight structures may be particularly difficult to erode, because they are linking firms from all over the world. There may be no reserve of independent potential entrants to threaten them in the future. Competition is being blocked out before it can begin, in scores of industries.

In addition to Eastern Europe's older manufacturing industries, the future will bring the growth of the newer information-based and electronics industries. To help make them competitive, eastern European countries need to avoid giving monopoly advantages to established western firms (e.g., IBM or AT&T) that are coming in. Again, the incentives favor monopoly, because monoply-seeking western dominant firms will be able to offer the highest bids.

In particular, claims for potential competition need to be reviewed skeptically. The theory of "contestability" has been shown to be faulty and of little relevance to real markets. It has also failed to give valid policy guidance in many important test cases, ranging from US airlines, telecommunications and railroads, to UK telecommunications and inter-city buses.

Altogether, these exciting transitional times contain large risks that monopolies will persist or be created on a grand scale, in hundreds of industries in Europe. When policy agencies do not exist or are embryonic, little clear, strong action can be expected.

But the policy lessons from the analysis of market dominance are reasonably straightforward. Dominance is a danger, and preventive actions taken ahead of time are more effective than corrective actions taken later.

If reasonable policies are developed, they will embody the realism and sophistication of de Jong's work. For the field of industrial organization in coming decades, as well as for real policies toward real markets, de Jong's contributions have set a high standard.

Notes

1. I am indebted to many colleagues for discussions on these issues over many years, but none more than Henk de Jong. Along with his skillful evaluation of technical ideas, he has instilled values of tolerance and scientific testing in dealing with professional matters. Though he vigorously defends points on which he finds the evidence convincing, he encourages an opennness to new ideas and approaches.
2 For historical reviews, see de Jong's chapter in de Jong and Shepherd, eds., *Mainstreams in Industrial Organization*, Books 1 and 2, Dordrecht: Kluwer Academic Publishers, 1986, vol. 1, pp. 69-112; Shepherd, *The Economics of Industrial Organization*, 3d ed., Englewood Cliffs, N.J.: Prentice-Hall, 1990, pp. 19-23 and 520-27; Almarin Phillips and Rodney E. Stevenson, "The Historical Development of Industrial Organization", *History of Political Economy*, 6 (Fall 1974), pp. 324-42; and George J. Stigler, *The Organization of Industry*, Homewood, Ill.: Richard D. Irwin, 1968.
3. In de Jong's chapter, ed. *cit.*
4. See also Joe S. Bain, *Industrial Organization*, rev. ed., New York: Wiley, 1968; John M. Blair, *Economic Concentration*, New York: Harcourt Brace, 1972; F.M. Scherer, *Industrial Market Structure and Economic Performance*, Chicago: Rand McNally, 1970; Carl Kaysen and Donald F. Turner, *Antitrust Policy*, Cambridge, Mass.: Harvard University Press, 1959, among many important works of the 1950s and 1960s.
5. De Jong and Shepherd, ed. *cit.*
6. The indispensable source (written in Dutch) is de Jong's *Dynamische markttheorie*, Leiden: H.E. Stenfert Kroese, 1985.
   Especially interesting recent samples of his work (written in English) are Chapter 1 in his *The Structure of European Industry*, 2d ed., Dordrecht: Kluwer Academic Publishers, 1988, pp. 1-39; "Competition Policy in Europe: Stimulus, Nuisance, or Drawback?" a chapter in K. Groenveld, J.A.H. Maks and J. Muyksen, eds., *Economic Policy and the Market Process: Austrian and Mainstream Economics*, Amsterdam: North-Holland, 1990, pp. 111-38; and "Free versus Controlled Competition", a chapter in Bo Carlsson, ed., *Industrial Dynamics: Technological Organizational, and Structural Changes in Industries and Firms*, Dordrecht: kluwer Academic Publishers, 1990, pp. 271-98.
7. For recent summaries of "new IO theory," see especially Jean Tirole, *The Theory of Industrial Organization*, Cambridge, Mass.: MIT Press, 1988; Michael Waterson, *Economic Theory of Industry*, Cambridge: Cambridge University Press, 1984; William Sharkey, *The Theory of Natural Monopoly*, Cambridge: Cambridge University Press, 1982; Lester Telser, *Theories of Competition*, Amsterdam: North Holland,1988; Joseph E. Stiglitz and C. Frank Mathewson, *New Developments in the Analysis of Market Structure*, Cambridge, Mass.: MIT

Press, 1986; and Alexis Jacquemin, *The New Industrial Organization*, Cambridge, Mass.: MIT Press, 1987.

8. Leading Chicago-UCLA writings include Stigler, *The Organization of Industry*, 1968; Yale Brozen, *Concentration, Mergers and Public Policy* (New York: Macmillan, 1982); John S. McGee, *In Defense of Industrial Concentration* (Seattle: University of Washington Press, 1971); Harold Demsetz, "Industry Structure, Market Rivalry, and Public Policy", *Journal of Law and Economics*, April 1973, pp. 1-9; and Demsetz, "Two Systems of Belief about Monopoly", a chapter in Harvey J. Goldschmid, H. Michael Mann, and J. Fred Weston, eds., *Industrial Concentration: The New Learning*, Boston: Little, Brown, 1974.

   Also John S. McGee, *Industrial Organization*, Englewood Cliffs, N.J.: Prentice-Hall, 1988; Sam Peltzman, "The Gains and Losses from Industrial Concentration", *Journal of Law and Economics* 20 (October 1977), pp. 229-63; John Carter, "Collusion, Efficiency and Antitrust", *Journal of Law and Economics* 21 (October 1978), pp. 435-44; and Richard A. Posner, "The Social Costs of Monopoly and Regulation", *Journal of Political Economy*, August 1976, pp. 807-27.

   For more extreme versions, see Robert H. Bork, *The Antitrust Paradox*, New York: Basic Books, 1978; and Dominick T. Armentano, *Antitrust and Monopoly: Anatomy of a Policy Failure*, New York: Wiley, 1982.

   The main papers have appeared primarily in one Chicago journal (the *Journal of Law and Economics*).

9. See especially Baumol, Panzar, and Willig, *Contestable Markets and the Theory of Industrial Structure*, 1982. For further praise of the theory, see Baumol and Willig, "Contestability: Developments Since the Book", *Oxford Economic Papers*, November 1986, Special Supplement.

   For critical assessments of the theory, see William G. Shepherd, " 'Contestability' versus Competition", *American Economic Review*, 74 (September 1984), pp. 572-87; and Marius Schwartz, "The Nature of Contestability Theory", *Oxford Economic Papers*, Special Supplement (November 1986).

10. See F.M. Scherer and David Ross, *Industrial Market Structure and Economic Performance*, 3d ed., Boston: Houghton Mifflin, 1990; Franklin M. Fisher, "Games Economists Play: A Noncooperative View", *Rand Journal of Economics*, 20 (Spring 1989), pp. 113-24; W.G. Shepherd, "Three 'Efficiency School' Hypotheses About Market Power", *Antitrust Bulletin*, 33 (Summer 1988), pp. 395-415; and Shepherd, "Efficient Profits versus Unlimited Capture, as a Reward for Superior Performance: Analysis and Cases", *Antitrust Bulletin*, 34 (Spring 1989), pp. 121-52.

11. Important forerunners include Alfred Marshall, in his *Industry and Trade*, London: Macmillan, 1920; and John Maurice Clark, *Competition as a Dynamic Process*, Washington, D.C.: Brookings Institution, 1962.

12. See especially Baumol, Panzar and Willig, *Contestable Markets and the Theory of Industry Structure*, op. cit.
13. An interesting recent analytical/empirical paper in de Jong's direction is Steven Klepper and Elizabeth Graddy, "The Evolution of New Industries and the Determinants of Market Structure", *Rand Journal of Economics*, 21, (Spring 1990), pp. 27-44. It finds predictable regularities in the evolving structure of a wide range of industries, of the sort stressed by de Jong.
14. De Jong, "Free versus Controlled Competition," *op. cit.*
15. Generally, effective competition requires a reasonable degree of parity among at least several comparable rivals. They will apply strong pressures on each other, forcing good performance. Moreover, each firm's moves will be responded to by others, in a sequence which elicits superior levels of effort and creativity as the struggle continues.

    Under dominance, the parity is absent. The dominant firm possesses much greater competitive resources, which it uses to apply pressures and tactics which its little rivals cannot match. Therefore the dominant firm is under only weak competitive pressure, and it is not forced to perform well in its cost-efficiency and innovation.

    In contrast, the little rivals face extreme pressure and risk, and they are subject to easy elimination by the dominant firm.

    Dominance therefore lacks the creative tension which is generated by effective competition. A majority of the market (the dominant firm) is free of "hard" competitive pressure. Competition is ineffective, with reduced efficiency, innovation, and equity.

    The normative burden of proof therefore is against high market shares, unless two pure (and extremely rare) conditions exist: 1) perfect-market conditions of knowledge and rapid adjustment, which prevent dominance from existing except from the firm's superior efficiency, and/or 2) "contestability", which makes market shares irrelevant to profits because no monopoly power can be exerted.

    See Shepherd, *The Economics of Industrial Organization*, 1990, Chapter 11; Dennis C. Mueller, *Profits in the Long Run*, New York, Cambridge University Press, 1986; and Donald Hay and John Vickers, eds/. *The Economics of Market Dominance*, Oxford: Basil Blackwell, 1987.
16. This dilemma has been urged particularly by the "efficiency school" wing of the Chicago-UCLA School. See especially Demsetz, *op. cit.*, 1973, 1974; McGee, *op. cit.*, 1974; and Bork, *The Antitrust Paradox*, 1978.

    In the earlier versions, the dilemma was ascribed solely to large economies of scale. But those were shown by 1975 to be a minor factor in explaining market dominance.
17. It first emerged in W.G. Shepherd, "The Elements of Market Structure", *Review of Economics and Statistics*, 54 (February 1972), pp. 25-35. See also my *The Economics of Industrial Organization*, 1990, for further discussion.

18. It is a partial relationship, assuming other structural elements and causative factors to be held constant.
19. See Shepherd, "Efficient Profits versus Unlimited Capture...", 1989, for further analysis showing that competitive profits are generally a sufficient reward for good performance.
20. Cheaper capital will be available when a higher market share reduces risk, so that the risk-adjusted cost of capital is lower.
21. See especially Scherer and Ross, *Industrial Market Structure and Economic Performance*, 1990, for summaries of the evidence on economies of scale.
22. This formulation of the vector of forces was first noted in W.G. Shepherd, *Market Power and Economic Welfare*, New York: Random House, 1970.
23. See Scherer and Ross, *Industrial Market Structure and Economic Performance*, 1990; Shepherd, "The Elements of Market Structure," *op. cit.*, 1972, *The Economics of Industrial Organization*, 1990, and "Tobin's *q* and the Structure-Performance Relationship: Comment," *American Economic Review*, 76 (December 1986), pp. 1205-10; Mueller, *Profits in the Long Run*, 1986; and Hay and Vickers, *The Economics of Market Dominance*, 1987.
24. Some individual-industry evidence (about the automobile, detergents and computer industries) further suggests that the cross-section A estimates are reasonably reliable.
25. That is because Chicago-UCLA analysts commonly regard competition as being effective even when a dominant firm has up to 80 percent of the market and only small rivals.
26. For reviews of the evidence, see Shepherd, *The Treatment of Market Dominance*, New York: Columbia University Press, 1975 (covering Japanese conditions 1952-66), and the summary in *The Economics of Industrial Organization*, 1990; and Paul Geroski's chapter in Hay and Vickers, *The Economics of Market Dominance*, 1987.
27. Cite my EIO 1990
28. George Pascoe and Leonard W. Weiss, "The Extent and Permanence of Market Dominance", Federal Trade Commission Working Paper, 1983.
29. "Corporate Takeover Battle Shaping Up Over East German Insurance Monopoly," *Wall Street Journal*, June 27, 1990, page A9.
30. Steven Greenhouse, "It's Sink or Swim in East Germany", *New York Times*, June 24, 1990, Section 3, pp. 1, 6.

3 MODELING ECONOMIC CHANGE AND RESTRUCTURING

The Micro Foundations of Economic Expansion

GUNNAR ELIASSON

1. Introduction

Three phenomena in particular are making life difficult for the economist today. *First*, inputs and outputs of the economic system are increasingly transacted in imperfect or regulated markets and/or are being dominated by quality components that we cannot easily measure. *Second*, production technology is increasingly moving economic activities across the statistical categories we have become accustomed to. *Third*, the economist's representation of a nation - a statistical system interacting with the statistical systems of other nations, each being autonomously controlled through a political authority - is being gradually diffused through the international integration of markets and the increasing presence of the multinational corporation. Thus, we are measuring less and less well what is becoming economically more and more important. A particularly tricky measurement problem is the presence of "tacit" knowledge or "human embodied capital".

I am beginning my story of a dilemma facing current economic analysis in terms of a statistical measurement problem. I do this for several reasons. It is particularly appropriate for IUI, the institute I come from, that has "spent its life" in applied economics trying to integrate theory and measurement. Neither theory nor measurement can develop without each other's support. It emphasizes not only the increasing awareness of knowledge-based information processing in economic activity (Eliasson 1986a, 1988a, 1990a). More important and interesting is that economic activity in general takes place far away from the classical state of perfect or almost full information. Rather than being asymmetrically informed, implying the possibility of becoming fully informed, agents are normally very ignorant about the content of the state space (of opportunities) within which they operate. Dynamic markets are characterized by a general lack of information and imply that an experimental organization of economic activity is needed to cope with uncertainty (Eliasson 1987, 1988c). The entrepreneur and dynamic markets is a theme that distinguishes continental European economic thinking from mainstream static industrial organization analysis (de Jong 1986). Dynamic industrial organization theory (de Jong 1989), hence, is an appropriate theme for this occasion, and a necessary starting point for any analysis of economic growth.

These introductory remarks move the focus of economic growth analysis into the imperfect parts of markets, notably *product markets*, more and more characterized by competition with technological product innovations (Eliasson 1987), the *labor market* more and more concerned with allocating human embodied competence - not labor (Eliasson 1988c) - and *the stock market end of the capital market* which exercises an increasing pressure on low performing business firms to structurally reorganize (Eliasson 1988b). This is where firms reside. This is where the core of the growth engine of the economy is.

The business firm lives on its competence to achieve synergy effects out of integrating markets through its administrative system. Sometimes the market is most efficient and firms break up, sometimes administrative systems outperform markets and larger and larger firms emerge. The relative rates of innovative activity in financial markets and in administrative technology determine the outcome. Hence, financial markets play a decisive role in restructuring the production system of an economy, through forcing institutional reorganization, thus underlining the unfortunate practice in economic theory to keep financial and real analysis separate. The interesting activity takes place in the intersection of the two dimensions; that is within the firm.

This presentation[1] introduces the theme of my paper, the firms in dynamic markets as the driving force behind firm formation, expansion and death, together constituting the growth engine of the economy that drives the macroeconomy through what Schumpeter called innovations, entrepreneurship and creative destruction. These economic processes are experimentally organized and largely unpredictable at the micro level, as they are represented for instance in the micro-macro simulation model of the Swedish economy, developed at the IUI. Economic growth ultimately rests on human based competence that has to be steadily upgraded and diffused through the economy. Therefore it becomes natural to begin to discuss economic growth under the heading of *The Knowledge-Based Information Economy* and then to proceed with the *aggregation problem* or the dynamic market processes that link competence based micro behavior with growth in macroeconomic output.

Concentration caused by economies of scale causes problems within the classical, static general equilibrium model. It is a theoretical concern there. It is a practical concern in U.S. anti-trust policy and German cartel legislation. It was a political problem for Joseph Schumpeter (1942) who saw the technology of routinized innovative activity breed superior firms that first took over markets, reducing or eliminating competition, then merging with Governments, destroying democracy. The political problem is gone, at least temporarily for two reasons. In the experimentally organized economy, no player, not even IBM is safe. The global integration of markets for technological competition has made market concentration a less relevant problem. Technology, furthermore, is pushing for smaller scale in a variety of markets, where economies of scale had earlier ruled. Technological competition in global markets currently is intensifying competition to the extent that whole industrial nations think of themselves as suffering. In this context it is interesting to observe Bo Carlsson's results[2] that while most industrial nations register a decline in the average size of their firms and manufacturing plants across industries, Sweden has been exhibiting exactly the opposite development, emerging out of the crisis years of the 70s with a small group of very large, and very competitive multinational firms dominating their segments of markets for mature products and together dominating the production system of the entire Swedish economy.[3] The knowhow to efficiently operate and to successfully reorganize large business enterprises is an important part of the industrial competence upon which advanced industrial nations base their economic wealth.

2. The Knowledge Based Information Economy

Classical economics is concerned with physical flows of production. As comprehensive, national statistical measurement systems were being designed and developed during and after the second world war, theories dealing with physical quantities that could be measured were refined to perfection both theoretically and in their empirical applications. Before, economics was very much social philosophy. It was concerned with, among other things, the nature of rational behavior in matters of economics. Measurement thus helped to turn economics into an almost "hard" science. Economics still, however, has an intellectual dimension. It can be viewed from two different angles. With intellectual processes imposed on, or integrated with the physical flows of production, it becomes difficult, perhaps impossible, or illogical to look at economics as a hardware-based, economic process. This is at least the case when you study the evolving organizational forms of an economy, which is what industrial economics has to be concerned with. The organizational structure very much controls the information processing of the economy, the mix between markets and hierarchies, the balance between goods production and marketing and distribution, etc. And the intellectual economic process draws significant resources. Hence, I want to approach my topic from both the intellectual ("information") and the physical sides simultaneously. This is almost the same as to say that I want the Austrian tradition back into economics.

Adam Smith (1776) coined the concept of productivity advance through division of labor. By breaking the work process down into finer and finer elements economies of scale in the small could be achieved. These scale effects became the drivers of the macro economy. Work specialization, however, came at a cost. It required *innovative knowledge* to be created.

The more elaborate work specialization the more resources needed to *coordinate* production. Hence, there are explicit transactions costs associated with organizing a specialized economy. Such organization can be achieved through the *market* by what Adam Smith called the invisible hand, and through the visible hand (Chandler 1977) of management or *administrative method* in production units. The relative efficiency of the two methods determines the size structure of hierarchies or firms in the economy, as suggested by Coase (1937), and hence the market structure. Determining the division of labor and thereby the information technology to coordinate economic activities is also a prime function of markets. This *choice of organization technology* is perhaps the most important choice of all, since it influences the properties of the entire economic system. This choice includes the entry and exit of firms, or the recombination of firms, the movement of people with unique competence between firms and within firms (internal labor markets). The complexities of the endogenous sorting and *selection* mechanisms of the markets are in a large measure *experimental* and characterize the dynamics of the economic system.

Finally, knowledge, once created (*innovation*) is diffused through the economy through imitation, or through various educational arrangements. *Learning*, is an important fourth category of economic activity that has to be considered to capture the whole economy at work (see Table 1).

The first conclusion coming right out of Adam Smith's original idea is that *macro-economic growth theory has to be based on a theory of organization of markets and of hierarchies* to capture what goes on in a growing economy. This theory has to be explicit about the relative efficiencies of coordinating economic activity through markets and through hierarchies, and, hence, also about the formation, the growth and the disappearance of market imperfections called firms; i.e., those "imperfections" that beat the market in coordination efficiency.

Having said this, I have placed the entity called a firm in the midst of a dynamic market process, making its ability to beat the market on innovative, coordination and learning accounts the source of economic growth. This firm will be a theoretical entity very differently organized from what you would expect to find within the general equilibrium framework.

Table 1 The elements of the knowledge-based information economy

1.	COORDINATION (organizational structure)	*The invisible and visible hands at work* - competition (in markets, Smith 1776) - management (of hierarchies, Chandler 1977)
2.	INNOVATION (exploring state space)	*Creation and exploitation of new business opportunities* (Schumpeter 1911) - innovation - entrepreneurship - technical development
3.	SELECTION (organizational change)	*Incentives for change* - entry - exit - mobility
4.	LEARNING	*Knowledge transfer* (Mill 1848) - education - imitation - diffusion

Source: Modified version of Eliasson, 1987, *Technological Competition and Trade in the Experimentally Organized Economy*, IUI Research Report No. 32, pp. 12 f.

I have furthermore made four information activities the dominant economic activity. Both the innovation and the selection activities cause theoretical trouble in the standard model. Economic *coordination* (item 1 in Table 1) - whether it occurs through the markets or through hierarchies - is controlled at each point in time by a structure; a "memory" that embodies the productive capacities of the economy. The properties of that "memory" are changed through "*innovation*" (item 2), through "*selection*" of organizational forms (item 3) and through *learning* (item 4). The development of that organizational memory occurs largely through the experimental organization of markets, and is hence "tacit". It makes the economic system path dependent, and gives economic historians a role to play in economic analysis.

The economics of knowledge and information has its origin in the Austrian School (von Hayek 1940, 1945). But the Austrian element of "unpredictability" was soon lost as "statistical decision theory" and the theory of communication of coded messages began to be formulated (Shannon-Weaver 1949, Marshak 1954, 1968, Stigler 1961, McCall 1982). Modern literature in the field takes "structure" for given (exogenous) and knowledge for codable (= information), and hence avoids both innovation and selection. The modern learning literature, hence, focuses on the gathering and use of asymmetrically distributed information for static coordination purposes. If innovation and selection occur simultaneously and are affected by coordination and learning activities the standard model gives a biased picture of economic processes. It is appropriate in this context, to discuss this particular element of process dynamics, since bringing the Austrian tradition back into economics also means bringing back some original ideas of the Stockholm School tradition, and in particular work by Myrdal (1927) and Svennilson (1938).

3. The Micro Foundations of Economic Growth

None of the information activities in Table 1 takes place without some resource use. It is therefore not satisfactory to assume - as has been common - that information costs are zero, or negligible or of some magnitude that can be perfectly known in advance. Information costs, see Figure 1, rather make up the bulk of costs applications in a modern manufacturing firm. They obviously cannot be perfectly known. With information use being the dominant resource use you have to accept that technological change in a major way originates as advances in the technology of using information. And *the technology of using information in a large measure depends on the organization of the economy.* To capture economic growth organizational change has to be modeled explicitly. This is part of the story of this paper. And technological advance is in a large measure unpredictable. Let me give two illustrations, one from within the firm and one from aggregating from micro to macro level. They both illustrate the micro foundations of economic growth.

Figure 1 *Distribution of labor costs. Large Swedish manufacturing firms. Global operations, percent*

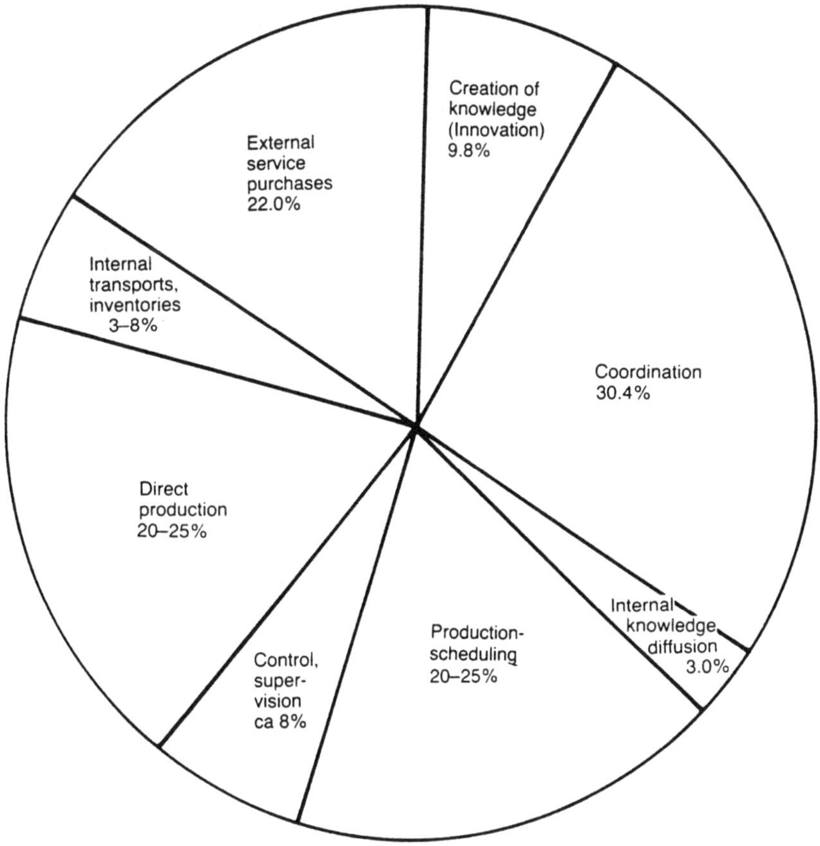

Total: 122%

Source: Eliasson, 1990a, The Knowledge Based Information Economy; in Eliasson-Fölster-Lindberg-Pousette-Taymaz (1990).

Example from within the firm

The dual (intellectual and physical) nature of economic activity means that all economic activity can be classified as knowledge based information processing (under one of the categories of Table 1) that controls the underlying physical flows. Think of factory automation. Before automation, work is performed at decentralized work stations, using the specialized knowledge of skilled workers. To automate the same production you have to retrieve and code the skills of the specialized workers - which is not easy, very costly and sometimes impossible (Eliasson 1980) - centralize the code and organize the machines and sensors such that the code can run production. What you have done is substitute one information technology for another through reorganizing production. This establishes three facts to keep in mind as we go along. Knowledge based, or information guided information processing runs production. Shifting from one production (or information) technology to another requires knowledge (or information) of a higher order. If it does not exist it must be created (innovation or selection) or learned. When seen in this perspective productivity advance at any level of aggregation, beginning at the factory level has its origin in productivity advance in information processing.

Example of going from micro to macro and back again (dynamic aggregation over Salter curves)

In the experimentally organized economy I have in mind, aggregation can be visualized (at least partly) through some well known concepts. At each point in time the capacities of the economic system (the "memory") can be seen as a set of potential Salter distributions of *productivities* and *rates of return*, very much like in Figures 2. At each point in time a firm is represented by a column on both of Figures 2, the height of the column telling its performance rate and the width of the column its size relative to all other firms.

To be complete (second) these distributions should include potential productivity (in Figure 2A), the result of potential entrants and the results of innovative activity in existing firms, but there are special problems here (see below).

Figure 2 *State descriptions of the Swedish economy*

Figure 2a *Potential and simulated value productivity distributions*

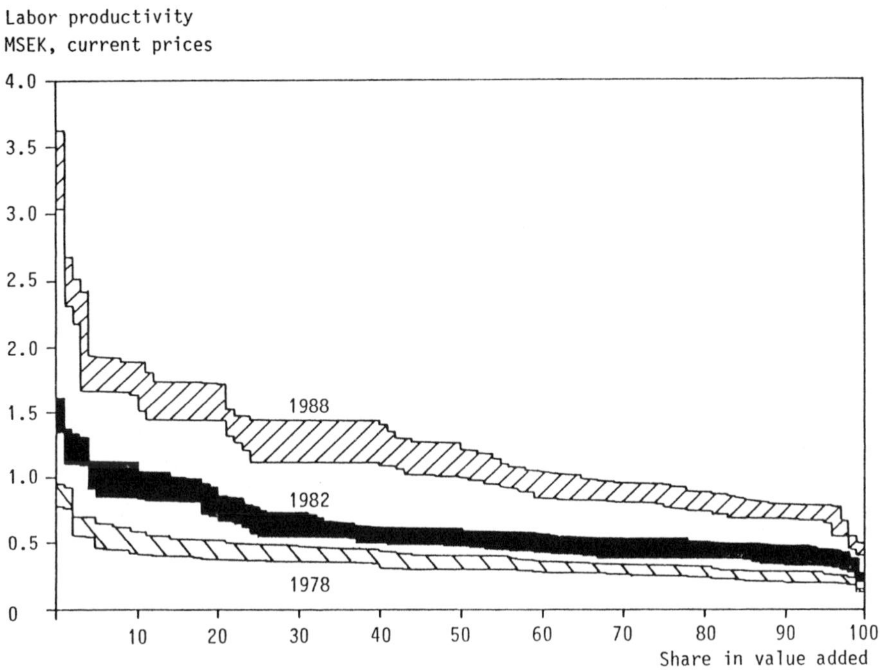

Note: Shaded areas show the difference between potential and actual distributions.

Source: Eliasson, G., 1990a, The Knowledge Based Information Economy; in Eliasson-Fölster-Lindberg-Pousette-Taymaz (1990).

The slope of the Salter distributions (third) represents *potential competition* in markets. The firms at the left part of Figures 2 can compete from a position very superior to those occupying the Salter right hand tail. More particularly, the best performers to the left have a considerable capacity to lower prices and/or raise wages to earn more profits and grow faster and put their left-hand competitors in an increasingly precarious position.[4]

We are talking both of earnings and financing capacity (in the capital market), wage paying capacity in the labor market and potential price competitiveness in the product market.

Figure 2b Rate of return distributions

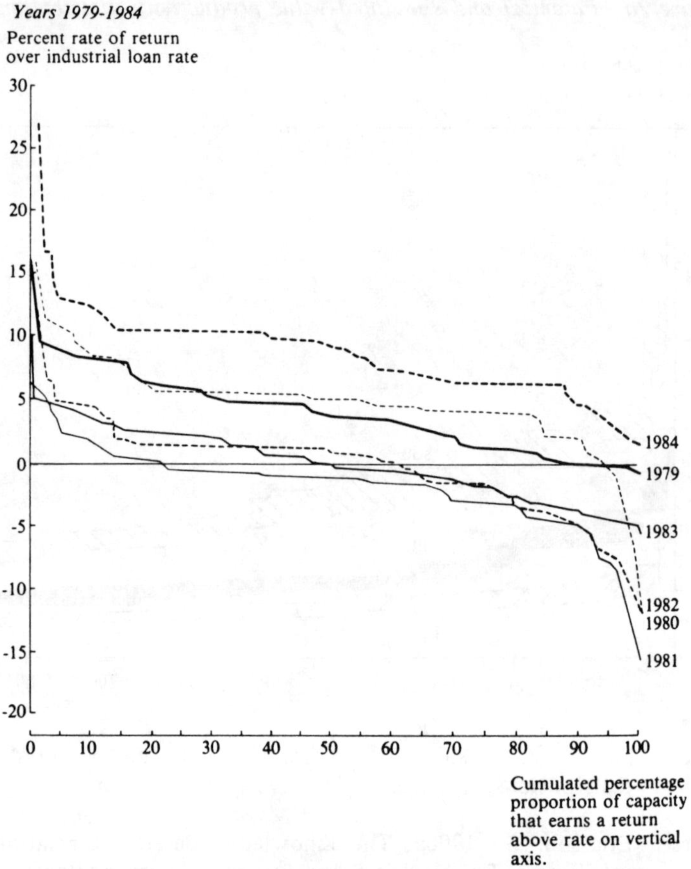

Source: Eliasson, G., 1988, Schumpeterian Innovation, Market Structure, and the Stability of Industrial Development; in Hanusch (ed.) *Evolutionary Economics, Applications of Schumpeter's Ideas*, Cambridge University Press, Cambridge (p. 162).

Each firm (fourth), however, is only fractionally informed about its competitors and engages in various forms of *learning* about the shape of the Salter curves in its neighborhood and also (of course) about demand conditions in the market. Firms in Figures 2 looking left at least know that it is feasible to perform up to the best standards they see on their left even though they may not know how. This they have to learn. I have already observed that this learning draws considerable resources, at least 50 percent of total labor costs in the large firms.

On the basis of its perceived performance relative to all other actors the firm (fifth) takes action (a) *in* the product, labor and capital markets and (b) *about* internal deficiencies in productivity performance. Ex ante price and quantity interactions occur and new prices and quantities are established.

Part of this reestablishment involves (sixth) updating the performance (Salter) distributions for the next period, including new competitive entry in response to perceived profit opportunities and forced exit. The "memory" is updated and the next step on the "path" taken.

So far this is only a description of what goes on in the Swedish micro-to-macro model within a quarterly framework (Eliasson 1977, 1978a, 1985, 1989b). The framework is that of asymmetric information on the "fundamentals" of the economy at each point in time, being represented by the Salter distributions.

One could say that the behavioral setting of the above Salter analysis responds to Arrow's (1959) plea for a generalized model of monopolistic competition in which agents act as both price and quantity setters on the basis of their local monopoly positions. The representation of the dynamic market process, however, is very much closer to Shubik (1959, 1960, 1975), which I prefer, since it opens up the classical model economy for my notion of mistaken decisions as the important mechanisms of learning at all levels. A number of very different problems, however, remains, at least, in the context of relating agent to macroeconomic behavior. This amounts to making dynamic aggregation explicit. The temporary monopoly positions upon which firms base their pricing behavior have to be explained, and I have concluded that the explanation should be looked for in a dominant organizational competence in agents (Eliasson 1986c, 1988c), that constantly reorganizes the institutional structure of the entire economy, generating macroeconomic growth in the process.

Another problem has to do with the time dimension of agent behavior, partly how the *future* bears on today and partly (a modeling and measurement problem) the *units of time* by which economic activity should be measured, problems discussed already by the Stockholm School economists. The first part of the time dimension incorporates the *ex ante ex post realization process*. On the second problem, an annual model of the economy and a daily (transactions) model of course have to be structured very differently. The finer the time units the more of economic structure represented by the sequencing of activity (as distinct from estimating lag structures in macro models) and the larger the measurement problem. Ideally all economic action should be represented by sequences of local interactions of agents in the markets, based on agents' perceptions of relevant current and future circumstances. Hopefully some systematic patterns ("theory") should exhibit themselves at that level. Rational expectations and efficient market theory invoke very strong such assumptions a priori. The Swedish micro-macro process model uses much weaker assumptions and relies on explicit price feedback through markets to control the macroeconomic process.

The technological memory

Information processing is controlled by knowledge. The information technology of an economy is largely embodied in its organizational structure, a "memory" of the model of the economy that organizes people with competence and information processing. The organizational structure has evolved historically, being influenced by the ongoing economic process. At each point in time the organizational structure sets the limits - very much like an operating language of a computer - on the innovative, coordinating, selecting and learning processes of the economy. The economic forces that push against these limits, and push them outwards, reside as human or team based competence endowments in business firms. It is very wrong to restrict this analysis to hardware embodied technology. Roughly one third of labor resources in an advanced industrial economy go into private service production, much of it being related to manufacturing goods production. The other third, public service production is not all consumption, as is often assumed but infrastructure inputs in goods production. Innovative activity occurs in all sectors. One of the most important sectors in need of innovation is the schooling system, all levels.[5]

Much of the competence I have referred to as growth creating, unfortunately is tacit and hardly communicable at all through regular educational channels. It is learned on the job, and is transmitted through the movements of people or groups of people in the job market or in the mergers and acquisitions markets. Such knowledge transmission mixes with job performance and is hardly measurable at all.

To understand technological advance in terms of the four activity types in Table 1, on the other hand, we need a measurable characterization of the organizational structure of the economy. Currently this is close to impossible. Whether we talk about competence at the firm (Eliasson 1988c) or industry levels, it is largely "tacit" and uncodable.[6] It develops through endogenous selection in the market process. The economy becomes - what I call (Eliasson 1986a,b, 1987) - *experimentally organized* or (Pelikan 1986, 1989) *self-organized*.

The organizational competence at various levels of aggregation both dominates and releases the productivity of physical factors. Hence, to explain macroeconomic growth one has to understand how changes in the organization of communication and information transfer that controls the physical flows in the economy generates productivity advance at the macro level. Aggregation requires a model of dynamic market processes. This makes it natural to see industrial economics as the *economics of innovation, coordination and learning*. These are all typical *information* activities. The way I have presented economic activity these information activities become the dominant drivers of the macroeconomic growth process. The dynamics of firm behavior in markets becomes the core of the growth engine of the macro economy.

Modeling dynamic competition and organizational change

The above principal analysis places the dynamics of firm (innovative) behavior in the core of the economic growth process. The Salter curve examples essentially remove the foundations for static aggregation. There is no stable macro theory of economic growth, beyond the descriptive value of production function measurement. Growth has to be built explicitly on micro behavioral assumptions, and aggregation in dynamic markets has to be an explicit part of theory. The minimum stable unit of measurement that can be measured in the sense that ready-made statistical systems exist is the firm or the division. This is the core unit of measurement in the IUI micro-to-macro model of the Swedish economy. It models firms as financially defined entities with financial objectives that operate on the basis of their own information systems, that serve as the statistical source for the model (Eliasson 1985, Chapter VIII).

Firms in the model occupy positions on the Salter curves. They learn about themselves and their environment. They invest and they make production and hiring decisions. In the process prices and quantities are set and the Salter curves (the organizational structure of the economy) are updated, thus setting the stage for price and quantity decisions in the next period and so on. A significant part of the performance upgrading of entire economies comes via the selection process (see Table 1) i.e. through entry of new firms and exit of inferior firms, together representing the Schumpeterian innovative and creative destruction processes. Business failures are part of the learning costs of the entire economic system. The outcome is a path dependent evolution of the economy, a development that exhibits phases of erratic or chaotic behavior, a development that is very difficult both to understand, to control and to manipulate centrally. To influence such an economy, or such a model of an economy, a very different "policy technology" than what is suggested by classical theory has to be designed. Above all the policy model has to be explicit about the lack of information on the part of policy makers and the risks for large scale policy failure that centrally directed policy action imposes on the economy. Large scale policy failure as a rule is not much of a learning experience for the failing economy, only for enlightened policy makers in other nations.

4. Economic Systems Properties

The dynamics of learning and competing that leads to the updating of the upper left hand section of the Salter curves and the creative destruction of its lower right hand tail is the essence of the growth machinery of the MOSES micro-to-macro model. The spread of the Salter curves determines the intensity of competition. The intensity of competition determines the macro productivity properties of the entire economy. This section presents the properties of the micro-macro model economy.

First I look at long-term growth and productivity performance of the model under stable market conditions, when quantity change does not disrupt the price system unduly and vice versa. I then investigate technical change under more or less rapid market regimes to see under what circumstances long-term, very rapid and stable macroeconomic growth can be achieved. This will all be a verbal summary of a large number of published studies. I conclude with some quantitative illustrations of the micro dynamics of variously designed macro growth processes.

Close to steady state growth experiments - the business cycle

To understand the relationship between technical change at the micro level, productivity growth and growth in output three distinctions have to be made.

First, technical change is *diffused gradually*. The market organization determines the time it takes for new, internationally available technology to be implemented locally and to affect productivity growth. A classical way of illustrating this is through measuring production at best-practice technology plants and compare with the productivity distributions of installed capacity (Salter curves). *Second*, aggregate productivity is not improved if best-practice technology is allocated in the wrong markets or in the wrong production lines. The efficiency of the *allocation* of investment matters. *Third*, productivity per se is not the right goal variable to be concerned with. Firms are not and economic advisors should not. Long-term economic growth is more adequately related to profitability, the competence to produce the right, highly priced goods and services for the right markets, and the ability to maintain a high rate of return and a high growth rate for long periods. The rate of return is in turn a price weighted productivity measure (Eliasson 1976, 1985).

To begin with, the diffusion of best-practice technology ("learning") depends on economic factors. It is asymmetric and usually slow (Eliasson 1980). *Increases* in best-practice technology take a long time to show up as productivity advance. Intensive market competition speeds up the process somewhat. In Eliasson (1987, Chapter IV) a domestic market protected from foreign price competition and a regime with price elastic foreign trade is compared, holding best-practice technology constant. The specialization effect on the macro economy from price elastic output competition is slow to be realized but very strong in the long run. If exogenous best-practice technology is *decreasing* in productivity (we can impose that unusual situation) the negative effects on productivity are much faster to come, everything else the same (Eliasson 1982, p. 86).

Rates of return are price weighted productivity measures. Hence, from an economic point of view the choice of right price environment (market, product) is as important for profit and welfare as productivity performance.

If firms overinvest in high productivity production techniques in the wrong markets a negative correlation between advance in best-practice techniques and aggregate productivity growth may occur. As Carlsson (1987) shows, the allocation of investment normally means much more for macro productivity advance than the increase in best-practice technology (the shifts of production frontiers). Generally speaking, from an economic growth point of view the economy should allocate its resources to areas where they produce maximum value to end uses, as they show up in relative product prices. From a welfare point of view it may be optimal to see growth occurring in typically low productivity service production, rather than in high productivity manufacturing.

Under normal circumstances (orderly pricing in markets) the model economy exhibits standard neoclassical behavior. Exogenous increases in interest rates (Eliasson 1984, p. 27), as expected, reduce long-term growth rates monotonically. The problem, however, is that interest rates are not exogenous, but depend on the overall organization and functioning of market competition. When market speeds have been calibrated such that the economy behaves well (the reference case) a typical business cycle is exhibited around the endogenously determined long-term growth trend.[7]

Structural diversity and stability of economic growth - the growth cycle

The Swedish micro-to-macro model is strongly non-linear and market prices are easily perturbed by sudden quantity adjustments, sending off trails of more or less dramatic price-quantity interactions through the economy. The size of quantity shocks and the speed of markets significantly affect long-run growth behavior of the entire economy. This means that the model exhibits, as a typical property, phases of seemingly unpredictable behavior ("chaos"). Individual business mistakes are a normal micro phenomenon and can be seen - in a macro context - as a normal cost of economic growth. Under disorderly market conditions, however, such mistakes can result in dramatic macro behavior.

If you attempt to remove mistakes by forcing markets to perform more efficiently in a static sense, through speeding up market transactions, you can - for long periods - increase productivity growth through eliminating slack and mistakes (Eliasson 1983, 1984, see Figure 5a in particular). However, the closer to a steady state characterization of the economy you gets the more potentially unstable the system. Wages become the same across the market; productivity rates are the same (the Salter curves become flat), rates of return are becoming equal across the markets and diversity of structure disappears. Diversity of structure in turn depends on both the competitive exit of low performers at the right end of the Salter distributions in Figure 2 and on innovative behavior at the upper left hand side of the Salter curves.

The less diversity in the economy the more sensitive it is to small adjustments at the micro level which push actors over broad flat surfaces with no natural stopping places. In a dynamic model diversity of structure corresponds to the convexity assumption in the static model. Once the extremely rapid macroeconomic growth rate achieved through fast market processes get slightly upset, a growing instability of the adjustment process, and possibly collapse, can be observed.

This macroeconomic behavior has been numerically simulated under various market regimes with no entry (Eliasson 1978, p. 105 ff, 1983, 1984, 1985, p. 292) and a half baked theoretical analysis is found in Eliasson (1985). The collapse means a temporary - a couple of decades - close down of large parts of the economy. Diversity of structure is restored and when prices have eventually been stabilized to reflect the new quantity structures of the system macroeconomic growth gradually resumes. In a historic perspective the long-term growth of this bumpy market regime appears to be inferior to a more constrained ("slower") market regime. Economic growth may in fact never really come back for very long. On the other hand if market competition is very much reduced, eventually the allocation machinery will become inefficient to the extent that long-term economic growth virtually vanishes. There is an *optimal intermediate growth path corresponding to an orderly experimental market process* (Eliasson 1983). The optimal growth path depends on the extent to which diversity can be maintained in the economy. New innovative entry is the most important diversity preserving factor in the long run (Eliasson 1990b).

With macro productivity and output growth mainly generated by economic forces, under the constraint of an upper technological best-practice limit, it becomes interesting to understand the dynamics of resource allocation that positions the economy somewhere underneath this maximum growth path.

In a first round of experiments (reported extensively elsewhere; Eliasson 1983, 1984), the state of technology - available best-practice technology - was held constant. A series of simulation experiments varying the "market regime" characteristics only were run. I found that the speed of adjustment to price signals was far more important for productivity performance than the parallel development of best-practice technology, since the economy was always operating far below best-practice capacity. This was so, however, only as long as price signals were reliable predictors of long-term future prices. This observation that markets and the allocation of investments matter more than pure technology has later been confirmed by Carlsson (1987).

This predictability depends on the existence of sufficient slack in resource use to smooth the adjustment process. When the speed of market allocation was increased the economy operated as a car on a narrow road; as long as it stayed on the road the point of destination got rapidly closer, but the faster the smaller the margin of errors. Flow performance of the economy could be increased until a small disturbance all of a sudden tipped the entire economy.[8] Once this had happened the price system was in complete disorder, price signals misguiding output and investment decisions causing further disorder. A period of some 10 to 20 years was needed to stabilize the price system, and in the meantime productivity and growth performance were down. Permanent damage to the economy could occur in the sense that firms that should have survived in an orderly market regime, were forced to exit. This is one example of the *path dependence* of the model economy.

Price instability, price reliability and efficiency

Efficiency of market coordination largely rests on the reliability of market price and quantity signals as predictors of future prices and quantities. Destabilized (relative) prices, prices that are systematically pegged differently from what a free market would set (regulation), or wedges due to taxes and subsidies distort allocation mechanisms and cause a deterioration in productivity performance of the model economy.

A particularly interesting case is to study the systems response to the price shock that occurs when a regulated price structure is removed and replaced by a free price adjustment. A case in point is the adjustment disorder that centrally planned East European and Russian economies are currently experiencing when being opened up to free market competition. Similar, but more gradual experiences occur when barriers to trade are removed and a common price system imposed on a wider area through competition.

Removing the constraint of regulated prices should generate a long-term improvement in allocative and process efficiency of the economy. However, during the intense period of adjustment when agents are experimenting with price, cost and quantity combinations to find an "equilibrium alignment", macro productivity might very well deteriorate. We have found (through simulation experiments) that this adjustment period is very long, that performance comes down on average, but not very much, but that quantity development is very unstable during the adjustment period. This instability is a parallel to the deficiencies in structural diversity discussed in the previous section.

The macroeconomic effects of three different kinds of price distortions have been analyzed on the model;

1) *tax wedges* in the investment allocation process (Eliasson-Lindberg 1981),
2) *industrial subsidies* (Carlsson 1983a, b, Carlsson-Bergholm-Lindberg 1981) and
(3) *price overshooting*, notably wage overshooting (Eliasson 1977, 1978a, b, 1983, Eliasson-Lindberg 1986).

These experiments fall into two categories, one where price distortions are *permanent*, and one where they are *temporary* and endogenously self correcting. Price overshooting is a temporary price distortion. A seemingly paradoxical result from model experiments is that the faster price adjustments in markets, the more prone to price overshooting the economy and the longer it takes for prices - after a disturbance - to return to normal, cost aligned (equilibrium) rates. The reason is that once the quantities of the model have been affected by "erroneous" price signals, then the entire price and quantity adjustment structure of the economy gets disorderly, and no "rational expectations" algorithms - that we have found - exist that allow the disorganized economic machinery to become dynamically transparent fast. In fact, once significantly disturbed by the cost crisis in the 70s the model economy took more than a decade to get the price system back in order. At the time we "learned that" this was not part of current economic wisdom. Since economists at large expressed disbelief, we were unduly cautious in formulating the results (Eliasson 1978a, b). The long adjustment period has been confirmed by empirical analyses on similarly structured price data (Genberg 1983).

The price adjustment of the Swedish economy was significantly aggravated by the industrial subsidies of the mid-70s, inserting temporary price wedges, especially on the wage setting mechanisms, but also in the mechanisms controlling the allocation of investment. Several different policy scenarios, the actual subsidization scheme being one, were reenacted on the model. The worst outcome in terms of long-term production growth and employment was - as expected - the actual subsidization scheme. The next best scheme would have been to lower wage taxes across the firm population, the total tax reduction being equal to total subsidies. There would have been local, intermediate and traumatic unemployment experiences when crisis firms were shut down, but most unemployed were reemployed in other firms after three to four years. The precision of the model is illustrated by the fact that crisis firms survived until "today" (the time of the experiment) on more or less exactly the "subsidy handout". With 10 percent less all subsidized firms were closed before "today". The best macro outcome came when subsidies where reallocated in favor of high profitability firms, signifying that high profits today increase the probability of a high rate of return tomorrow. Allocating subsidies in favor of firms with fast export growth did not increase macroeconomic growth as much, indicating that rapid export growth is not necessarily a good predictor of future high rates of return and productivity growth.

We thought of an additional scenario, implementing the phasing out of crisis firms more slowly, to smooth the local unemployment situation, but still very much faster than what actually occurred. We thought that some intermediate rate of phase out would be optimal, with a minimum of price disturbances, but were unable, at the time to design the appropriate experiment.

Finally, the allocative effects of the plow back features characterizing corporate income tax systems of most industrial economies were tested on the model (Eliasson-Lindberg 1981). The intention was to evaluate the negative effects on internal rate of return targets and investment allocation of the corporate income "tax wedge". Results were as expected. The tax stimulated retained earnings (as against dividends) in firms where profits had been generated. As long as relative (product) prices did not change, this policy was clearly growth stimulating, since a high rate of return today was on the average a signal of future high rates of return. The slow pivoting of relative prices in favor of engineering firms, but against basic industries compared to an alternative scenario with unchanged relative prices, generated a slow deterioration in macroeconomic growth, and the more so the higher the tax wedge. The reason, of course, was that firms that had become profitable in the past were stimulated by the tax system to plow profits back into now relatively less profitable investments.

This effect became dramatic when we reenacted the cost crisis years of the 70s. As a result of high corporate income taxes basic industries entered the second half of the 70s with new, modern production capacity to face a catastrophic market slump. In retrospect, the best scenario would of course have been to have the resources invested elsewhere. A strong revaluation of the currency or even a floating rate, would probably have helped eliminate some of the temporary inflation profits in basic industries 1973/74 and hence, also reduce investment spending there. However, as we learned from the experiments, *from an economic point of view it was alright to invest in the wrong markets - the actual investment was a minor cost to the economy. The large macroeconomic effects came from carrying on production in the new factories, locking up labor in the wrong industries and significantly increasing the general wage level.* This detrimental effect on economic growth from price wedges that raise the general wage level has been reconfirmed in later experiments. We have in fact found (Eliasson-Lindberg 1986) that the high real interest rate, partly propped up by Swedish exchange controls (Oxelheim 1988) lowers investment and raises profit margin targets in firms. The latter means that wage inflation and wage overshooting tendencies are checked by the discipline of the capital market. (It also means that partial wage setting models, neglecting to account for the influence of the interest rate and the rate of return or profits are misleading.) The negative investment effect is minor, since the allocation of investments is improved by the high interest rate.

Is big bad or good?

Economies of scale is an old problem in economics. The classical static model was phrased in terms of atomistic competition. In "applications" like computable equilibrium models the size of firms is concealed through aggregation, or controlled through convenient assumptions, as in contestable market theory, to overcome the problem that the design of the static general equilibrium model does not naturally accomodate economies of scale or scope on the firm.

Scale introduces the firm as a market imperfection or as a (temporary) monopoly, and requires explicit modeling of markets with competition among the few. In MOSES firms scale effects originate in superior organizational competence (Eliasson 1988c). Competition (among the few) through learning and upgrading of competence, checks excessive monopoly profits and concentration tendencies endogenously.

Size and concentration is the classical problem in industrial organization theory. Facing severe problems of laggard industrial competitiveness a discussion of whether big is good or bad has been carried on in business journals. One argument is that "oversized" firms have become sloppy because of past successes, and can live far too long because they are protected by accumulated financial wealth.

This issue cannot be resolved within the framework of the micro-to-macro model. The model, however, features a competitive dynamic market process, that checks concentration tendencies, which are not matched by superior competitive performance.

Model firms operate as temporary monopolies on the basis of their ability to maintain scale advantages. Scale advantages in turn arise out of their ability to create new competence (innovation) or through rapidly imitating new technology created elsewhere. This is the essence of technological competition and economic growth. Such a model specification requires an explicit market process that checks (bounds) concentration endogenously. This is the needed substitute mechanism for the convexity assumption in the static model.

With no new entry and only exit the model simulation generated a steady concentration of output to a smaller and smaller number of firms, even though this process turned out to be very slow. Concentration is checked by competition which in turn depends on the spread of the Salter curves, the high end producers competing with lower prices to the detriment of the tail end of the Salter curves. In the end the initially superior producers *tend* to take over. New entry, however, prevents the flattening of Salter distributions. And entry is stimulated in markets where monopoly profits are earned (Eliasson 1990b).

Economies of scale can be demonstrated to exhibit superior process performance in existing lines of business, but large firms tend to be less efficient innovators, even though the definition of innovative performance remains to be operationally defined (see Eliasson 1989b). Conventional wisdom would suggest, that allowing scale ("bigness") to take over through forcing low end producers to *exit* would enhance medium-term process efficiency, but reduce the long-term creation of innovative, new best-practice production techniques.

The static antitrust position would be to prevent large scale operators to become monopolists. Increased competition by a larger number of firms would increase efficiency and lower prices, through reducing short-term slack in the economy. This might, however, reduce profits to the extent that innovative activity ceases.

To prevent that, *markets have to be organized such that short-term efficiency and incentives to innovate are balanced* to generate the desired, sustainable rate of growth. We currently do not have a theory in which this balancing occurs endogenously and in which policy parameters are explicit. I have just illustrated, however, that my micro-to-macro model allows this balancing to be achieved through experimenting with various market regime determining parameters. The empirical evidence is pointing in the direction of innovation being more efficient in a small scale organization than in a large one. New technology, furthermore, is making small scale production profitable where huge scale once dominated (e.g. in steel production). The general tendency (Carlsson 1988) among industrial countries - except Sweden - is a lowering of average firm and establishment size. We find that some large and very successful firms, engaged in volume production, shop around in the market for small innovative firms, that have come up with something new in the product range of the large firm (Eliasson 1986c). The reason is that the large firm is organized for efficient large scale volume production, being often an inefficient innovator.

We also find that small units, with high knowledge intensive production, usually engaged in service production tend to separate off from the big firms (Eliasson 1986d). This is one reason for the rapid growth of the business service sector. The increase in capital market efficiency, furthermore, has forced a number of large and not well managed firms to sell off parts or divisions or subsidiaries, illustrating the point made earlier, that organizational change really should be treated as endogenous and market determined. This closes the circle and takes us back to the notion of the experimentally organized economy in which the organizational memory that controls all information processes in the economy develops along a "path" that is endogenously determined by the ongoing dynamic market activity. Until we have managed to work that awareness into economic theory we will, as economists, remain grossly ignorant of the nature of economic growth.

Bibliography

Arrow, K.J. (1959). Toward a Theory of Price Adjustment, in Abramowitz, M et al., *The Allocation of Economic Resources*, Stanford, Calif.

Carlsson, B. (1983a). Industrial Subsidies in Sweden; Macro-Economic Effects and an International Comparison, *The Journal of Industrial Economics*, Vol. XXXII, No. 1, September.

Carlsson, B. (1983b). Industrial Subsidies in Sweden. Simulations on a Micro-to-Macro Model, in *Microeconomics, IUI, Yearbook 1982-83*, Stockholm.

Carlsson, B. (1987). *Investment and Productivity Change in Manufacturing: A Micro-to-Macro Perspective*, IUI Working Paper No. 181, Stockholm.

Carlsson, B. (1988). *The Evolution of Manufacturing Technology and Its Impact on Industrial Structure: An International Study*, IUI Working Paper No. 203. Published in *Small Business Economics*, Vol. 1, No. 1, 21-37, 1989.

Carlsson, B. (1989b). Industrial Dynamics: An overview, in Carlsson.

Carlsson, B. (ed.) (1989b). *Industrial Dynamics*, Kluwer Academic Publishers, Boston/Dordrecht/London.

Carlsson, B., F. Bergholm, T. Lindberg (1981). *Industristödspolitiken och dess inverkan på samhällsekonomin* (Industry Subsidy Policy and its Macroeconomic Impact), IUI, Stockholm.

Carlsson, B., G. Eliasson, I. Nadiri (eds.) (1978). *The Importance of Technology and the Permanence of Industrial Structure*, IUI Conference Reports 1978:2.

Chandler, A.D. Jr. (1977). *The Visible Hand - the Managerial Revolution in American Business*, Harvard University Press, Cambridge Mass. and London.

Coase, R.H. (1937). The Nature of the Firm, *Economica*, Vol. IV (November), 13-16.

Day, R.H., G. Eliasson (eds.) (1986). *The Dynamics of Market Economies*, IUI, Stockholm, North-Holland, Amsterdam.

Day, R.H., T. Groves (1975). *Adaptive Economic Models*, Academic Press, New York.

Eliasson, G. (1976). *Business Economic Planning - Theory, Practice and Comparison*, John Wiley & Sons, London, New York, Sidney, Toronto.

Eliasson, G. (1977). Competition and Market Processes in a Simulation Model of the Swedish Economy, *American Economic Review*, No. 1.

Eliasson, G. (1978a). *A Micro-to-Macro Model of the Swedish Economy*, IUI Conference Reports 1978:1.

Eliasson, G. (1978b). *Relative Price Changes and Industrial Structure - the Norwegian Case*, in Carlsson-Eliasson-Nadiri (eds.), 1978:2.

Eliasson, G. (1980). *Electronics, Technical Change and Total Economic Performance*, IUI Research Report No. 9, Stockholm.

Eliasson, G. (1982). Electronics, Economic Growth and Employment - Revolution or Evolution, in Giersch (ed.), *Emerging Technologies, Consequences for Economic Growth. Structural Change and Employment*, Kiel.

Eliasson, G. (1983). On the Optimal Rate of Structural Adjustment, in Eliasson, Sharefkin, Ysander.

Eliasson, G. (1984). Micro Heterogeneity of Firms and the Stability of Industrial Growth, *Journal of Economic Behavior & Organization*, Vol. 5, Nos 3-4. Also in Day, R.H, G. Eliasson (eds.) (1986).

Eliasson, G. (1985). *The Firm and Financial Markets in the Swedish Micro-to-Macro Model - Theory, Model and Verification*, IUI, Stockholm.

Eliasson, G. (1986a). A Note on the Stability of Economic Organizational Forms and the Importance of Human Capital, in Day, R.H., G. Eliasson (eds.).

Eliasson, G. (1986b). The Economics of Institutions and Markets - The Organization of Research at IUI, in *IUI Yearbook 1986-1987, The Economics of Institutions and Markets*, Stockholm.

Eliasson, G. (1986c). International Competition, Productivity Change and the Organization of Production, in De Jong, H.W, W.G. Shepherd.

Eliasson, G. (1986d). *Innovative Change, Dynamic Market Allocation and Long-term Stability of Economic Growth*, IUI Working Paper No. 156, Stockholm.

Eliasson, G. (1987). *Technological Competition and Trade in the Experimentally Organized Economy*, IUI Research Report No. 32, Stockholm.

Eliasson, G. (1988a). Schumpeterian Innovation, Market Structure and the Stability of Industrial Development. Published in Hanusch, H. (ed.) *Evolutionary Economics, Applications of Schumpeter's Ideas*, Cambridge University Press.

Eliasson, G. (1988b). Ägare, entreprenörer och kapitalmarknadens organisation - en teoretisk presentation och översikt (Owners, Entrepreneurs and the Organization of Capital Markets - Theory and Empirical Research); Chapter II in Örtengren et al.

Eliasson, G. (1988c). *The Firm as a Competent Team*, IUI Working Paper No. 207, Stockholm, published in *Journal of Economic Behavior & Organization*, July 1990.

Eliasson, G. (1989a). The Dynamics of Supply and Economic Growth, in Carlsson, B (ed.), 1989, *Industrial Dynamics*, Kluwer Academic Publishers, Boston/Dordrecht/London.

Eliasson, G. (1989b). *Modeling Long-term Macroeconomic Growth as a Micro-based, Path Dependent, Experimentally Organized Economic Process*, IUI Working paper No. 220, Stockholm.

Eliasson, G. (1990a). The Knowledge-Based Information Economy, in Eliasson-Fölster-Lindberg-Pousette-Taymaz (1990), *The Knowledge Based Information Economy*, IUI, Stockholm.

Eliasson, G. (1990b). *Deregulation, Innovative Entry and Structural Diversity as a Source of Stable and Rapid Economic Growth*, forthcoming IUI Working paper.

Eliasson, G., T. Lindberg (1981). Allocation and Growth Effects of Corporate Income Taxes, in Eliasson-Södersten (eds.).

Eliasson, G., T. Lindberg (1986). *Economic Growth and the Dynamics of Wage Determination - a Micro Simulation Study of the Stability Consequences of Deficient Variation in Factor Prices and Micro Structures*, IUI Working Paper No. 170, Stockholm.

Eliasson, G., M. Sharefkin, B.C. Ysander (eds.) (1983). *Policy Making in a Disorderly World Economy*, IUI Conference Reports 1983:1, Stockholm.

Eliasson, G., J. Södersten (eds.) (1981). *Business Taxation Finance and Firm Behavior*, IUI Conference Reports, 1981:1, Stockholm.

Genberg, H. (1983). *Overshooting and Asymmetries in the Transmission of Foreign Price Shocks to the Swedish Economy*, in Eliasson-Sharefkin-Ysander.

Hanusch, H. (ed.) (1988). *Evolutionary Economics - Applications of Schumpeter's Ideas*, Cambridge University Press, Cambridge, New York etc.

Von Hayek, F.A. (1940). Socialist Calculation, *Economica*, Vol. VII, No. 26.

Von Hayek, F.A. (1945). The Use of Knowledge in Society, *American Economic Review*, Vol. XXXV, No. 4, 519-530.

De Jong, H.W. (1989b). Free versus Controlled Competition, Chapter 12 in Carlsson.

De Jong, H.W., W.G. Shepherd (1986). *Mainstreams in Industrial Organization*, Book I, Kluwer Academic Publishers, Dordrecht/Boston/Lancaster.

Marshak, J. (1954). Towards an Economic Theory of Organization and Information, in Thrall-Coombs-Davies (eds.), *Decision Processes*, Wiley, New York.

Marshak, J. (1968). Economics of Inquiring, Communicating, Deciding, *American Economic Review; Papers and Proceedings*, Vol. 58, No. 2, 1-18.

McCall, J.J. (1982). *The Economics of Information and Uncertainty*, University of Chicago Press, New York.

Myrdal, G. (1927). *Prisbildningsproblemet och föränderligheten*, Uppsala and Stockholm.

Örtengren, J. et al. *Expansion, avveckling och företagsvärdering i svensk industri* (Expansion, Exit and the Valuation of Firms in Swedish Manufacturing), IUI, Stockholm.

Oxelheim, L. (1988). *Finansiell integration* - en studie av svenska marknaders internationella beroende, IUI, Stockholm.

Pelikan, P. (1986). Why Private Enterprise? Towards a Dynamic Analysis of Economic Institutions and Policies, in *IUI Yearbook 1986-1987*, The Economics of Institutions and Markets, Stockholm.

Pelikan, P. (1989). *Markets as Instrument of Evolution of Structures*, Paper prepared for IUIs 50'th Anniversary Symposium, November 15-17, Stockholm.

Radner, R. (1986). The Internal Economies of Large Firms, *Economic Journal* (January).

Schumpeter, J.A. (1942). *Capitalism, Socialism and Democracy*, Harper & Row, New York.

Shannon, O.E., W. Weaver (1949). *The Mathematical Theory of Communication*, University of Illinois Press, Urbana.

Shubik, M. (1959). Edgeworth Market Games, in Tucker, A.V., D.R. Luce (eds.), *Contributions to the Theory of Games*, Vol. IV, 267-278, Princeton University Press, Princeton.

Shubik, M. (1960). Simulation of the Industry and the Firm, *American Economic Review*, Vol. L, No. 5.

Shubik, M. (1975). The General Equilibrium Model is Incomplete and not Adequate for the Reconciliation of Micro and Macroeconomic Theory, *Kyklos*, Vol. 28, 545-573.

Stigler, G.J. (1961). The Economics of Information, *Journal of Political Economy*, Vol. LXIX, No. 3.

Svennilson, I. (1938). *Ekonomisk planering* (Economic Planning), Almqvist & Wiksell, Uppsala.

Notes

1. My essay draws directly on several studies at the IUI, most importantly a forthcoming IUI book under the title *The Knowledge Based Information Economy*, but also Eliasson, *Technological Competition and Trade in The Experimentally Organized Economy*, IUI Research Report No. 33, Stockholm 1987, Eliasson, *The Firm as A Competent Team*, IUI Working Paper No. 207, 1988, Eliasson, *Modeling Long-Term Macroeconomic Growth*, IUI Working Paper No. 220, 1989 and Eliasson, *The Economics of Coordination, Innovation, Selection and Learning* - a theoretical framework for Research in Industrial Economics, IUI Working Paper No. 235, 1989.
2. See Carlsson 1988, *The Evolution of Manufacturing Technology and Its Impact on Industrial Structure, An international study*, IUI Working Paper No. 203.
3. See *De svenska storföretagen* (The Swedish giant corporations), IUI, Stockholm 1985 and Eliasson (1986c).
4. It is interesting to study the macroeconomic consequences of differently tuned competitive regimes simulated on the IUI micro-to-macro model. See e.g. Eliasson 1984, 1989b, 1990b.
5. Eliasson G., *The Knowledge Base of an Industrial Economy*, IUI Research Report No. 33, 1988.
6. Remember (see above) the difficulties of coding even simple machining and assembly sequences at the workshop level.
7. The coefficients have been calibrated such that the model tracks historic macroeconomic variables. See Eliasson (1985, chapter VIII).
8. This is one way of explaining the "collapse" of the economies of advanced industrial nations in the wake of the oil crises of the 70s (Eliasson 1983). Excess demand policies in the postwar period speeded up flow performance, reducing diversity of structure and introducing structural rigidities, thus making the economies increasingly sensitive to disturbances of the price coordination mechanisms.

4 GROWTH OF LARGE ENTERPRISES AND THEIR MARKET ENVIRONMENTS*

RICHARD E. CAVES

1. Introduction

The study of competition in its European setting has traditionally emphasized dynamic processes and institutions rather than equilibrium models (de Jong, 1986). One prominent subject has been the growth of large firms, its causes, and its contribution to the concentration of control overall as well as in particular markets. De Jong (1988) pointed out the considerable increase that had occurred during 1962-1986 in the largest firms' share of gross domestic product in economies other than the United States. He mentioned a number of factors contributing to the relative growth of the largest firms, such as diversifying mergers and changes in the relative sizes of their base sectors and in their competitive positions within these sectors. He also noted the close ties between the growth rates of large firms and of their national economies, which in the 1970s led the large European firms to gain on their mature British counterparts (Jacquemin and de Jong, 1977, pp. 97-101).

Another process studied extensively has been the turnover of large firms. Concern has been voiced over a possible decline in their turnover, implying that large size might somehow be yielding increased invulnerability to displacement by competitors. Turnover was reported to decline in both the United States (Stonebraker, 1979) and United Kingdom (Hannah and Kay, 1977, p. 103). The turnover of large companies, like the increase in their shares of economic activity, raises the question of the reliance of their positions on the fates of the economic bases (sectoral and national markets) from which they operate.

This paper addresses the turnover process by observing how the changing positions of large firms based outside the United States are related to the growth rates and structures of the markets in which they operate. The growth or success of large firms can be studied in both the macroeconomic context of national development and the microeconomic context of market

* Grateful acknowledgment is made to Denise Neumann for research assistance and the Division of Research, Harvard Business School, for support.

competition. Robert Rowthorn's *International Big Business 1957-1967* (1971) emphasized the macroeconomic environment. Rowthorn found that the largest firms' growth rates were related to the growth rates of their national economies but with that link weakened by foreign trade and investment. The microeconomic context embraces a large literature founded on random processes as an explanation for the concentration of firms. The random-process literature has emphasized tests of the assumption underlying Gibrat's Law of Proportionate Effect (the independence of firms' sizes and growth rates) or its main prediction (lognormality of firm sizes). With a few notable exceptions such as Nelson and Winter (1978), the statistical processes presumed to govern the distribution of firm sizes have not been linked to the structural traits of markets in which that growth was occurring.[1]

The set of large industrial firms analyzed here is *Fortune's* list of the largest 300 based outside the United States in 1973 and 1988. These are classified by country of origin and by sector, and for each sector the proportional change is observed of the share of each country's firms in total sales by *Fortune* 300 firms in that sector. The resulting rate of share change for each country and sector is then related to the growth of real output in that country, both within the sector and overall. This simple relation serves to revisit the questions addressed by Rowthorn (1971), de Jong, and others. How closely changes in large firms' positions are related to the growth of their national "platforms" then is probed to test further hypotheses. We expect that closeness to vary with characteristics of the national economy and the sector's technology and market structure. These hypotheses are tested by means of differences in the magnitudes and goodness of fit of slope coefficients.

2. Analytical Framework

How can we think about the linkage between national economic growth and the growth of the economy's largest firms? Growth rates of firm and nation are the same if national economic expansion entails adding resources in identical proportions to every existing firm's flow of inputs. Alternatively the output of a single sector and of each of its member firms may grow at the same rate. The difference between the sectoral and national reference cases points to the possibility that large firms' growth rates differ because their base sectors grow at different rates and thus account for changing shares of the nation's resources. Besides that, we focus on three other sources of divergence between the growth rates of leading firms and of their home sectors or nations:

1) Market growth changes the number or size distribution of firms. Many studies show a close relation between the net entry of firms and the industry's rate of growth.[2] A large firm's growth rate falls short of its market's growth to the extent that entrants recruit the additional resources entering the industry (Hause and Du Rietz, 1984). Large firms' growth rates also diverge from their market's growth when they gain or lose shares in competition with their existing market rivals. Some market models offer specific predictions about changes in (arbitrary) initial shares; the familiar Cournot model predicts reversion of competing firms' sizes toward the mean, while other models predict the enlargement of a dominant position (Ghemawat, forthcoming).

2) A firm's growth rate can diverge from the growth rate of its platform because the firm's activities spill beyond the platform that represents its principal operating base. Industry shipments differ from domestic purchases due to exports and imports, and the growth of a large firm's consolidated sales can differ from the growth of its national economy or market because of changes in its nondomestic sales (exports or foreign subsidiaries); in the case of the national platform, changes in import penetration are also a source of discrepancy.[3] Large firms are diversified in product as well as geographic space. Product-market diversification severs the link between the firm's growth and its base market's growth in the same way as geographic diversification (trade and foreign investment).

3) Growth rates of large firms and their markets can diverge due to random factors not (primarily) related to the mode of competition. This possibility is the domain of the random-process models mentioned above that interject variance due to stochastic elements between the growth rates of large firms and of other firms sharing their platforms. The attraction of the random-process model lies in the strong predictions that it obtains from the assumption that firms' growth rates are independent of their initial sizes: the concentration of the size distribution increases with the variance of the growth-rate distribution and with the autocorrelation of successive disturbances. Unlike the many papers stimulated by these predictions, we shall not be concerned with

testing directly either the assumption or the predictions that it supports. Rather, we draw on the approach for hypotheses (developed below) about the probable divergence of large firms' growth rates from the growth rates of their platforms.

3. Growth of Large Firms and Their Platforms

Like previous researchers on large firms' growth we draw upon *Fortune* magazine's annual listings of the largest enterprises. Wishing to focus on competition in Europe, we made the somewhat arbitrary decision to exclude United States firms and analyze only large firms from other industrial nations. *Fortune's* list of the largest non-U.S. firms has been expanded over the years from 50 to 500 enterprises. We chose to work with lists of the largest 300, which have been compiled since 1973. By observing their changes in position between 1973 and 1988, we pick up the effects of turbulence and change that followed the collapse of the Bretton Woods system of fixed exchange rates (early 1970s) and the oil shock (1973).[4] This turbulence extended to the flows of international trade and restrictions thereon, providing a desirably stringent test of the degree to which the relative sizes of the largest enterprises depend on the fates of their national platforms. Furthermore, the period is long enough that sustained differences in markets' growth rates should assert their effects.

Fortune also provides total sales and other main financial data for each firm converted to U.S. dollars at the current exchange rate. It classifies each company as to country of origin and assigns it to one of 26 base industries in manufacturing, a classification system conforming to the two-digit level of the U.S. Standard Industrial Classification with a few three-digit categories broken out. Nonmanufacturing firms were omitted from our analysis to facilitate controlling for market-structure characteristics not readily defined outside of manufacturing. After some hesitation we retained in the list non-U.S. firms that are subsidiaries of U.S. multinational enterprises. For our purposes their reactions to market opportunities should not exhibit first-order differences from those of independent enterprises, and we feared that an attempt to purge subsidiaries might cause errors from failing to identify some control linkages.

In each year we consolidated firms classified to the same country and industry and expressed sales for each industry-country cell (S_{ic}) as a fraction of sales of all *Fortune* 300 companies classified to that industry ($S_{i.}$). A rate of change of each share was then calculated as:

$$GSIC = 2(S_{ic}88/S_{i.}88 - S_{ic}73/S_{i.}73)/(S_{ic}88/S_{i.}88 + S_{ic}73/S_{i.}73)$$

GSIC is affected both by the entry of firms into and their departure from the list, and by differential growth of firms on the list in both years. GSIC is of course not the growth rate of the individual firm or of firms classified to a given sector-country cell. If we relate it directly to growth rates of sector and country platforms, the regression coefficients will not have any direct interpretation. Therefore those growth rates are expressed as deviations from appropriate sample averages so that their units are roughly comparable to those of GSIC and the regression coefficients can be given approximate direct interpretations.[5] When a firm moves into (out of) the *Fortune* 300, we set its 1972 (1987) sales value at zero. This is of course a source of noise in the regession analysis through overstatement of the change in the firm's position. However, we preferred it to attempting to locate data on firms before they entered the list or after they departed.

The breadth of the platforms from which these firms operate can receive various definitions, and we selected two that bracket the plausible choices. The first is the sector as defined in *Fortune's* classification, for which real output indexes can be obtained from United Nations sources.[6] Indexes of real output were used to construct a measure of the growth of industry output (GIND) parallel to GSIC, namely twice the change in the index divided by the sum of the beginning and ending index values. The period covered is 1972 to 1987, the years to which the data accompanying the 1973 and 1988 *Fortune* lists actually pertain. The broad measure of the growth of the firm's platform is simply the growth of real gross domestic product for 1972 to 1987. This rate, GCO, is expressed in the same proportional form as GSIC and GIND. GIND and GCO were then finally expressed as deviations from sample averages.

Because some countries contribute many large firms to the *Fortune* 300, others only one, a question arose whether to retain all available country/-industry cells in the analysis. Nothing in the research design requires a complete enumeration, and the adequacy of data for GIND becomes increasingly problematical as one proceeds beyond the OECD countries. Therefore we chose to retain only those countries shown in Table 1. The omitted countries not only contribute to just one or two cells but also tend to move into or out of the *Fortune* list, making their observations particularly noisy in the regression analysis that follows.

Table 1 *Number of large companies and sectoral and national growth rates by country*

Country	Number of companies		Mean GSIC[a]	Mean GIND[a]	Real GDP growth
	1973	1988			%
Australia	4	5	0.079	0.072	44.8
Belgium	6	3	-0.929	0.146	31.2
Canada	15	14	0.094	0.335	54.0
France	31	27	-0.540	0.048	34.7
Italy	9	6	-0.448	0.296	45.2
Japan	85	96	0.291	0.421	57.9
Luxembourg	1	1	0.542	0.345	38.3
Netherlands	9	8	-0.528	0.174	32.5
South Korea	0	9	2.000	1.560	112.6
Spain	6	5	-0.319	0.236	36.8
Sweden	11	12	0.403	0.088	29.6
Switzerland	8	11	0.695	0.066	17.1
United Kingdom	55	45	-0.239	0.149	30.8
West Germany	40	32	-0.501	0.151	29.9
Total[b]	280	274			

[a] Unweighted average of growth rates expressed as the difference between final and initial size divided by one-half of the sum of initial and final sizes.

[b] Totals are less than 300 because of the omission of enterprises classified to extractive sector and to countries omitted from the analysis.

Before exploring the relation of GSIC to GIND and GCO we describe the sample of companies that was obtained. The 280 out of 300 companies retained in the analysis for 1973 fell into 127 industry/country cells. For 1988 274 companies were classified to 134 cells. Table 1 lists the countries represented and shows the number of sectors represented in each year. Also shown are the average rates of change of the sectoral shares claimed by each country's large firms, the (unweighted) average rate of growth of its manufacturing sectors, and its rate of growth of real GDP. The table confirms a general association between a country's size and its number of large enterprises and between national economic growth and changes in both the number of large companies and their shares. Although the correlation between mean sectoral and GDP growth rates is high (0.949), some independence between the two is evident. Most countries' manufacturing sectors grew a good deal slower than their GDP levels, especially the "Dutch disease" countries such as Australia and the Netherlands; the fast-growing Asian economies were the exceptions.

With the statistical materials in hand we analyze the relation of large companies' relative positions to the growth rates of their platforms. The framework set forth above raises several questions. First, how tightly do changes in the positions of large firms depend on the respective growth rates of their platforms? Sources of discrepancy between company and platform growth were identified above, but the fact of their existence leaves open the degree to which they actually liberate the fates of large firms from those of their operations bases. At the simplest level, this question is addressed by examining the significance of the slope coefficients in the regression:

$$GSIC = a_0 + a_1 GIND + a_2 GCO + u$$

Second, does more explanatory power repose in the broadly or narrowly measured platform (country or sector)? Rowthorn (1971, pp. 66-73), worked with value added in manufacturing and mining as his broad measure of the national platform. Although he did not seek to answer exactly this question, his analysis clearly suggests that the relation between a large firm's growth and the growth rate of its broadly defined platform is a close one. When Rowthorn (1971, pp. 41-58) regressed firm growth rates on sector and country dummies, country effects accounted for the bulk of the variance, and not much industry-country interaction was evident. Recent evidence supports the expected dominance of country effects by showing a convergence of industry productivity levels and factor-cost structures among the industrial countries (Dollar and Wolff, 1988; Mohktari and Ressekh, 1989), implying the absence of strong comparative-advantage differences among countries to create variance in the growth rates of a country's individual sectors. We compare regressions of GSIC on the two exogenous growth rates together and separately:

$$\underset{}{GSIC} = \underset{(0.81)}{0.094} + \underset{(2.08)}{0.802}\ GIND + \underset{(1.01)}{0.878}\ GCO \qquad \bar{R}^2 = 0.110$$

$$\text{GSIC} = \underset{(0.94)}{0.108} + \underset{(3.91)}{1.075}\ \text{GIND} \qquad \bar{R}^2 = 0.110$$

$$\text{GSIC} = \underset{(0.12)}{0.006} + \underset{(3.12)}{1.899}\ \text{GCO} \qquad \bar{R}^2 = 0.059$$

Contrary to Rowthorn's findings GIND has more explanatory power than GCO. Each taken by itself is highly significant; although the explanatory power of either (as expected) is low, the relation based on 116 observations is significant overall at the 1 percent level. The large coefficient of GSIC on GCO in the third equation suggests that fast-growing countries in this sample have had especially fast-growing manufacturing sectors, no surprise with Korea and Japan attaining the highest growth rates.

The sector and country growth rates are correlated, of course, and to establish their respective influence we defined GDIF = GIND - GCO and substituted GDIF for GIND in the model:

$$\text{GSIC} = \underset{(0.81)}{0.094} + \underset{(2.08)}{0.802}\ \text{GDIF} + \underset{(2.54)}{1.680}\ \text{GCO} \qquad \bar{R}^2 = 0.110$$

The distinct influences of country and sector are shown both to be significant when their overlap is eliminated.

4. Differences among Countries

The dependence of large companies' fates on the development of their national platforms should vary among countries. Several distinctions among countries hold interest:

1) The larger the country, in general the smaller is the proportion of its economic activity represented by international transactions. We expect companies' fortunes to be linked more tightly to their national markets in large industrial countries than in small, open ones.[7] With the United States excluded from the analysis, however, variations in the size and openness of the other OECD countries may not be large enough to expose the effect. We formed a dummy variable (DLG1) set equal to one for France, Japan, United Kingdom, and West Germany, zero otherwise, and a second dummy (DLG2) set equal to one for mid-size industrialized countries Canada, Netherlands, and Italy, zero otherwise.

In Table 2, equations 2.1 and 2.2, we allow slope and intercept shifts for the coefficients of GDIF and GCO. In 2.1 the dependence of GSIC on GDIF is statistically significant (one-tail test) for the large countries but for no others. In 2.2 the pattern is similar but less decisive. The countries designated by DLG2 are not distinct from the omitted group.

Table 2 Regression models testing effects of differences among countries

$$2.1\quad \text{GSIC} = \underset{(1.83)}{0.412} + \underset{(1.71)}{0.935}\,\text{GDIFDLG1} + \underset{(0.06)}{0.058}\,\text{GDIFDLG2} + \underset{(0.86)}{0.601}\,\text{GDIFOTHER}$$

$$+ \underset{(2.27)}{1.734}\,\text{GCO} - \underset{(1.39)}{0.386}\,\text{DLG1} - \underset{(1.62)}{0.565}\,\text{DLG2} \qquad \bar{R}^2 = 0.105$$

$$2.2\quad \text{GSIC} = \underset{(1.84)}{0.402} + \underset{(1.96)}{0.812}\,\text{GDIF} + \underset{(1.82)}{2.224}\,\text{GCODLG1} + \underset{(1.31)}{3.557}\,\text{GCODLG2}$$

$$+ \underset{(1.48)}{1.253}\,\text{GCOOTHER} - \underset{(1.38)}{0.386}\,\text{DLG1} - \underset{(1.63)}{0.579}\,\text{DLG2} \qquad \bar{R}^2 = 0.108$$

$$2.3\quad \text{GSIC} = \underset{(2.54)}{0.470} + \underset{(1.84)}{0.963}\,\text{GDIFDEC} + \underset{(1.360)}{0.755}\,\text{GDIFOTHER} + \underset{(0.84)}{0.683}\,\text{GCO}$$

$$- \underset{(2.46)}{0.692}\,\text{DEC} \qquad \bar{R}^2 = 0.149$$

$$2.4\quad \text{GSIC} = \underset{(0.70)}{0.089} + \underset{(0.31)}{0.352}\,\text{GDIFJAPAN} + \underset{(2.06)}{0.877}\,\text{GDIFOTHER} + \underset{(0.88)}{1.682}\,\text{GCOJAPAN}$$

$$+ \underset{(2.12)}{1.593}\,\text{GCOOTHER} \qquad \bar{R}^2 = 0.095$$

2) Since its formation during the 1960s the European Community's (EC) common market is known to have promoted increased intra-industry trade and foreign investment among EC-based firms. It created opportunities for successful enterprises to break through into operations on much greater scales uncoupled from the confines of their base markets (Owen, 1983). We therefore hypothesize that the positions of firms

based on EC countries (for this period, the original six plus Britain) were less closely tied to their national markets than were those of other countries. We formed the dummy variable DEC, set equal to one for EC members and zero for others. In equation 2.3 the hypothesis is not confirmed for GDIF, and it also fails when the treatment is applied to GCO (not shown).

3) Because of its extraordinary rate of development Japan and its large firms automatically call for a test of differential behavior. Because Japanese *Fortune* 300 firms appeared in 20 industries in 1973 (21 in 1988), we have some statistical leverage on the question. The dummy DJAPAN is set equal to one for Japanese cells, zero for others. In equation 2.4 GDIF takes a different slope for Japan, and the dummy on GCO functions as an intercept shift. The growth of Japan's successful large firms has apparently been less closely tied to their sectors' growth rates than have the growth rates of other countries' large firms.

We note another hypothesis that is important though infeasible to test. The more competitive the national economy, it has been suggested (e.g., Prais, 1976, pp. 150-155), the less persistent should be the success of any one large company. Concern was expressed by de Jong (1989) that the increasing incidence of controls within the European Community is freezing the existing structure of large firms and deterring the influx of new enterprises. A significant line of reseach has sought to test this hypothesis by investigating the persistence of abnormal profitability in large companies.[8] It has generally failed to find strong intercountry differences. This conclusion, coupled with the difficulty of identifying a reliable structural indicator of an economy's competitiveness, caused us reluctantly to lay this hypothesis aside.

5. Differences among Sectors

If countries' characteristics can affect the turnover of the largest firms, so can those of the industries in which they are based. We are interested here not in shifts of technology, tastes, or comparative advantage that cause differential growth rates of sectoral outputs within countries; these are controlled by the variable GDIF. Rather, we consider how differences in the structures of markets affect the degree to which the individual large firm's growth is tied to or liberated from the growth of its national market. The analytical reference point is the random process model, noted above, with the variance of the distribution of firms' random drawings assumed to depend on elements of market structure.

As we noted above, in the random-process model independence of a firm's growth and initial size and an absence of serial correlation in firms' "draws" of growth rates suffice to predict steadily rising concentration. This prediction holds even if there is also a tendency toward regression to the mean among the distribution's outliers (Kalecki, 1945). The expected level of concentration increases with the variance of growth rates and the magnitudes of their serial correlation (Ijiri and Simon, 1977, pp. 159-165), and of course would also be increased (reduced) if mean growth rates are positively (negatively) correlated with initial size.

These propositions are relevant to explaining why some sectors, given whatever constraints of minimum efficient scale set lower bounds on firms' sizes, evolve higher levels of concentration than others. Our objective is not to explain sector-level concentration or what sectors are represented among the largest firms, however, but to understand how closely the (already) largest firms' growth rates are aligned with the mean growth rates of their sectors. Assume that the variance of firms' growth rates in a research-intensive sector is higher than in one based on a mature technology. For one period of time any particular firm in the high-technology industry, including its largest, is more likely to draw a growth rate exceeding any given divergence from the industry mean. It is thus less well predicted by that mean, which corresponds to the growth rate for its sector as a whole.

Other predictions of this sort can be advanced. The variance of growth rates for a sample of firms has often been found to decrease with their initial sizes (Singh and Whittington, 1975). That relation (cet. par.) reduces the potential divergence of large firms' growth rates from their sector's mean. Competitive conditions matter for this relation, as Nelson and Winter (1978) pointed out. The more aggressively does a firm compete to exploit the advantage of a "good" drawing, the more does its size increase; conversely, a leading firm disinclined to spoil an oligopolistic market will hold back on the maximal pursuit of its opportunity, which behavior contributes to a negative relation between the variance of growth rates and the sizes of firms. Finally, the higher (more convex) are the adjustment costs associated with changing a firm's scale or market share, the less will the maximum efficient growth rate for firms in the sector diverge from the sector's average.

The following market-structure elements can be linked to differences in these variances:

1) Research and development activities represent a pure type of random factor (Nelson and Winter, 1978), and the proposition's force is readily seen in the present-day large or dominant firms that seized their leading positions on the basis of innovations, perhaps discovered long ago. The positive correlation between the long-run progressiveness of various United States industries and the levels of concentration that prevail in them (Phillips, 1956) supports the proposition. To measure research-intensity and other structural traits of sectors we employ United States data, as representing the experience of the nation with the most successful long-run track record for industrial development as also as exogenous to the growth patterns of the companies in our sample. The specific variable employed is the ratio of company-financed research and development outlays to sales for all lines of business classified to the sector, 1977 (RDS). We expect the fates of large companies to be predicted less well by the growth of their industries in research-intensive sectors.

2) An analogous source of variance in success lies in the potential inherent in a market for the firm to develop a durable goodwill asset or first-mover advantage on the basis of some brand name or product reputation. This case clearly overlaps with that of research and development, because the goodwill asset is often based on some sort of innovation, possibly in marketing or the configuration of product attributes rather than in any technological sense. Sutton (forthcoming) demonstrated the extent to which the structures of differentiated food-products markets reflect firms' past successes in breaking out of market equilibria in which the number of competitors was tied only to the effective size of the market. These market situations are, from another perspective, the ones identified with product-differentiation barriers to entry in the literature of industrial organization. The ratio of media advertising to total sales (ADS) for the sector in the United States captures this influence.

3) Closely related to the preceding two forces is the incidence of foreign direct investment, which serves prominently to allow firms to maximize

the value of proprietary intangible assets (product innovations, brand names, etc.) by means not only of home production and exports but also by administrative coordination of production facilities located in foreign markets. Empirical research on multinational enterprise makes it clear that the incidence of foreign investment will be highly correlated among industries with the extent of R&D and of the sales-promotion activities that generate and sustain goodwill assets. The question is whether a sector's revealed opportunities for foreign investment, given these inducing factors, increase the variance of opportunities and predict a further decoupling of large firms' fortunes from general developments on their platforms. The variable used is global sales by subsidiaries of U.S. enterprises classified to the sector as a percentage of total shipments by the U.S. domestic industry, 1977 (FDI).

4) Capital-intensive technologies should (other things equal) reduce the variance of firms' fortunes and tighten the relation between firms' sizes or market positions and the sizes of their base markets. If firms' levels of revenue productivity depend on the performance of capital goods bought at arm's length from a supplying industry, there is little reason why those levels should vary except due to vintage effects, which are themselves tied to (proxied by?) the growth of the base market. Learning by doing is important in capital-intensive process industries, but firms' apparent inability to preserve it from appropriation (Lieberman, 1984) drains the potential it would otherwise have for generating turnover among leading firms. Several studies of the determinants of market structure suggest that the variance of firm sizes tends to be small in industries limited to few member companies by scale economies in production. A binding minimum efficient size can itself account for this pattern, but either diseconomies of large scale or the infeasibility of rapid bursts of growth by the firm may also contribute. We employ the variable gross book value of capital stock divided by total annual payroll for U.S. business units classified to the sector, 1977 (K/L).

5) The constraint on the divergence of company and industry growth may come not from large plant scales and the costs of adjusting them but from the scales of business organization that are efficient in an industry. The fact that the variance of firms' growth rates decreases with their absolute sizes (Singh and Whittington, 1975) implies a closer

alignment of firm and market growth in large-firm industries. Company size is measured by the estimated size of total dollar sales by the enterprise accounting for the U.S. industry's median dollar of sales, 1977, when firms are ranked from largest to smallest (SIZE). Another measure is the proportion of the U.S. industry's shipments accounted for by the 456 largest U.S. companies that were required to report to the Federal Trade Commission's Line of Business program, 1977 (LOB). The influence of LOB may be ambiguous, however, because it is also associated with the diversification of firms active in an industry.

6) Other things equal, the competitiveness of a market is likely to affect the variance of growth rates of large firms. With Cournot rivalry the higher is the share of the largest firm, the more does its pursuit of some advantage or opportunity face the hazard of driving down market price and its marginal profitability. Considerations of spoiling the market thus can attenuate the variance of the growth rates of large firms. Also, one mode of cooperative behavior among large firms is to adopt reaction functions that maintain constant market shares (Osborne, 1976). The common measure of the fraction of industry shipments accounted for by the largest four companies (C4) is employed. Taken from the United States for 1977, it should apply to industries in other countries as well on the basis of Pryor's (1972) findings.[9] Where C4 is high, a firm's growth should be tied to its sector's more tightly and/or with a lower slope coefficient.

The market-structure variables just set forth are all continuous. They can be integrated in several ways into the model employed in this paper. We can use the continuous variable to sort industries into groups above or below the variable's mean value, then analyze differences in coefficients and significance levels in the same manner employed for difference among countries. Or the continuous market-structure variables can be used directly in interactive specifications. In practice the former procedure provided much more insight and will be reported below. It yields a direct indication whether the explanatory power of sectoral growth for large companies' shares is less where structural conditions liberate the typical firm's growth potential from the growth of its competitors.

It also allows the comparison of slope coefficients of GSIC on GDIF for high and low values of the structural variable, although no clear prediction pertains. Consider high-R&D and low-R&D industries. The typical firm's growth should be more independent of average experience in high-R&D industries, and thus the t-statistic lower. If the typical firm's success is uncorrelated with its initial size, we should also expect the slope coefficient to be lower for high-R&D industries. If the largest firms in the high-R&D industries were also the most successful over the period of observation, however, the slope coefficient could be larger. Thus, we take notice of the ranks of slope coefficients as well as t-statistics.

Table 3 shows the results of allowing the coefficient of GDIF to vary between sectors with values of each structural variable above and below its mean (an intercept shift is also included).[10]

Table 3 *Regression models showing effect of market-structure differences on dependence of large firms' growth on sectoral growth*

Equation No.	Structural variable (S)	Coefficient of GDIF		Coefficient of GCO	Intercept	$\bar{R}^2$
		S high	S low			
3.1	RDS	0.235 (0.45)	1.119 (1.88)	1.738 (2.64)	0.292 (1.20)	0.120
3.2	ADS	1.801 (1.12)	0.695 (1.70)	1.860 (2.77)	0.393 (1.21)	0.107
3.3	FDI	0.494 (1.08)	1.527 (1.96)	1.789 (2.71)	-0.021 (0.08)	0.106
3.4	K/L	1.085 (1.91)	0.531 (0.97)	2.008 (2.87)	0.474 (2.02)	0.128
3.5	SIZE	0.520 (0.93)	0.972 (1.85)	1.724 (2.61)	0.087 (0.37)	0.100
3.6	LOB	0.689 (1.56)	1.564 (1.73)	1.866 (2.81)	-0.452 (1.72)	0.119
3.7	C4	0.589 (1.14)	1.378 (2.17)	1.785 (2.70)	-0.310 (1.26)	0.112
3.8	DIV	0.821 (1.46)	0.698 (1.34)	1.702 (2.58)	-0.207 (0.87)	0.102

Consider first the related structural variables RDS, ADS, and FDI, for which results appear in equations 3.1, 3.2, and 3.3. In each case the link between firm and sector growth is statistically significant (one-tail test) in sectors with low values of these variables but not for high values. The slope coefficients themselves exhibit the same ranking except for ADS, and that exception disappears when the regressor GIND replaces GDIF.[11] Next consider K/L, SIZE, and LOB (equations 3.4, 3.5, and 3.6) each representing a different form of sunkenness or inflexibility that should tie the firm's growth to its sector's more closely when these variables take high values. The hypothesis is supported for K/L but not for SIZE or LOB. The hypothesis about adjustment speeds and costs in sectors with scale economies and sunk assets is at best weakly supported.[12] We wondered if we had erred in neglecting the influence of diversification, which liberates large firms' growth rates from their base markets more than it does for specialized small firms' growth. With some qualms (because corporate diversification patterns seem to differ strongly among countries), we formed a measure of diversified sales as a fraction of total sales for companies classified to the U.S. industry (DIV). We estimated equation 3.8, which fails to confirm the expectation of a weaker tie of companies' changes to their base industries' in sectors prone to heavy diversification. Overall, the questions raised about the flexibility of large firms receive no clear answers.

Although the results on sectoral structures are mixed, they certainly give some support to the hypothesis that the variance of firms' opportunities is related to the structure of the market.

6. Summary and Conclusions

This paper presents an exploratory investigation of the factors influencing the turnover of position of large industrial enterprises, in particular the 300 largest firms based outside the United States in the years 1972 and 1987. The population of large enterprises gets attention from economists for two reasons: its aggregate size as a measure of the overall concentration of business activity, and its turnover as an indicator of the vigor of competitive processes. This paper has investigated the turnover process not to measure its extent but to identify its foundations: the dependence of differences in large firms' growth (and thus their shares of activity in their

industrial sectors) on the growth of the sectoral and national "platforms" from which they operate.
Growth rates of both the sectoral and national platforms influence the fortunes of large enterprises, as one would expect. More interesting analytically is the factors that govern the varying closeness of that relation. Large companies' changing shares are more closely tied to their national platforms in large and relatively closed economies, as predicted. The European Community's development, however, has not voided the dependence of large EC firms on their sectoral and national platforms.

We invoked the random-process model to devise hypotheses about the closeness of the link between the large firm and its sectoral base. The ties should be tighter, the smaller the variance of the random opportunities open to firms and the greater the adjustment cost associated with seizing a particularly good opportunity. The former hypothesis is strongly supported by the data, while the latter yielded unclear results. No influence could be identified for competitive conditions, perhaps because the analysis is decidedly coarse for that purpose.

One wonders what the future will bring for the turnover of large companies, both absolute and relative to their respective platforms. As we noted at the beginning, de Jong (1989) expressed concern about regulation-driven ossification in the European Community that would reduce the turnover of large companies and their abilities to detach their fates from those of their platforms. On the other hand, an optimist could see in "Europe in 1992" and the striking changes in Eastern Europe a combination of opportunities and prosperous circumstances that would support a more favorable outcome.

Bibliography

Davies, Stephen W. and Bruce R. Lyons (1982). "Seller Concentration: The Technological Explanation and Demand Uncertainty", *Economic Journal* 92 (December), 903-919.

Jong, H.W. de (1988). "Market Structures in the European Economic Community", in De Jong H.W. (ed.) *The Structure of European Industry*, 2nd ed., Dordrecht, Kluwer Academic, 1-39.

Jong, H.W. de (1989). "Free versus Controlled Competition", in Carlsson, Bo (ed.) *Industrial Dynamics: Technological, Organizational, and Structural Changes in Industries and Firms*, Boston, Kluwer Academic, 271-298.

Dollar, David and Edward N. Wolff (1988). "Convergence of Industry Labor Productivity and Advanced Economies, 1963-1982", *Review of Economics and Statistics*, 70 (November), 549-558.

Geroski, Paul and Alexis Jacquemin (1988). "The Persistence of Profits: A European Comparison", *Economic Journal*, 98 (June), 375-389.

Ghemawat, Pankaj. "A Model of Market Dominance", *International Journal of Industrial Organization* (forthcoming).

Hannah, Leslie, and J.A. Kay (1977). *Concentration in Modern Industry: Theory, Measurement and the U.K. Experience*, London, Macmillan.

Hause, John C. and Gunnar Du Rietz (1984). "Entry, Industry Growth, and the Microdynamics of Industry Supply", *Journal of Political Economy*, 92 (August), 733-757.

Ijiri, Yuji and Herbert A. Simon (1977). *Skew Distributions and the Sizes of Business Firms*, Amsterdam, North-Holland.

Jacquemin, Alexis P. and Michel Cardon de Lichtbuer (1973). "Size Structure, Stability and Performance of the Largest British and EEC Firms", *European Economic Review*, 4 (December), 383-408.

Jacquemin, Alexis P. and Henry W. de Jong (1977). *European Industrial Organization*, London, Macmillan.

Kalecki, Michael (1945). "On the Gibrat Distribution", *Econometrica*, 13 (April), 161-170.

Kumar, Manmohan S. (1984). *Growth, Acquisition and Investment: An Analysis of the Growth of Industrial Firms and Their Activities Overseas*, University of Cambridge, Department of Applied Economics, Occasional Paper No. 56, Cambridge, Cambridge University Press.

Lieberman, Marvin B. (1984). "The Learning Curve and Pricing in the Chemical Processing Industries", *Rand Journal of Economics*, 15 (Summer), 213-228.

Mansfield, Edwin (1962). "Entry, Gibrat's Law, Innovation, and the Growth of Firms", *American Economic Review*, 52 (December), 1023-1051.

Mokjtari, Manouchehr and Farhad Rassekh (1989). "The Tendency Toward Factor Price Equalization among OECD Countries", *Review of Economics and Statistics*, 71 (November), 636-642.

Nelson, Richard R. and Sidney G. Winter (1978). "Forces Generating and Limiting Concentration under Schumpeterian Competition", *Bell Journal of Economics*, 9 (Autumn), 524-548.

Odagiri, Hiroyuki and Hideki Yamawaki (1985). *A Study of Company Profit-Rate Time Series: New Results for Japan and an International Comparison*, Centre for European Policy Studies, Working Document No. 17.

Orr, Dale (1974). "The Determinants of Entry: A Study of the Canadian Manufacturing Industries", *Review of Economics and Statistics*, 56 (February), 58-66.

Osborne, D.K. (1976). "Cartel Problems", *American Economic Review*, 66 (December), 835-844.

Owen, Nicholas (1983). *Economies of Scale, Competitiveness, and Trade Patterns within the European Community*, Oxford, Clarendon Press.

Phillips, Almarin (1956). "Concentration, Scale and Technological Change in Selected Manufacturing Industries 1899-1939", *Journal of Industrial Economics*, 4 (June), 179-193.

Porter, Michael E. (1990). *The Competitive Advantage of Nations*, New York: Free Press.

Prais, S.J. (1976). *The Evolution of Giant Firms in Britain: A Study of the Growth of Concentration in Manufacturing Industry in Britain, 1909-70*, Cambridge: Cambridge University Press.

Pryor, Frederic L. (1972). "An International Comparison of Concentration Ratios", *Review of Economics and Statistics*, 54 (May), pp. 130-140.

Rowthorn, Robert (1971). *International Big Business 1957-1967: A Study of Comparative Growth*, University of Cambridge, Department of Applied Economics, Occasional Paper No. 24, Cambridge, Cambridge University Press.

Singh, Ajit and Geoffrey Whittington (1975). "The Size and Growth of Firms", *Review of Economic Studies*, 42 (January), 15-26.

Stonebraker, Robert J. (1979). "Turnover and Mobility among the 100 Largest Firms: An Update", *American Economic Review* 69 (December), 968-973.

Sutton, John. *Sunk Costs and Market Structure*, Cambridge: MIT Press (forthcoming).

Yamawaki, Hideki (1989). "A Comparative Analysis of Intertemporal Behavior of Profits: Japan and the United States", *Journal of Industrial Economics*, 37 (June), 389-410.

Notes

1. See, for example, Ijiri and Simon (1977). Empirical papers that sought to place random processes in a market-structure context include Mansfield (1962) and Davies and Lyons (1982). We also take note of Porter's (1990) study, which addresses the link between the successful firm and its platform in terms of fundamental attributes of the platform's endowment of factors of production and traits of economic, legal, and social organization. His interpretation allows room for random factors, but in a truly long-run context.
2. Orr (1974) was an important stimulus for a number of studies at the level of the individual industry, and these have been undertaken for many countries and time periods. For recent examples see Yamawaki (1989) and the papers appearing in *International Journal of Industrial Organization*, March 1987.
3. The analyses of national and sectoral growth would be fully parallel if "domestic disappearance" (production minus exports plus imports) were measured at the sectoral level rather than total sales. The unavailability of suitable matched data on trade and production ruled out parallel treatment in the empirical analysis that follows.
4. The *Fortune* list for a given year is based on financial reports of the firms for fiscal years ending in the preceding calendar year, so the effective period is considered to be 1972 to 1987.

5. GSIC's particular form, the change normalized by the average of initial and terminal values, was chosen to avoid the asymmetry between the ranges of positive and negative percentage changes that otherwise results when the percentage changes are not small. Its range is from +2 to -2.
6. Details on sources and construction of the data set appear in an appendix.
7. Kumar (1984) found that for large British firms the growth of export sales was uncorrelated with the growth of domestic sales.
8. Studies promoted by Dennis Mueller. Odagiri and Yamawaki (1985) found greater persistence of large firms' abnormal profitability in the United States and no great differences among other countries. Geroski and Jacquemin (1988) found greater persistence in the United Kingdom than in France and the Federal Republic of Germany.
9. Relevant to the preceding series of hypotheses are findings about how the persistence of profits of large companies depends on the structures of the markets in which they operate. See Geroski and Jacquemin (1988) and Yamawaki (1989).
10. It makes a slight difference whether the sectoral growth variable employed does (GDIF) or does not (GIND) have the country's growth rate (GCO) subtracted from it. We note where the conclusions are affected.
11. The significance of differences in the slopes was tested in a separate procedure by estimating models that permit a slope shift for the above-mean observations from the whole sample. None of the slope shifts proved statistically significant.
12. The 15-year time period covered by this study is probably too long for optimal testing of a hypothesis based on short-run inflexibilities and adjustment costs. One can think of major changes in the structure of international trade in products of "heavy industry" that have occurred in shorter periods.

Appendix: Sources of Data

As indicated in the text, the population of leading companies was obtained from the *Fortune* listings for 1973 and 1988, which rest on information for fiscal years ending in 1972 and 1987 respectively. *Fortune* states that its industry classification is based on the United States Standard Industrial Classification; the concordance is largely obvious, but we checked the classifications of selected companies with known principal activities to verify certain features. For 1973 *Fortune* did not report industrial classification numbers, so we assigned these ourselves on the basis of information in *Fortune* and standard directory sources. The few binational companies appearing on the list were allocated in equal proportions to their parent countries. To calculate a given country's share of a sector's sales, we used for the denominator sales by all firms classified to that sector in the *Fortune* list, including any based in countries omitted from the analysis.

Information on rates of growth of sectors (GIND) is currently published in United Nations Statistical Office, *Industrial Statistics Yearbook*, Vol. I. *General Industrial Statistics* (formerly *Yearbook of Industrial Statistics* and *Growth of World Industry*). The UN data are based on the International Standard Industrial Classification (ISIC). At the rather aggregated level used in this study the concordance between the ISIC and the U.S. SIC (and *Fortune*) classifications does not involve serious problems. The UN source provides indexes of real output that can be chained together to cover the 1972-1987 period when the data are reported at an appropriate and unchanging level of aggregation. The amount of sectoral breakdown reported varies from country to country, reflecting distributions of real economic activity as well as the quirks of national record-keeping. For some countries and sectors it was necessary to use an industry category broader than the sector defined in the *Fortune* list or to splice narrower onto broader indexes as the reported detail changed over time. Data missing from the source for the United Kingdom were estimated using production data from the *Report on the Census of Production* and price series from Central Statistical Office, *Annual Abstract of Statistics*, Part 18; various years were utilized to chain together the price series that are frequently rebased in this source.

Data on rates of real growth of gross domestic product were obtained from Organization for Economic Cooperation and Development, *OECD Economic Outlook*, and United Nations, *National Accounts Statistics: Main Aggregates and Detailed Tables, 1986*, Part II (New York: United Nations, 1989).

Exact definitions of the market-structure variables, based on United States data, are as follows:

K/L — Gross book value of capital stock divided by annual payroll, 1977, for business units reporting to the Federal Trade Commission Line of Business program.

RDS — Company-financed R&D outlays as percentage of total sales and transfers, 1977, for business units reporting to the Federal Trade Commission Line of Business program.

LOB — Ratio of total sales and transfers by business units reporting to the Federal Trade Commission Line of Business program to value of industry shipments estimated by U.S. Bureau of the Census, 1977 (a measure of the prevalence of the 456 large companies reporting to the LOB in total industry activity).

C4 Percentage of industry shipments accounted for by the four largest enterprises, 1977.

SIZE Estimated size, based on total sales within the four-digit industry, of the company acounting for the median dollar's worth of shipments in the 4-digit industry when companies classified to the industry are ranked from largest to smallest, 1977.

FDI Global sales by foreign subsidiaries of U.S. enterprises divided by domestic industry shipments estimated by U.S. Bureau of the Census, 1977.

DIV Shipments by establishments controlled by enterprises classified to this industry, divided by total shipments by enterprises classified to this industry, 1982.

All data bearing on Line of Business companies were taken from U.S. Federal Trade Commission, Bureau of Economics, *Annual Line of Business Report, 1977* (1985), Table 3-13 (for LOB) and Master Table (all other information). Ratios ADS and RDS for individual LOB industries were weighted by industry sales and transfers for aggregation to the *Fortune* classification, as were individual industries' rates of participation of firms reporting to the Line of Business program in total industry shipments. Several different participation rates are quoted; we used ADJ-B, which makes adjustments for both plant diversification and vertical integration. Values of certain variables, especially R&D expenditures, were not disclosed for some industries. Such industries were left out in the aggregation process (the fraction of the *Fortune* industry's total sales affected thereby is quite small in every case). Industry ratios of capital stock to value of payroll were weighted by value of payroll.

Data for C4 and SIZE were taken from U.S. Bureau of the Census, *1977 Census of Manufactures*, Vol. 1, *Special Report: Concentration Ratios in Manufacturing*, Table 7. Median company size was estimated as follows. Average company size (shipments) can be calculated from this table for the largest 4, next largest 4, next largest 12, next largest 30, and all remaining enterprises classified to each industry (subject to the limitation of the total number of firms so classified). We identified the group containing the firm that accounts for the median dollar of industry shipments (i.e. 50%) when companies are ranked (by shipments) from largest to smallest. If the 50% point fell roughly in the middle of one of the classes identified in the table, we took the average size (shipments) of firms in that class to approximate the median. If it was near one end of a class, we calculated average company size for that class and its neighbor and made a judgmental interpolation between them to obtain median company size. In the few cases where the four-firm concentration ratio was suppressed because of disclosure, an accurate guess about its value could be made from other data. Both SIZE and C4 were aggregated to the *Fortune* classification using value of industry shipments as a weight.

FDI's numerator was taken from the 1977 Benchmark Survey of foreign investment by the U.S. Department of Commerce, specifically *U.S. Multinational Companies: U.S. Merchandise Trade, Worldwide Sales, and Technology-Related Activities in 1977*, p. 33. Industry shipments were taken from U.S. Bureau of the Census, *1977 Census of Manufactures*, Vol. 1, *Summary and Subject Statistics*, Table 1 (General Summary). The industry classification system used in the Benchmark Survey is rather coarse for some sectors in which foreign investment is unimportant. It was necessary to apply a single value for textiles and apparel to both industries, to assume that the figure for forest products can be represented by furniture and forest products, and to make educated guesses about *Fortune* industries 31, 46, and 47 (all of which fall into the Benchmark Survey's miscellaneous category).

DIV is taken from U.S. Bureau of the Census, *1982 Enterprise Statistics*, with industry shipments used as weights in aggregating to the *Fortune* classification.

5 INDUSTRIAL AND MARKET CONCENTRATION IN EUROPE

REMO LINDA

1. The Markets

1.1 The Problems and their Approaches

Have industrial concentration and market power of enterprises increased in Europe during the eigthies? Certainly, as we will see later on. Which are the resulting effects for the working of competition? They are different, according to the sector and market considered. However, a trend towards the domination of some markets seems to appear. To analyse these phenomena, we have several approaches, methods, indicators at our disposal. We will choose two complementary approaches, respectively based on samples of (a) product markets and (b) industrial mega-firms, distinguishing the sector specificity. Generally, the former ones are more and more oligopolistic and the mega-firms are more and more diverse and multinational.[1]

For what concerns the approach (a), we will base ourselves on the quantitative analysis of the market shares belonging to each of the three main firms, operating on a market for a certain product, in a certain territory (national, European, world). Of course, the growth of this market share expresses a proportional increase of the existing concentration in the market considered, but this does not necessarily lead to an increase in market power and a weakening of the dynamics of competition.[2]

The choice of the indicators analysed aims at demonstrating the different aspects of concentration and of market power (as well as their mutual relationships).

1.2 The Quantitative Analysis of Market Structure

To analyse market structures, we do not use the system of the Linda indices, nor the chromatic zonal approach.[3] To simplify the quantitative synthesis, we limit ourselves to three indicators, which are easily transparent and interpretable; they are defined in Appendix 1.

1) The concentration ratio C_3, measuring the cumulative concentration;
2) The index 2L, i.e. the market power of the "leader" vs. the next firm in the classification of the market shares;
3) The index NIL_2 (new index L), which is the "power of the compound market", belonging as well to the "leader" as to the "conventional oligopolistic arena", made up of the first three firms operating on the market *de quo*.

The hypothesis of the "conventional arena" is realistic, since the market structures of the nineties will be more and more dominated by a nucleus of 2 or 3 diversified mega-firms, having a cumulative market share of more than 50% on most of the markets of industrial products (or "relevant markets").[4] In this context, both indicators 2L and NIL_2 are very fruitful to compare and follow the evolution of market power in the modern market structures.[5]

Let us take the examples of 2 structures A and B, with a C_3 of 56%, market shares being as follows:

A) x_1 = 20% x_2 = 20% x_3 = 16%
B) x_1 = 50% x_2 = 5% x_3 = 1%

In the first case, we have 2L = 100% and NIL_2 = 314, whereas in the second, we have 2L = 1000% and NIL_2 = 3136.

1.3 Producers' Concentration and the Working of Competition

Nevertheless, it must be noted that even if it is admitted that the first firm holds a *very large share of the considered market or sector* (more than 30% for example), one may not infer straight away that:

- this firm has an oligopolistic (even monopolistic) *market power*
- this firm takes advantage of this *by imposing excessive prices* and realising monopolistic profits in this way.

The manufacturer or producer cannot reach the final consumers directly, but he must sell his products to retailers, or to wholesalers (sometimes importers and exporters). His selling-price will thus be determined by the contractual strength he will be able to force on his buyers. In this respect it must be noted that:

- there exist some purchase-groups and large retailers (supermarkets) which have a very strong bargaining power
- that bargaining power is not only measurable at the level of national concentration, because the strength of these large retailers depends on:
  a) their dominating position concerning retail-sales in some regions and towns;
  b) the sizeable impact of their cumulative centralised demand, which no manufacturer or producer could ignore;
  c) their ability to buy enormous quantities anywhere and from anyone.

1.4 Relation between the Level of Concentration and Price Evolution

It follows from the preceding that in order to appreciate the working of competition, we must know:

- not only the degree of market power hold by a producer, but also:
- the *selling-prices* to retailers, in the meaning of the *effective purchase prices* that the retailers have managed to negotiate;
- a significant and objective "*parameter*" to estimate the *relevance of the observed prices*, i.e. to confirm that these prices indeed reflect the existence of a large contractual power of the seller (manufacturer or producer), or of the buyer (large retailer or wholesaler, importer or exporter).

In fact, owing to the availability of international - and interregional data - we can make relevant comparisons, such as:

- the comparison of levels of concentration and especially of market powers relative to the industry in the various countries, and, particularly, the comparison of market shares between important manufacturers or producers in each country,
- the comparison of producers' price-levels (transaction prices) and wholesalers' price-levels in each country and region,
- the comparison of retail price-levels
- the comparison of the evolution of all these data.[6]

One can at least deduce in which regions and countries, as well as for which products, the existence of dominating positions and contractual power with respect to certain manufacturers can be identified.

1.5 The Results of an Empirical Research on 200 Product Markets in the FDT Sector (Food, Drinks and Tobacco)

We will discuss an empirical research on a sample, relatively representative of 200 national markets of products, belonging to the food, drink and tobacco industries and a few consumption products commonly sold in supermarkets.[7] Naturally, these results may not be extended to the whole of this sector. The following conclusions were reached:

1) The highly concentrated markets (C_3 larger than 70%) concern more than 50% of the cases studied.
2) In 26% of the cases the dominating power of the "leader" is very high (2L larger than 300%).
3) The oligo-monopolistic domination and concentration is apparent in 29% of the cases (index NIL_2 larger than 1500).

This trend towards domination seems to increase steadily since 1985 as a result of the wave of take-overs, mergers and joint ventures. This survey should therefore underestimate the power of domination, because most of the cases considered belong to the period before 1985.

2. The Actors

2.1 The European Industrial Mega-Firms

The "market structures" approach developed in par. 1.1 to 1.5 is an essential tool to analyse the basics of the working of competition. However, this analysis must be inserted in the context of global competition. Therefore we study:

- the principles and the effects of new strategies
- a recent file of facts concerning the principal operations of concentration
- some sectoral samples of European industrial mega-firms to quantify their evolution (b approach of par. 1.1).

In this way, having studied the logics of the modern oligopolistic markets, we examine the logics inspiring the strategies of the mega-firms which dominate and shape these markets.

2.2 The Logics of Growth-Strategies[8]

Growth-strategies are the distinctive characteristic of an increasing number of European companies and especially of multinational mega-firms.

The current dynamic context is characterised by the emergence of the new post-industrial society, generated by *long waves*:

- of technological and especially commercial *innovations* touching all aspects of economic, social and cultural life;
- of *operations of restructuring competition*, centered around mergers, take-overs and joint ventures between European, American and Japanese firms.

Global competition is the global result of new growth-strategies and particularly of the process resulting from *new restructuring forms of competition*. Their appearance initiates a lasting change, i.e. precisely a "new structuring" of arrangements, functions and positions which are characteristic of the numerous systems of units and enterprises concerned. They really are "new forms of competition" as well with respect to the globally pursued objectives as regarding the enormous dimensions, even planetary, implied by such strategies. New organisational articulations are also - and necessarily - developed by similar strategies and operations.

The negotiation between firms becomes an engine for modern competition, being an essential condition, not only for the growth - as well of these firms as for the whole European economy - but even for the *survival* of these firms. As a result of concentrations, fusions, joint ventures, the firms succeed to equip themselves with long-distance strategic arms necessary to face the growth of global competition which is, at the same time, a multidimensional, multiple and planetary competition.

The joint ventures are a powerful and often necessary tool to simultaneously *realise strategic innovations, functional diversifications, sectoral and geographical synergies*!

The important novelty of the nineties is that we can no longer discuss concentrations without studying *the four linked phenomena*, which are at the same time the components and the effects of concentration:

1) The "joint venturisation", i.e. the generalisation and dynamisation of the "structured and systematic collaboration" between companies and groups which are sometimes, or even often, competitors in other branches and activity areas.

2) The diversification, which tends to become "functional", allowing the realisation of scale economies and multiple synergies.
3) The "mobility" of the firms, whose control and ownership often passes from one group to another.
4) The process of internationalisation of sectors, markets, firms, management.

2.3 The Two Poles of Behaviour: Rivalry and Negotiation

The essence of the concept of competition, or of "restructuring competition" consists in the opposition between two "poles of behaviour":

1) the rivalry between the firms
2) the negotiations, or, better, the cooperation and coordination.

These cooperations and coordinations increase the power of the firms concerned and allow to face better the rivalry of the other firms. Without the existence of negotiation, cooperation, coordination, agreements, (often involving the effects of specialisation and/or the structural allocation of the markets), competition would become impossible on the oligopolistic markets, in which the competitive dynamics are precisely accelerated by the evolution of the balance (or the unbalance) of power between the firms.

The modern entrepreneurs use the motto of a latin pact: "*Rivales sociei*", freely translated: "Associated to compete" - with the other entrepreneurs, but also to compete against each other. This is not surprising. One can very well cooperate to enhance common industrial research and then face each other, very agressively, on the final markets where agents sell the competitive products, resulting from the joint research, each for his own account. The example of the "compact discs", fruit of a creative initiative of a bold European giant (Philips), associated to a Japanese mega-firm (Sony), illustrates very well the binomial (or dualism?) "rivalry" (fight) and "coordination" (or association, negotiation, planification in common). In fact, this binomial-dualism tends to develop a chain process of industrial growth, of innovation and of industrial and social mutation.

2.4 The Operational Objectives of the Mega-Firm

Four *instrumental objectives* are not easily separable in the strategy of the large multinational firms:

a) entering *new markets and sectors and/or countries*,
b) *increasing market shares* in the traditional fields of activity,
c) *realising scale economies* at different levels and in many aspects, technical, commercial, organisational, R&D, financial and/or more generally economies of infrastructure resulting from the *geographical spread and concentration*,
d) *maximising diversified growth* of the firm in the long-term to stabilise returns at a reasonably high long-term level.

There exists a link between the triad "concentration-domination-diversification", resulting of these four objectives, and the already described behaviours in par. 2.2 (four points) and par. 2.3 ("rivalry-negotiation").

From this point of view, *diversification also becomes, in many cases, a tool of domination*, as it stimulates the growth of the global market power.[9] All this will be illustrated in par. 2.6 and may reduce the dividing line between the sectors and especially between the traditionally engaged firms in different sectors. The approach in terms of "*sectoral samples of large firms*" must not be left because each of these generally operates in a privileged area of activities. Similarly the multinational mega-firm keeps its roots and its sectoral impact within its global and consolidated activity.

2.5 The Sectoral Files

How could one analyse the phenomena of sectoral concentration and of market power held by the large European enterprises?

We have selected a number of large sectors of the manufacturing industry, characterised by a high degree of concentration and, except for oil refineries and petrochemical industry, by a dynamic rate of growth.[10] It is clear that the growth of a firm may be measured by the evolution of its consolidated turnover, for example from 1983 to 1988. The sectoral sample of these large firms is thus also a gross and indirect indicator of the trend of the concentration as well as a kind of "thermometer" giving the variations of "temperature" of the market power held by the principal mega-firms, operating in the same sectors and markets.

We considered only 67 groups, appearing in Tables 1 to 5, which have obtained a global and consolidated turnover of almost one thousand billion of US $ in 1988 (exactly 988.097 million $), employing 6,6 million people.

In most sectors, mega-firms have more than doubled their consolidated turnover (CT) between 1985 and 1988, a period characterised by a high degree of price stability in Europe. But how have they realised that uncommon growth? Through mergers, buy-outs, joint ventures, with the internal growth playing a background role.[11]

2.6 The Firms of the Sample from the Food, Drinks and Tobacco Industries

The world record of the group size growth and of concentration, between 1983 and 1988, has been recorded in Europe in the food and drink sector. Some groups have more than fourfold increased their consolidated turnover, expressed in $ and about threefold in ECU, as can be read in Table 1. But this table does not mention the operations of 1989/1990, which have been uncommonly important. We mention *only* a few marking examples:

1) Four of the most important Italian companies of the food sector have entered the club of the multinationals: Galbani, Star and Agnesi were bought by the French-Italian conglomerate BSN-IFIL, and Negroni by the American Philip Morris-General Foods-Kraft, which already controls important trademarks in Italy (Invernizzi, Simmenthal, Fini, Crippa & Berger).[12]
   The BSN-group has also bought the "biscuits" network of the American Reynolds-Nabisco, with well-known trademarks in Europe (such as Jacob's, Belin, Saiwa), and also the German "leader" in pasta, Birkel (the latter joining Sonnen Bassermann, which was already controlled by BSN), not mentioning other less important take-overs.[13]
2) Unilever has made a huge number of take-overs, for example: Boursin in France, Homann in West-Germany, Dante and S. Giorgio in Italy, Fabergé, Elizabeth Arden, Calvin Klein and others in the United States.[14]
3) Grand Metropolitan and Hillsdown Holdings have also realised an important succession of take-overs in Europe and on the American continent, not mentioning other very dynamic groups which do not appear in the very restricted sample of Table 1 (Cadbury, Schweppes, United Biscuits, Whitbread, Albert Fischer, and so on).[15]

One can foresee that when the 1990 data will be available, the 50 largest food, drink and tobacco mega-firms of Europe will totalise a consolidated turnover of more than 300 billion $.[16]

Concerning this, it could be mentioned that generally the enormous size growth of the European groups has also increased their degree of internationalisation, because several foreign firms have been taken over.[17] The growth of the market strength is thus tied to the globalisation and internationalisation of the markets, with all the consequences resulting from this.

Table 1 Europe - FDT (Food, Drinks and Tobacco Industries), Sample of major industries (R = net profit on turnover)

No.	Corporation	R in %		$ USA	
		1983	1988	1983	1988
1.	Bat - GB	3,9	9,0	12.033	31.436
2.	Unilever - GB/NL	2,9	5,1	20.292	31.303
3.	Nestlé - CH	4,5	5,2	13.304	27.827
4.	Gruppo-Ferruzzi (1) - I	--	4,1	5.892	25.490
5.	Hanson Trust - GB	7,6	15,2	2.316	13.158
6.	Grand Metropolitan - GB	5,4	11,8	6.045	10.726
7.	Allied Lyons - GB	4,1	8,1	3.694	8.006
8.	Dalgety - GB (1)	1,0	1,8	4.598	8.000
9.	BSN - F	3,0	5,4	3.265	7.085
10.	Bass - GB	7,7	8,9	2.295	6.644
11.	Hillsdown Hold - GB (1)	2,6	6,2	1.471	6.320
12.	Guiness - GB	4,0	16,5	908	4.944
13.	Berisford Int. - GB	--	2,7	6.486	4.706
14.	Rothmans Intern. - GB	4,8	15,2	2.448	4.521
15.	Associated British Foods (A.B.F.) - GB	3,0	5,2	3.979	4.398
	Total (2)			89.076	194.564

1 The following corporations have ceased to exist as independent corporations since 1983. Between brackets are the names of the acquiring corporations

a)	Impérial Groups - GB	Turnover 1983	$ 3,850 milliards	(Hanson Trust - GB)
b)	Rowntree Mc Intosh - GB		$ 1,443 milliards	(Nestlé - CH)
c)	Beghin Say - F		$ 1,393 milliards	(Ferruzzi - I)
d)	Brooke Bond Liebig - GB		$ 1,474 milliards	(Unilever - GB/NL)
e)	Distillers - GB		$ 1,368 milliards	(Guiness - GB)
f)	Lesieur - F		$ 1,007 milliards	(Ferruzzi - I)

2.7 The Firms of the Samples from Pharmaceuticals, Petrochemical Industry

Most of the mega-firms considered in the Tables 2a-b-c and 3 have used internationalisation strategies. The United States have been the aim. If we look at the list of the 10 most important chemical companies of the United States, we see that four of them are in fact European subsidiaries: the German Hoechst Celanese, Bayer and BASF, the English Hanson Ind.[18]

It seems obvious that the chemical industry of the European giants is by far first in the world, if we except the phenomena Du Pont (E.I.) De Nemours. Concerning pharmaceuticals, there exists some balance between both coasts of the Atlantic, especially if we take into account the fact that many mega-firms of Table 2a are also very important pharmaceutical producers: Hoechst, Bayer, ICI, Ciba-Geigy, Rhône Poulenc, etc.[19]

But we must add other groups, not appearing as very large scale items in Table 2a, in some segments of the chemical industry: for example Unilever and Ferruzzi, the latter controlling Montedison, and also several large ones in the petroleum industry of Table 3: Shell, BP, ENI (taking part, whether they like it or not, with Montedison of the common subsidiary Enimont) and especially the French ELF Aquitaine, which, owing to Sanofi, is engaged in "pharma" (particularly the American Pennwalt bought in 1988) and in cosmetics (Yves Rocher). Besides, Elf Aquitaine (controlled by the French state) will buy in 1990 (eventually in cooperation with Total (FR)) Orkem, last on the list of Table 2a.

We only mention some of the mega-take-overs which have characterised the sector.

1) BASF-D bought a.o. the Inmont Corp. USA and American Enka-USA. Maybe it is still the European "leader" for magnetic tapes and audio-video cassettes, notwithstanding the more and more agressive competition of the Japanese and South-Coreans.
2) Hoechst-D bought the enormous Celanese-USA (for almost 3 billion $). It controls the French Roussel-Uclaf.
3) ICI-GB bought the agro-chemical division of Stauffer Chemicals-USA (Chesebrough Pond's USA group, bought in 1987 by Unilever), and also other companies, such as the chemical division of Beatrice-Co-USA and Glidden Corp.-USA, the latter sold by the Hanson Trust. With its take-overs ICI has become the world "leader" in paint.[20]
4) Rhône-Poulenc-F. After having retaken the whole chemical industry of Saint-Gobain and Pechiney, this Group has bought divisions of Union

Carbide and of Stauffer Chemicals-USA, and also of the German Stettner. In June 1990, in turn, an important American pharmaceutical producer comes under the control of the French group, Rorer.

Table 2a Europe - Diversified chemicals

No.	Corporation	R in %		$ USA	
		1983	1988	1983	1988
1.	BASF - D	1,5	3,2	13.250	24.961
2.	Hoechst - D	0,9	4,4	14.558	23.308
3.	Bayer - D	2,0	4,6	14.616	23.026
4.	ICI - Imperial Chemical Industries - GB	4,5	7,1	12.750	20.839
5.	Montedison - I	-3,0	5,9	7.014	14.477
6.	Ciba - Geigy - CH	5,3	7,5	7.018	12.060
7.	Rhône Poulenc - F	0,2	5,6	5.657	10.971
8.	Saint-Gobain - F	0,7	8,7	7.596	9.890
9.	Norsk Hydro - N	1,6	5,7	4.077	9.202
10.	Pechiney - F (1)	--	4,8	3.997	8.619
11.	Akzo - NL	2,8	5,1	5.284	8.388
12.	Solvay - B	2,2	5,3	3.886	6.893
13.	Henkel - D	1,7	3,1	1.744	5.833
14.	DSM - NL	0,8	6,1	6.926	5.120
15.	Huls - GB	--	1,6	2.020	4.685
16.	Pilkington - GB (2)	0,1	8,8	1.707	3.973
17.	Courtaulds - GB	0,2	5,9	3.184	4.123
18.	l'Air Liquide - F	5,7	6,2	2.243	4.304
19.	Boc - GB	2,5	8,6	2.656	3.756
20.	Orkem - F	--	11,6	---	3.617
	Total			120.183	208.045

1 1985 instead of 1983

2 Different sources show different figures: $ 4.350 or 3.973 million?

We shall also mention:

a) the merger of the English Beecham (Table 2b) with the American Smithkline Beckman[21]

b) the purchase by Pechiney of the American Triangle Industries, and also its offensive in the packing sector (operation American Can or ANC-USA), where it has become the world leader

c) the growing wave of common companies, joint ventures, alliances and more generally, (re)structuring agreements, with the participation of most of the companies of Tables 2a-b-c and 3.

Table 2b Europe - Pharmaceuticals (1)

No.	Corporation	R in %		$ USA	
		1983	1988	1983	1988
1.	Sandoz - CH	4,9	7,5	3.116	6.937
2.	Hoffmann - La Roche (Roche - Sapac) - CH	4,4	7,4	3.575	5.939
3.	Beecham - GB	8,8	9,6	2.845	4.224
4.	Glaxo - GB	11,2	28,3	1.659	3.609
5.	Schering - D	1,9	3,0	1.677	3.000
6.	Boehringer Ingelheim - D	2,1	1,7	1.034	2.362
7.	Wellcome - GB	5,6	10,2	1.064	2.212
	Total			14.970	28.283
	Total 2a + 2b			135.153	236.328

1 A number of firms of the sector of various chemicals of Table 2a are also important producers of pharmaceuticals

Table 2c Europe - Oil refineries and Petrochemical industry

Corporation	R in %		$ USA	
	1983	1988	1983	1988
Total 2c Sample of 7 méga-firms (2)			204.295	201.196
Total 2a + 2b + 2c			339.448	437.524

2 1) Shell, 2) BP, 3) Eni, 4) Elf Aquitaine, 5) Total CFP, 6) Petrofina, 7) Neste - FN

Table 3 more particularly requires a few comments. It is a sector in stagnation, the index of consolidated turnover (CT) of 1988 (base 1983 = 100) is smaller than 100 and this notwithstanding the devaluation of the dollar. Meanwhile the index R (net profit on turnover) has risen in a very considerable way, compared to 1983. What is the explanation? New economies of scale, rigidity of oligopoly prices, more or less tacit negotations, public planification, a more favourable fiscal regime? The answer would need a deeper analysis. In any case, most of the groups of Table 3 have developed their process of diversification and internationalisation. So, BP has become the undisputed European and world leader in animal food, after several take-overs, for example in 1986 Purina-Mills-USA.[22]

But we cannot quote all the European and world leaders, in their respective markets of activity, which figure in our tables. Bayer, ICI, Hoechst, St Gobain, Pilkington, Pechiney, Solvay, Rhône-Poulenc, and so on.

Table 3 Europe - Oil refineries and Petrochemical Industry

No.	Corporation	R in %		$ USA	
		1983	1988	1983	1988
1.	Royal Dutch Shell - GB/NL	5,2	6,7	80.557	78.381
2.	BP - British Petroleum - GB	3,2	4,7	49.195	46.174
3.	Eni - Ente Nazionale Idrocarburi - I	-3,7	+3,7	25.022	25.227
4.	Elf Aquitaine - F	2,7	5,7	18.188	21.175
5.	Total - F	0,5	1,8	18.350	13.987
6.	Petrofina - B	3,2	5,5	8.718	9.899
7.	Neste - FN (Finland)	0,3	5,0	4.265	6.353
	Total			204.295	201.196

2.8 The Firms of the Samples from the Car and Electrical Manufacturing Sector - Some Common Points

During the eighties the European companies in these two sectors have installed an enormous network of joint companies, joint ventures and other (re)structuring agreements, increasingly international, even transcontinental.[23]

This network of restructuring agreements has accompanied and sometimes prepared mergers and absorptions, which have changed the sectoral structures.[24] In fact, in both sectors, the obvious imperative is to realise all conceivable scale economies and synergies, to stay or become competitive and to win from the competitors. The alliance and collaboration of some of these may help to beat, even to eliminate others.

Three strategies, and strongly linked factors play the major role: (1) first of all, the competition of the Japanese and of the manufacturers of the newly industrialised countries (South-Corea for example), (2) the creation of excess capacities in production, (3) the functional diversification of several groups.

Concerning this, we must emphasize the natural linkages, sometimes disturbed or biased by other factors, existing between:

1) oligopolistic strategies
2) growth of the companies and concentration of power
3) creation of excess capacities of production (i.e. excess supply of goods)
4) increased and agressive oligopolistic competition
5) changes in the social-economic structures, following from above-mentioned dynamics
6) search for political solutions as well as agreements and arrangements between the mega-multinationals (European, American and Japanese).

The use of "scale economies", after adopting new innovating technologies, leads to increased production capacities of the involved companies and thus to larger global supply on the market, thereby directly threatening the market shares of less competitive and less innovating producers. It is only after the elimination of these that it will be possible to reach a more reasonable balance between global supply and demand.[25]

Concerning this, it must be admitted that there are economic laws which tend to appear continuously and almost unavoidably, in the presence of certain conditions and data of the context. It is economically perfectly logical to proceed to concentration of firms and to develop structuring agreements in order to meet those crises of excess capacity of industrial production. The considerable increase in concentration and in market power is inherent in the evolution of the internal European market of 1993. Notwithstanding the numerous common points, there subsists nevertheless an important difference between the two sectors.

The car industry is an industry which has reached its phase of maturity and saturation (this explains the strategy of diversification of Daimler Benz, as we will see in par. 2.9), while several segments of the electrical industry represent new and promising markets, animated by the dynamics of revolutionary innovation (we are not exaggerating: the video tape recorders, the compact discs, the high definition television, the camerascopes). On these promising markets, the battle of global competition seems already to be won by the Japanese (par. 2.10 and 2.12).

2.9 The Structural Mutations in the Car Industry - the Case of Daimler Benz

The most important mutations of the eighties have been characterised by:

1) the crisis of the English industry, followed by the development of and the cooperation with the Nippon constructors (in particular Honda) and the transfer of Rover to British Aerospace[26]
2) the construction of new production units in Great Britain by Japanese firms[27]
3) in 1989, the buy-out of Jaguar by the American Ford Company Company
4) in Italy, the buy-out of Alfa Romeo by Fiat, following those of Lancia and Ferrari
5) the buy-out of the Spain Seat by the German Volkswagen, not mentioning other mega-initiatives of this group (for example, in Latin America, in collaboration with the American Ford)
6) in 1990, the structuring agreement - with cross participations - between the French Renault and the Swedish Volvo, and the participation of the American General Motors in the Swedish Saab
7) the strategy of diversification of Daimler Benz.

Table 4 Europe - Automobile Industry

No.	Corporation	R in %		$ USA	
		1983	1988	1983	1988
1.	Daimler-Benz - D	2,6	2,3	15.660	41.818
2.	Fiat - I	2,6	6.8	14.466	34.039
3.	Volkswagen - D	-0,3	1,3	15.693	33.696
4.	Renault - F	-1,4	5,5	14.468	27.110
5.	Peugeot - F	-3,0	6,6	11.244	23.250
6.	Volvo - S	0,2	3,6	12.963	15.752
7.	Robert Bosch - D	1,4	2,0	5.618	15.747
8.	BMW - D	2,4	1,6	4.675	11.763
	Total			94.787	203.175

As it appears from Table 4, several European mega-groups have realised a considerable growth. Concerning Daimler Benz, it must nevertheless be emphasized that its exceptional growth is the result of a succession of strategic mega-purchases, outside the automobile sector, concretisising a process of functional diversification.

Which is the first West-German industrial group? Daimler-Benz of Stuttgart (the manufacturer of Mercedes) which started a very large process of functional diversification in 1985 by the purchase of four large German firms:

1) the "sick" giant of electronics: AEG
2) the aviation motorist MTU (Machinen und Turbinen Union)
3) the second of the German aeronautics: Dornier
4) the constructor of MBB airplanes, member of the AIRBUS consortium.[28]

This process of diversification has been marked by the late M. Alfred Herrhausen of the Deutsche Bank, the most important shareholder of Daimler-Benz, with 28% of the equity. Note that the Deutsche Bank is also present in the Board of Directors of the other giant of the automobile industry, Volkswagen. But the new strategy has caused controversies within the Board of Directors, which reached its peak on the 13th of July 1987 when the official announcement was made of the resignation of M. Werner Breitschwerdt and of his replacement by M. Edzard Reuter.

As a result of this change in the direction, the strategy of diversification will certainly be pursued further, because the previous boss (who was at the origin of the success of the 190 serie) wanted to limit the activity of the group to the sector of the automobile industry. Concerning this, the position of M. E. Reuter, a law-graduate, is totally clear: "Daimler-Benz has become another company. Before, it was a vehicle manufacturer. Today, it is a world-wide concern operating in many new fields".

The purchases of AEG, MTU, Dornier and MBB should allow the realisation of important synergies in the field of high technology. Indeed, we foresee that in the year 2000 revolutionary progress in the electronic and new materials for the car industry will be made. Reuter even mentions that "the best example is the move towards an integrated electronic control system for motor vehicles - the heart of the vehicle of the future".[29]

The aeronautics - military branche - counts for about 10% of the turnover, electronics for 16%, car industry and commercial vehicles for about 70%, since Mercedes is the European leader for commercial vehicles.[30]

Several joint enterprises and joint venture projects are written into the programs of the group: with the French Aerospatial and with the Japanese Mitsubishi,[31] as well as with other partners such as the American General Electric and Pratt & Whitney.[32] Lastly:

1) The German BMW has recently begun the construction of airplane engines in a joint venture with the British Rolls-Royce.[33]
2) The world leader in tyres, Michelin, has recently purchased the American giant Uniroyal-Goodrich.[34] The market share of the French group should be about 50% on the European and world market.

And the German Bosch is the leader on several markets of car equipment. The Bosch universe, including the joint ventures in which it takes part, needs an ad hoc study!

2.10 The Electrical Industry in Europe and in the World

It concerns a set of very large and differentiated sectors. On the one hand one can distinguish the construction of equipments and the electrical installations (and similar) for public services and enterprises, and on the other hand, the mass electronics, with its white and brown products. We refer to Table 5, with these remarks:

1) Several actors of the sixties and the seventies do no longer appear in Table 5 because they were absorbed by other greater groups in the meantime, as mentioned between brackets: the Italian Zanussi (Electrolux) and IRE-Ignis-Borghi (Philips), the German AEG (Daimler-Benz) and SEL-Standard Lorenzt (Nokia-FN), Grundig (Philips), Plessey (Siemens-D and GEC-GB).
2) Philips has recently taken a participation of 25% in the Danish Bang & Olufsen.
3) An increasing part of products, as well white as especially brown, are imported from East-Europe.

Table 5 *Europe - Electronical Industry*

No.	Corporation	R in %		$ USA	
		1983	1988	1983	1988
1.	Siemens - D	1,9	2,3	15.724	34.129
2.	Philips - NL	1,4	1,9	16.177	28.371
3.	CGE - F	0,6	3,2	8.195	21.488
4.	Asea Brown Boveri	2,8	2,3	5.074	17.562
5.	Thomson - F	-2,2	3,2	6.493	12.567
6.	Electrolux - S	1,0	2,3	4.190	12.055
7.	GEC - GB	8,4	8,2	7.731	9.457
8.	Schneider - F	--	2,3	---	6.800
9.	Thorn Emi - GB	1,5	5,6	4.539	5.201
10.	Nokia - FN	1,4	4,9	1.249	5.204
	Total			69.372	152.834

* Schneider is excluded in calculating the index of 1988 on the base of 1983 = 100

4) In any case, the front of the world scene is from now on firmly occupied by the Japanese and South-Coreans. Indeed, the world classification of Table 6 sees the European leader, Siemens, only in 3rd position and the mega-firms of the EEC only count for 30% of the consolidated turnover in 1988 of the 20 most important world electric manufacturers. If we consider the index of growth of the consolidated turnover in 1988 (base 1983 = 100), we may conclude that Europe, notwithstanding the process of concentration, is until now the loser in the global competition battle. The recent crisis of Philips shows a worsening of the situation.[35]

Table 6 World - The 20 largest corporations in the electronic industry in 1988

No	Corporation	Turnover in $ bn	R in %	Index 1988 base 1983 = 100
1.	General Electric - USA	49,4	6,9	154
2.	Hitachi - JAP	41,3	2,4	262
3.	Siemens - D	34,1	2,3	217
4.	Matsushita Elec. Ind. - JAP	33,9	3,5	203
5.	Philips - NL	28,4	1,9	175
6.	Samsung - SUD COR	27,4	1,7	382
7.	Toshiba - JAP	25,4	1,7	267
8.	CGE - F	21,5	3,2	262
9.	NEC - Jap	19,6	9,3	339
10.	Asea Brown Boveri - CH	17,6	2,3	346
11.	Mitsubishi Elec. - JAP	16,9	9,5	275
12.	Thomson - F	12,6	3,2	194
13.	Westinghouse - USA	12,5	6,6	128
14.	Electrolux - SU	12,1	2,3	287
15.	Sony - JAP	10,1	2,6	223
16.	Lucky-Goldst. Ar - SUD COR	9,9	0,8	138
17.	GEC - GB	9,5	8,2	122
18.	Sanyo Elec. - JAP	9,4	0,5	196
19.	Daewoo - SUD COR	8,7	0,6	430
20.	Sharp - JAP	8,6	1,7	250
	Total	408,9		
	of which in the EC	123,7		
	Rest	285,2		

2.11 The Sector of the White Products - the Giant Electrolux

A rapid growth in the sixties, then a stagnation in demand, and now a wave of concentrations and restructuring. It is the recent history of the sector of the white products, notably of the larger electric domestic appliances (refrigerators, washing-machines, micro wave ovens, and other cooking equipment). The world leader is the Swedish Electrolux, who has obtained control on the Italian Zanussi (23% of the European market), followed by Philips (12%), the German Bosch-Siemens (9%), the Italian Merloni (Ariston and Indesit, with 8%) and the French Thomson (between 5 and 7%).

The Swedish Electrolux has also made a name in the United States by buying factories on the spot. This country being the first world producer with 18,5 million electric household devices a year, followed by Italy, with 13 million devices.

But who is Electrolux? It is one of the spearheads of the Wallenberg empire (the Swedish family), particularly powerful in the electrical industry, because it also controls LM Ericsson (consolidated turnover: $ 5,1 billion) and partly the giant ASEA Brown Boveri (of Table 5). The group also controls Stora Kopparbergs Bergslags (paper: consolidated turnover 1988: $ 5,6 billion, engaged in a take-over of the German paper manufacturer Feldmoehle Nobel - consolidated turnover 1988: $ 4,5 billion), SKF (consolidated turnover 1988: $ 3,5 billion) and Scania/Saab (their agreement with General Motors was already mentioned in par. 2.9).

But it must also be noted that the position of Philips in the sector becomes more and more fragile, because the American leader Whirlpool (consolidated turnover 1988: $ 4,4 billion) bought in 1988 a participation of 53% in the subsidiary of the Dutch giant, producing "domestic appliances" keeping the right of option for the residual capital at a price fixed beforehand. In May 1990, Whirlpool seems to want to use this right to become the exclusive owner of the joint venture.[36]

2.12 The Brown Products and the "Tornado" from the Far East

The European markets are more and more invaded by the well-known Japanese trademarks, at the avant-garde of technology and especially of marketing, the latter being particularly efficient.

How did things get that far? We shall mention two important lost occasions for the Europeans, the first one concerning (a) the choice of the color-TV-system and the other concerning (b) the choice of the video-recording. Concerning (a), the debate between the supporters of the PAL and of the SECAM system has not permitted to choose a unique system in the EEC, with some desastrous consequences from all points of view (losses of enormous scale economies, double uses, political and social consequences, brake at the R&D, and so on). The effects of that Franco-German debate have reflected on the other European countries. So the Italian electronic industry, which used to be very prosperous and agressive, has been paralysed and punished by the hesitant and the inadmissible shilly-shally of the Italian government about the choice of the color-TV-system. This has caused the disappearing of the most important Italian groups, which have passed under foreign control much more easily.[37]

Concerning (b) the history is more complicated and interesting. At the beginning of the video recorders, in the early eighties, there were three different recording systems, two Japanese, VHS of JVC ("the winner") and BETAMAX of Sony, and one European, V2000 of Philips. The Europeans have finally overwhelmingly chosen for the VHS system and Philips, after its defeat, has manufactured, under licence, video recorders based on the Japanese system. Why has Philips been dropped by the other Europeans? For technological reasons? Certainly not, because it seems that the V2000 system was particularly sophisticated and efficient. But it was too expensive relatively to its Japanese competitor, notwithstanding that Philips had considered the introduction of a cheaper model. But since May 1981, three European giants of the electronic construction concluded an important agreement on TV tubes and video recorders, with the Japanese firm JVC. These three giants were the French Thomson, the English Thorn-Enu and the German AEG-Telefunken.

That agreement has then been contested by the French government, who wanted to develop cooperation between the European mega-firms. So a new formula was invented involving the entry of the French Thomson in the German firm Grundig, in which the Dutch Philips already held 24,2% of the capital.

In this way, a fruitful collaboration between French and Dutch should have been realised through Grundig, the Dutch having in this way a chance to compete with their V2000 system and the new form of cooperation with Thomson against the Japanese dominating system of JVC.

On his side, Thomson would strengthen its presence on the German market, where it already occupies an important position, due to the purchase of well-known and famous TV trademarks.

After all, it was a good solution for everybody, even Europe, with one exception. This exception made the project collapse because in March 1983 the German office of cartels (Bundeskartellamt) showed its perplexity about this operation, which should have created a bloc Thomson-Philips-Grundig dominating more than 50% of the German market for mass electrical manufacturing.

In other words, the operation could only be admitted if Philips renounced its participation in Grundig, which was unacceptable. At last, the winner was JVC, the Japanese!

JVC means Japanese Victor Corporation, of which the world giant of mass electronics, the Japanese Matsushita detains 51%.

2.13 New Perspectives and Common Initiatives

It is impossible to quote all mega-operations of the past years. Siemens, with the absorbing in 1989/90 of Plessey (with the collaboration of General Electric-GB) and Nixdorf and the French "ALCATEL ALSTROM - Compagnie Générale d'Electricité (new social name of the CGE group), with the restarting of some activities of the American ITT in Europe (others have been restarted by the Finnish Nokia) and Thomson, with the constitution of a joint venture with the Italian public sector (SGS-Thomson) have been the most active.[38]

The big hope of mass electronics in Europe is now the HDT (High Definition Television), a potential market of 100 billion ECUS. Since October 1986, 3 European giants have come together within the EUREKA project: Philips, Thomson and Bosch.[39] On the 16th of May 1990 comes the turn. An agreement is announced of integrated collaboration between Philips and Thomson on the most important technological aspects, to improve manufacture and sell the HDT at the end of the nineties. The project, supported by the French state, provides for 20 billion francs to invest from now to 1995, of which 11 billion by Philips.[40] When and how will the money be found? What will be the attitude of the Germans towards this initiative? Will we end up with a unique European HDT-system? Or will the egoism and national glamour beat the European solidarity? And yet this initiative of Philips-Thomson seems to be the last chance.

3. Public Policies - Conclusions

3.1 The Logic of Concentration in the Perspective of 1993

The completion of the European internal market for 1993 represents:

1) The most important strategic innovation of the last twenty years.
2) The very likely convergence of the European structure towards the North-American model of production, distribution and consumption.

Relative to this, one can conclude that one will increasingly be confronted with the following phenomena:

3) The increasing acceleration of the process of internationalisation of firms and mega-firms, both for the industrial sector, the commercial distribution and the service sectors.
4) Consequently, the increase of the global size of these firms and mega-firms, forces them to adapt to the new musts, dimensions and constraints of a single market of 320 million consumers.
5) The intensification of global competition with the elimination of marginal companies.
6) The considerable increase in concentration at the European level may sometimes break positions of market domination and barriers to competition of a local nature, but will therefore be not less harmful to the objectives of the single market.

In fact, there exists a real risk that the mega-firms of other countries will take advantage of the divisions and rivalries between the Europeans and also of the mistakes of the governments to conquer all markets of large consumption in the future.

3.2 The Role of the Anti-Trust Policy - Objectives and Instruments

Two fundamental priorities emerge from the analysis:

1) To adapt the antitrust policy of the EEC, as well as the policies of the member-states, to the requirements and constraints of global competition and of the European internal market of 1993.[41]
2) To fund the application of the new regulation No. 4064/89 of 21st of December 1989, coming into effect on the 21st of September 1990, in order to control the operations of concentration between enterprises:
   - on the transparency,
   - on the global, systematic and periodic information, to the benefit of the European Parliament and of other institutions, associations, organisations, enterprises and consumers.

Therefore, we shall recommend the installation of a European Global Observatory[42] with three windows, with as objects:

- the market structures (and particularly the market shares)
- the price structures

- the enterprise structures, with a periodic updating of an inventory of all mergers, take-overs, creation or modification of joint ventures, joint companies as well as more generally all restructuring alliances or agreements.

Of course, the Observatory should only take into consideration the operations having an effect in the Common Market and in which mega-firms are involved (even of other countries) with a consolidated annual turnover above a given level (but certainly not the level of 5 billion ECU).[43] The files and the results of the "observatory with three windows" should be published.[44]

Bibliography

Bonfour, A. (1985). Les Accords de Coopération entre les Firmes Automobiles américaines et japonaises, *Chroniques de la SEDEIS*, no. 7 (Juli).

Bonfour, A. (1987). L'Avenir de l'Industrie Automobile mondiale, *La documentation française*, série: *Notes et Etudes documentaires*, Paris no. 4831.

Burns, J. (1983). Mc Inerney, Swinbank (eds.), *The Food Industry*, Heineman, London.

Camagni, R., G. Martelli (1979). *Ricerca sulla distribuzione ed i prezzi dei prodotti elettrodomestici, elettroacustici, radio e televisori e sulla concentrazione industriale*, Série "Evoluzione della concorrenza", no. 40, Commission de la CEE, Bruxelles (Juillet).

Carabini, O. (1979). Caravita, Nuove strategic per gli elettrodomestici, *Mondo Economico*, no. 17 (Avril).

Caves, R.E. (1982). *Multinational Enterprise and Economic Analysis*, Cambridge University Press.

Dunning, J.H. (1981). *International Production and the Multinational Enterprise*, G. Allen & Unwin, London.

EEC Commission, Rapports sur la politique de concurrence (IIIème partie): publiés de l'avril 1977 à l'avril 1980.

1 - 6ème rapport, Bruxelles/Luxembourg par. 288/319.
2 - 7ème rapport, Bruxelles/Luxembourg par. 283/324.
3 - 8ème rapport, Bruxelles/Luxembourg par. 266/296.
4 - 9ème rapport, Bruxelles/Luxembourg par. 218/259.

EIU (The Economist Intelligence Unit), *Marketing in Europe*, several reports, 40 Duke Street, London W1A1DW.

Fortune, Several Issues

F.T. = *Financial Times*

Galizzi, G. (1985). Problemi e prospettive dell' industria agro-alimentare nelle economie sviluppate, Istituto di Ricerche *Il Poliedro*.

Hartley, K. Aerospace, in De Jong /4/ 329/352.

Jacquemin, A. (1979). *Economie Industrielle Européenne*, Paris, Dunod.

De Jong, H.W. (1) (1971). *Marktanalyse en markttheorie*, Leiden.

De Jong, H.W. (2) 1972[1], 1981[2], 1985[3]). *Dynamische markttheorie*, Leiden.

De Jong, H.W. (3) (1986). European Industrial Organization: Entrepreneurial Economics in an Organizational Setting, in De Jong, H.W. and W.G. Shepherd (eds.), *Mainstreams in Industrial Organization*, Kluwer Academic Publishers, Dordrecht, Boston, Lancaster.

De Jong, H.W. (4) (1988). *The Structure of European Industry* (ed.), Kluwer Academic Publishers, Dordrecht, Boston, London.

Kumps, A.M., P. Druylans, L. Tempels (1989). *L'évolution de la situation concurrentielle consécutive à certaines fusions dans les secteurs de l'automobile et des télécommunications*, Commission CEE.

Linda, R., (1) (1972). Concurrence oligopolistique et planification concurentielle internationale, in *Economie Appliquée*, Librairie Droz, Geneva, no. 2-3.

Linda, R. (2) (1976). Methodology of concentration analysis applied to the study of Industries and Markets, ECC Commission, Bruxelles-Luxembourg (September).

Linda, R. (3) (1977). Domination, Concurrence et Concentration des marchés, in Van Damme, J.A., De Tempel (eds.), *La Réglementation du comportement des monopoles et entreprises dominantes en droit communautaire*, Semaine de Bruges, Cahier de Bruges N.S. 36.

Linda, R. (4) (1984). *Crise industrielle européenne*, IICC, Bruxelles.

Linda, R. (5) (1987). European industry on the March, in *European Affairs* no. 3, Elsevier, Amsterdam.

Linda, R. (6) (1988). Strategie di sviluppo delle imprese dell' industria agro-alimentare, in *Strategie e adattamenti nei sistema agro-industriale*, Atti XXIV Convegno SIDEA, Il Mulino, Bologna.

Linda, R. (7) (1988). The food and drinks industry: large firm strategies, in (see De Jong, H.W., ed.) *The Structure of European Industry.*

Linda, R. (8) (1988). Strategie de croissance diversifiée de quelques géants européens de l'industrie alimentaire dans *Chronique de la SEDEIS*, no. 11.

Linda, R., (9) (1989). *La Distribuzione commerciale in Europa*, Etas Libri, Milano.

Linda, R. (10) (1989). L'antitrust européen et les concurrences de la dernière génération, dans *Chroniques de la SEDEIS*, no. 11, Paris (November).

Linda, R. (11) (1990). Les bases théoriques et factuelles de la Perestroïka, dans *Chroniques de la SEDEIS*, no. 2, Paris (Mars).

Linda, R. (12) (1990). *Quelles stratégies pour les coopératives agro-industrielles européennes face à la croissance diversifiée des multinationales*, étude réalisée pour le COGECA de Bruxelles, rue de la Science 23/25, Bruxelles-1040, doc. no. 1432 du 30 avril.

Marfels, C. (1988). *Recent trends of concentration in selected industries*, Commission CEE.

Maunder, P. (1983). Competition Policy in the Food Industry, in Burns, J. and others (eds.), *The food industry.*

Pardos, Marketing, (1979). *Etudes sur l'évolution de la concentration dans l'industries des plastiques en France*, Série "Evolution de la concentration", no. 37, Commission de la CEE, Bruxelles (Mai).

Pearce, J., J. Sutton (1986). *Protection and Industrial Policy in Europe* (with R. Batchelor), RIIA, Routledge & Kegan Paul, London, Boston & Henley.

Pellicelli, G. (1989). *Imprese multinazionali*, Etas Libri, Milano.

Ravenscraft, D.J., F.M. Scherer F.M. (1987). *Mergers, Sell offs and Economic Efficiency*, The Brookings Institute, Washington.

Shepherd, W.G. (1) On the core concepts of Industrial Economics, in De Jong /3/ - Shepherd /3/.

Shepherd, W.G. (2), Public Enterprise; see De Jong /4/ pp. 355/385.

Shepherd, W.G. (3), See De Jong /3/.

Stopford, Turner (1985). *Britain and the Multinationals*, J. Wiley & Sons, Chichester.

Tecnetra, (1982). *Evoluzione delle telecomunicazioni negli anni '80*, a cura di Umberto Pellegrini, Edizioni Sarin, Rome.

Notes

1. In 1988, 847 European enterprises have been bought for a value of $ 31,6 billion. In 1989, the number of international take-overs in Europe rose to 1314 for a value of $ 50 billion. In the United States we recorded in 1988 1257 international take-overs for $ 75,2 billion and in 1989, 926 for $ 68,8 billion. The global number of international take-overs has been 2408 for $ 117,8 billion in 1988 and 2599 for $ 129,3 billion in 1989. Our source is KPMG Peat Marwick (Mondadori Business Information 1990). Other sources say that in 1989, the Europeans have made 5558 take-over operations for $ 114 billion, the Americans 2366 for $ 221 billion, the Japanese 298 operations for $ 17,8 billion.
   For the first time, the amount at take-over prices of the foreign assets in the United States ($ 390 billion) is larger than the amount of the American assets abroad ($ 359 billion). But the latter may be estimated at $ 785 billion at market prices, for $ 466 billion for the foreign assets in the US.
2. De Jong /1/ /2/ /3/ /4/ and Linda /7/ /9/ /10/.
3. EEC Commission /1/ /2/ /3/, De Jong /3/, Book 2, pp. 287/307.
4. Linda /a/ pp. 53/60, 275/294, 362/364 and Linda /2/ /3/ /7/.
5. De Jong /3/, Book 2, pp. 287/307.
6. For example, at the beginning of the nineties, several department stores in Germany have reduced the retail prices of coffee with 20% or 25% so that their clients could benefit of the fall of the coffee prices at the production. Other sellers in other countries and especially in public establishments (restaurants etc.) did not follow this example.
7. Linda /9/ pp. 275/294 and 363/364.

8. Linda /12/.
9. Linda /9/ pp. 28/29, 288/292.
10. R is the net profit after taxes in % of the consolidated turnover.
11. Linda /8/ /9/ /10/ /12/.
12. The Americans seem to aim mainly at the rate of return, notwithstanding that RJR Nabisco has lost $ 1149 million $ in 1989 on a consolidated turnover of $ 15,2 billion, after the take-over of Kohlberg, Kravis, Roberts. The consolidated turnovers of the most important American groups in 1989 are: Philip - Morris - General Foods - Kraft: $ 44 bn, Pepsico 15,4, Sara Lee: 11,7, Conagra 11,3 (but, after the outstanding mega-operations the purchase for example of several activities of Beatrice Co. could reach $ 20 bn in 1991), Anheuser Busch 9,5 and then, very active in Europe and in the world, Coca-Cola, Borden, Ralston Purina, Quaker Oats, Campbell Soup, CPC, Kellogg.
13. Linda /8/ /9/ pp. 260/262.
14. Linda /7/ /8/ /12/.
15. We may note the uncommon increase of the consolidated turnover (after take-overs) between 1987 and 1988, even in ECU, for some English companies of medium-large size: Albert Fisher + 116%, Polly Peck + 89%, Booker + 45%, Premier Brands + 45%, Hazlewood + 26%. The increase 1988/1989 of the consolidated turnover in ECU was larger than 20% even for the giants Hillsdown Hold. (+ 24%), Cadbury Schweppes (+ 74%), United Biscuits (+ 30%), Tate & Lyle (+ 31%). The list of their take-overs is spectacular.
16. The process of take-overs has continued in 1989 and 1990.
17. Linda /5/ /9/ /12/, Burns & others, Galizzi, Marfels, Maunder.
18. On the first place of the American list we find Du Pont (E.I.) De Nemours (consolidated turnover 1989: $ 35 bn, of which about $ 5 bn made in Europe), followed by Dow Chemicals ($ 17,7 bn), Union Carbide ($ 8,7 bn), Monsanto ($ 8,7 bn), without mentioning the giant diversified Procter & Gamble ($ 21,7 bn).
19. In 1989, the USA leaders of the pharma have made the following consolidated turnovers: Johnson & Johnson $ 9,8 bn, Bristol-Myer Squibb 9,4 bn, American Home Products 6,7 Merck 6,7 Pfizer 5,9. For the European industry, De Jong /4/ pp. 209/235.
20. ICI is followed in the world classification of paint by the Germans BASF and Hoechst. F.T. of 16/8/86.
21. After this operation, the world classification of the first 10 pharmaceuticals would be: (1) Merck-USA, (2) M-B-Squibb-USA, (3) Glaxo-GB, (4) Beecham Smithkline-GB/USA, (5) Ciba-Geigy-CH, (6) Rhône-Poulenc-Rorer-F, (7) Hoechst-D, (8) Bayer-D, (9) Johnson & Johnson-USA, (10) American Home Products-USA. (La Tribune of 22/1/1990 and, with a few differences, Frankfurter Allgemeine of 29/1/1990).
22. Another older purchase made by BP the American giant of petroleum: "Standard Oil Co.".
23. Par. 2.1 - 2.3 of this report.

24. Linda /5/ /9/ /10/ /12/.
25. Linda /1/.
26. Bonfour /2/, Marfels & Kumps & others.
27. See note 30.
28. MBB is the most important partner of the European Consortium of aeronautical construction AIRBUS, with 37,9% ex aequo with the French Aerospatiale, followed by British Aerospace (20%) and the Spanish Casa (4%). See also Hartley in De Jong /4/.
29. In June 1990, Daimler-Benz announced it had programmed an investment in the "automotive" of 13 bn DM in R&D. A new generation of the luxe serie S will be launched on the market (FT of 20/6/90 p. 21).
30. In 1988, Mercedes made in Europe a market share of 25% on the markets of lorries of more than 3,5 ton, followed by IVECO (Fiat) with 21%, Renault-F with 12%, DAF-NL with 9,5%, Volvo-S with 9,2%, MAN-Volkswagen-D with 7,7% (FT of 23/11/89). We understand the perplexities which bring the joined initiatives of Daimler-Benz and MAN to buy the Spanish ENASA in 1990, the latter already controlling 3,5% of the European market. And also in 1990 Volvo tries to obtain the total control on DAF, of which they hold a minority participation. Let us also recall that the scale economies at the level of the maintenance and the assistance play an enormous role for the lorries. This also explains the reasons of the alliance of Volvo and the French Renault in 1990.
31. For example JV Eurocopter and Aerospatiale (La Tribune 9/4/90, FT 7/4/90). For the projects with Mitsubishi: Le Monde 8/3/90, Der Spiegel 23/3/90, La Tribune 24/4/90. See also Hartley, L'Aerospace in De Jong, /4/ pp. 329/352. For the initiatives in USSR: FT 23/5/90, Linda /11/.
32. We recall that Pratt & Whitney is a subsidiary of United Technologies (consolidated turnover 1989 $ 19,8 bn), competitor of General Electric on the markets of airplane engines (La Tribune 25/5/90).
33. FT 4/5/90, L'Echo de la Bourse 4/5/90.
34. On the difficulties of Michelin to finance this purchase, see: le Fig.-Eco (le cahier saumon) of 22/6/90 p. 1 and 21/2/90.
35. La Tribune 14/5/90: Cor van der Klugt, President of Philips, has resigned.
36. La Tribune of 9/5/90, FT 10/5/90.
37. Carabini-Caranita, Camagni-Martelli and especially Pearce-Sutton, ch. 1.
38. FT 23/3/87, with articles of P. Betts, T. Dodsworth, A. Friedman.
39. La Tribune 26/4/90, 16/5/90, Le Monde 17/5/90, FT 16/5/90.
40. See notes 39, 41 and 43.
41. For a critical note on the philosophy of the article 85: Linda /9/ and /10/.
42. On several counts the *OGE* merits the name of being global:

    1) by its worldwide objectives
    2) by the increasing importance of diversified groups

3) by the relationship it establishes between market shares and price-strategies and operations in terms of joint ventures, mergers and take-overs;
4) by its global logic, because the OGE wants to emphasize the numerous factors which determine the evolution of the markets. We will add relative to this:

   a) there does not exist an automatic relationship between the degree of concentration and its evolution, on the one hand, and the fixation of domination-prices and the realisation of domination-profits on the other hand;
   b) nevertheless, to allow for the existence of monopoly prices and profits, we must know if there does or does not exist dominant positions;
   c) consequently, the analysis of the degree of producers' concentration is a prior condition to make it possible to interpret the results of the analyses of the evolution of the different prices;
   d) particularly, the knowledge (and its measure) is essential to explain and understand the followed price-policy,
      - by the most important manufacturers and producers;
      - by the most important retailers;
   e) the OGE becomes in this way also a factual basis and a necessary precondition to apply the article 86 of the Treaty. We may estimate that the IIIrd parts of the 4 reports of the EEC Commission on the policy of competition (the 6th, 7th, 8th and 9th) represent fruitful landmarks for the installation of this observatory, of which the urgency seems obvious. Indeed, the increasing diffusion of new dominating positions on the markets urge some companies to use all their efforts to block the information and the analysis on the matter. And this to avoid providing munition to the companies' (potentially) competitors, to the consumers and to their associations, and to the governments.

43. At the first stage of the data-collection and at the informational elaboration, no threshold may be fixed, because of the relations between the trademarks, subsidiaries and joint ventures operating in the context of global competition.

44. Why? For numerous reasons and in particular to strengthen the impact of the Communities policy and its credibility, due to the control and the support of the consumers, the public opinion, the national authorities, the concerned circles. Indeed, in the context of global competition, the European anti-trust policy is becoming less and less efficient facing the mega-operations of the foreign mega-multinationals. At another occasion (Linda /9/ pp. 53/60) we have studied, with documental evidence, the business of the Swiss Nestlé and of the American Philip Morris - General Foods - Kraft. But the latter has recently bought in 1990, after the take-over of the Italian

Negroni, the second Swiss group in food (after Nestlé), this is Jacob Suchard (chocolate and coffee). The subsidiaries in the EEC of these 2 extra-community groups which from now on will become one, are numerous and occupy very important, even dominating positions and market shares on several national product markets in many countries of the EEC. It is global market power that increases in a considerable measure. Which real power does in fact the antitrust of Brussels possess facing such mega-operations? How could we slow down firm concentration when mega-companies like Philip Morris with a consolidated turnover beyond the $ 50 bn are involved?
The debate is open.

Appendix 1

Definition of indicators of concentration

C_3 : summation of market shares of the three biggest firms

X_i : market share of firm i

$$2L = \frac{X_1}{X_2} \times 100$$ the ratio between the market shares of the first firm and the second firm

$$NIL_2 = \frac{(C_3 \times 100)^2 \cdot 2L}{10}$$ index of market power

6 EFFICACY AND FREEDOM OF MERGERS AND ACQUISITIONS

PIETER W. MOERLAND

1. Introduction

Mergers and acquisitions are both interesting and intriguing for a variety of reasons. First, these external forms of corporate restructuring seem to be more popular or at least more prevalent in some periods of time than in others. Second, different branches of economic science, such as industrial organization, strategic management and financial economics try to bring about plausible and testable explanations for these phenomena. This has already generated a multitude of theories and hypotheses, postulated from various angles, each of which only provides a partial approach to this complex problem. Third, the subject of mergers and acquisitions is much more than merely an economic problem. Especially, historical, cultural, juridical and institutional aspects deserve sufficient consideration when one studies the causes and consequences of these transactions.

In his very productive scientific career Professor De Jong has shown a broad and profound interest in a variety of economic problems, such as innovation, competition and concentration, both on the level of individual firms and of industries. His approach to these and other aspects of industrial organization is continually and consistently anchored in his well-known dynamic market theory. He always displays a strong preference for an integral and comprehensive approach by combining theory and practice, structure and process, generality and specificity, and so on. This also applies to his approach to the subject matter of mergers and acquisitions. On the one hand, he develops a general view on the origins of merger waves by way of abstraction, referring to severe fluctuations in competitive intensity throughout the world, which herald massive corporate restructurings in many countries and in many industries. On the other hand, he excites the admiration of his audience again and again by his impressive knowledge of and insight into an endless variety of individual cases and circumstances. In his unique way, Professor De Jong made many contributions, also on the subject of mergers and acquisitions. I do not attempt to review all of them here, since consultation of the original sources will be much more valuable (e.g. De Jong (1989a, 1989b, 1990)). However, at the end of this article I shall pay special attention to some of his recent research findings.

Economic theory generally offers two competing approaches as to the efficacy of mergers and acquisitions. On the one hand, students of financial economics, relying on stock market data and the efficient market hypothesis view mergers and acquisitions as value-enhancing activities in which managers work to maximize shareholder wealth. This value creation may come from all sorts of advantages like synergy, economies of scale, increased market power and replacement of inefficient management. The gains from this restructuring are evidenced in the large increases of stock prices of acquisition targets (Franks and Harris (1989)). On the other hand, students of industrial organization, on the basis of accounting data and models of market structure, are rather skeptical of the efficiency gains on account of mergers and acquisitions. They claim that most acquisitions are unsuccessful in terms of increasing profitability and market share. Industrial organization economists often suggest that managerial empire-building rather than efficiency gains, constitutes a driving force to mergers and acquisitions (Browne and Rosengren (1987)).

In this article, we shall try to shed some light on the observed controversy in views with respect to the alleged efficacy of mergers and acquisitions. Thereby, attention will be paid to the impact of differential institutional characteristics regarding the freedom of the takeover market in different countries of the world. Especially, a distinction is made between takeover regimes in Anglo-Saxon countries and Continental European countries, disposing of rather liberal versus rather restrictive takeover markets, respectively. According to De Jong (1990) a parallel distinction might be made between profit maximizing behaviour in Anglo-Saxon countries and growth maximizing behaviour in Continental European countries (and Japan). Our discussion will be concluded by relating managerial behaviour to differences in disciplinatory power of the market for corporate control in the above mentioned two geographical blocks. Eventually, convergence of takeover regimes will emerge since the recently proposed E.E.C.-regulations rest heavily on the present English model. When adopted, this implies reduced possibilities for managerial entrenchment, and more freedom on the market for corporate control in Europe is to be expected.

2. Separation of Ownership and Control: an Agency Problem

Mergers and acquisitions take place through the exchange of property rights between different groups of shareholders. This involves a transfer of control with respect to the governance of business firms by accomplishing some transaction on the takeover market. However, the firm cannot be simply conceived as ordinary negotiable commodity. Thinking about the concept and the nature of the firm has a long history in economic science. For a proper assessment of the causes and consequences of phenomena like mergers and acquisitions a clear understanding of some important features of the firm may be useful. Therefore, without aiming at completeness, a brief review of some relevant aspects of the firm will be given.

First, there is the well-known neo-classical theory of the firm. In this view, the firm is conceived as a profit maximizing entity, consisting of a production function which exhibits the transformation of inputs into output. This is a rather mechanical and static view which pays no adequate attention to multiple objectives of different stakeholders and to entrepreneurial activities like discovering hitherto unnoticed opportunities. The latter aspect has been dealt with eminently by authors like Schumpeter (1934), Kirzner (1973), and, of course, De Jong himself (1989a).

As to the former aspect of different stakeholders in the firm, the relationship between managers and shareholders is of special interest. Except for those cases where ownership and control are united in one person (manager-owner), that relationship poses an agency problem which asks for a solution. Whereas the development of agency theory is rather new - it actually goes back to the seventies - the problem of potential divergence in economic interests between managers and financiers has been recognized much earlier. Illustrative of this is what the father of economic science, Adam Smith (1776), wrote with respect to the joint-stock company (p. 741): "(T)he directors of such companies, however, being the managers rather of other peoples money than of their own, it cannot well be expected, that they should watch over it with the same vigilance with which the partners in a private copartnery frequently watch over their own. (...) negligence and profusion, therefore, must always prevail, more or less, in the management of the affairs of such a company."

In their famous book on the modern corporation, Berle and Means (1932) express a fear of "corporate plundering" due to a separation of ownership and control. Jensen and Meckling (1976) were the first to put this problem systematically within the framework of agency theory. Managers are seen as agents who act on behalf of shareholders being the principals. The latter delegate decision making authority over the money they provide to the managers under conditions of uncertainty and asymmetric information. This poses an agency problem, as it is unlikely that the managers will only act in the shareholders' best interest. Rather, one might expect the agents will try to maximize their own utility functions, by pursuing perquisites, restraining their efforts, and stressing their own attitudes towards risk. In order to solve, or at least to mitigate this agency problem, the principals should provide appropriate incentives to the agents such as stock option plans, bonuses, and so on.

Furthermore, various forms of monitoring can be applied by auditing financial statements, reviewing of perquisites, limiting of decisions, and so on.

In addition to this, the functioning of markets too may have a disciplinatory power to make the managers behave as closely as possible in accordance with the maximization of shareholder wealth. Fama (1980) suggests that managers are primarily monitored by the managerial labour market. If this market is competitive both within and outside the firm, it serves as a disciplinatory mechanism to the managers. If this market is not very competitive, then there is still another disciplinatory mechanism, namely the market for corporate control, or the takeover market. Jensen and Ruback (1983) view this market (p. 6) "as a market in which alternative managerial teams compete for the rights to manage corporate resources." Hence, they conceive the takeover market as an important component of the managerial labour market. When the incumbent management team does not perform very well, its position is at risk by the threat of a takeover implying the replacement by another management team. This argument has become to be known as the improved management hypothesis, which goes originally back to Marris (1963) and Manne (1965). Of course, this hypothesis pertains to the management team of a target firm. It is equally interesting to investigate whether the management team of the bidding firm acts in the best interest of its own shareholders when it is planning and realizing some particular merger or acquisition. Do mergers and acquisitions virtually generate positive net private returns and how are they distributed? The next section is devoted to considering this intriguing and controversial question.

3. Controversial Assessment Methods

There are at least two, more or less competing, approaches for the assessment of the financial effects relating to mergers and acquisitions. Generally speaking, students of industrial organization habitually analyse changes in profitability, market shares and productivity following mergers and acquisitions. On the other hand, students of financial economics usually analyse stock market reactions to announcements of mergers and acquisitions. When comparing the empirical results of both research approaches, one cannot but observe much disagreement and controversy: researchers in the realm of industrial organization and those in the realm of financial economics differ in the research methods they apply and in the conclusions they reach. Without pretending to solve this puzzle, I should like to highlight some of its intriguing elements.

In financial economics, a customary approach to estimate the effects of mergers and acquisitions is to focus on the behaviour of stock prices of bidder and target firms around the time of announcement (Jensen and Ruback (1983)). These so-called "event studies" use estimates of the abnormal stock price changes around the offer announcement date as a measure of a merger or takeover. Abnormal returns are measured as differences between actual and expected stock returns. A correction is usually made for the influence of market-wide events which would otherwise also take place, mostly with the help of the so-called market model. The vast empirical literature in the United States, applying event studies, indicates that target shareholders generally earn high abnormal returns of 20 per cent (mergers) or 30 per cent (tender offers). However, the abnormal returns to the shareholders of the bidding firms are much less convincing, namely zero (mergers) or 4 per cent (tender offers). Furthermore, according to Jensen and Ruback (p. 20), "several studies show indications of systematic reductions in the stock prices of bidding firms in the year following the event." Thus, the evidence regarding abnormal returns to bidders exhibits a somewhat mixed picture.

As far as all shareholders, i.e. of both the target and the bidding firms, gain positive abnormal returns the transaction is said to be value-enhancing, and therefore privately and socially desirable. When reviewing the empirical literature, Jensen and Ruback (1983) incline to the favourable conclusion that corporate takeovers generate positive gains. However, Roll's review (1986) of this literature yields a more skeptical conclusion, namely that (p. 198) "takeover gains may have been overestimated if they exist at all." Nevertheless, most students of financial economics tend to draw the conclusion that mergers and acquisitions are in general value-enhancing. One might put the question whether or not stock price movements adequately reflect the possible advantages that are to be expected from a merger or acquisition.

In financial economics, it is widely accepted that financial markets are highly efficient. This means that, for instance, security prices reflect all available information about the economy, about financial markets and the specific company involved. Security prices adjust rapidly to the release of new information. As a consequence, security price reactions to the announcement of a merger or acquisition are conceived as the market's consensus estimate of the significance and value of such events. Numerous studies estimate the effects of mergers and acquisitions on stock prices of bidding and target firms around the time of announcement. The outcomes of these "event studies", as mentioned before, heavily depend on the validity of the so-called efficient market hypothesis.

Several authors (e.g. Summers (1986)) have expressed doubt on the tenability of the efficient market hypothesis. Black (1986) describes market efficiency in the following terms (p. 533): "we might define an efficient market as one in which price is within a factor of 2 of value, i.e., the price is more than half of value and less than twice of value." Thus, Black accounts for temporary undervaluation of corporations which might induce potential acquirers who possess specific superior information about that corporation or about its industry to make a takeover attempt. Then, a premium can be offered without a corresponding perspective on new value creation.

More radical critics of the efficient market hypothesis come from experts in industrial organization. Scherer (1988) rejects the relevance of this hypothesis, since in his view it is uncapable of demonstrating whether or not mergers and acquisitions are in fact efficiency-enhancing.

Also, a heavy assault on the concept of market efficiency has been made by Du Boff and Herman (1987), posing (p. 2): "Our thesis is that the vision of the merger process associated with efficient market theorizing is largely irrelevant to the explanation of merger movements (...). The four major outbursts of merger activity between 1897 and 1987 occurred in periods of economic expansion, high liquidity and buoyant stock markets, introduction of new security market instruments and techniques, and an influx of new participants into financial markets. These markets were characterized by varying but significant degrees of misinformation, manipulation, the outcropping of facts, euphoria, and speculation. (...) It is not surprising that each merger movement was terminated by a stock market crash or a recession, or both. This suggests that a disequilibrium system, not an informed and efficient market, provides the institutional basis for merger movements."

All this criticism on the efficient market hypothesis touches the relevance of using event studies as a method for measuring wealth effects as indicators for value creation. Some caution should be exercised when interpreting stock price reactions during a relatively short period of time (window) surrounding an announcement of some particular event, such as a merger or acquisition. We cannot be sure that the stock market (the investors) is capable of estimating the long run economic gains resulting from such events to perfection. Especially, industrial economists are skeptical of the efficiency gains that financial economists often claim for corporate restructurings. They emphasize again and again that acquirers and investors overestimate the potential gains, contending that most acquisitions are unsuccessful in terms of increasing profitability and market share. Hoped-for gains tend to be reduced by transaction costs associated with the integration. Caves (1987) reviews a number of studies that are particularly negative on mergers and acquisitions (p. 164): "The thrust of evidence accumulated in the past on the ex post profitability of mergers is that the average acquiring firm at best realizes no net profit on its consolidated assets." One might argue against these types of studies in the sense that their use of accounting data is at least as questionable as relying solely on stock price movements. Accounting data largely depend on depreciation practices, treatment of goodwill, reserves and so on. Furthermore, it is probably hard to discern, over a longer period of time, the effects on profitability that are due to one or perhaps more acquisitions from other causes that occur simultaneously, such as changing competitive pressure, new technological developments, and so on.

Nevertheless, there seems to be a discrepancy between the favourable ex ante expectations regarding mergers and acquisitions as reflected by stock price movements on the one hand, and disappointing ex post performance as measured by profitability and market share outcomes on the other. This constellation elicits the question by what motives and considerations managers are driven when selecting and assessing a target firm. Do the poor returns to shareholders of acquiring firms reveal managerial behaviour that diverges from maximization of shareholder wealth? Are managers bent upon empire-building and increasing market power, rather than efficiency gains? The next section pays attention to the puzzling question why, as it seems to be, management of acquiring firms on the average pays too much for its targets.

4. (Why) do Acquirers Pay too Much for their Targets?

Standard financial economics assumes that corporate management acts as if it maximizes its present shareholders' wealth. However, sometimes it looks as if the reverse is true. Consider the case of Du Pont's acquisition of Conoco in 1981 (Weston and Copeland (1986), p. 903). As is well-known, Du Pont won the take-over battle eventually by surpassing other bidders (Seagram, Mobil Oil) through a threefold revision of its offer. The total amount of its final offer was $ 7.5 billion, i.e. $ 3.2 billion more than the pre-offering period market value of Conoco. The latter's shareholders realized an abnormal return of 71 per cent during a six weeks period, while the equity value of the winning bidder, Du Pont, was reduced by about 10 per cent, corresponding to a dollar loss of $ 0.8 billion. Was this action by Du Pont's management in the best interest of its own shareholders? It certainly was in the best interest of Conoco's shareholders! Obviously, Du Pont's shareholders were not sure of the attractiveness of the deal. When we subtract the $ 0.8 billion wealth loss to the shareholders of the bidding firm from the $ 3.2 billion gain to the shareholders of the target firm, can it then be maintained that this transaction is a $ 2.4 billion value-enhancing one? In answering this question one should keep in mind the previous discussion about the validity of the efficient market hypothesis. So, the answer might at best be: possibly. Ruback (1982) has made an interesting attempt to identify the sources of the revaluation that occurred. He explored a variety of different explanations, such as synergy, the release of new information, undervalued oil reserves, replacement of managers, but none of these factors provided a satisfactory explanation. So, it seems to be difficult to give a clear answer to the question whether Du Pont has paid too much for Conoco. One can only say that the available evidence points into that direction. As we have seen before, the average takeover premiums over a large sample of cases, are generally relatively high, if not too high from the bidder's shareholders' point of view. There is a number of possible explanations for this unsettling finding. Roughly speaking, these explanations can be classified into two broad categories, viz.,

a) management aims at other objectives than maximization of its own shareholders' wealth;
b) management does aim at maximization of its own shareholder wealth, but encounters serious problems in accomplishing this.

a) *Management aims at other objectives*

Industrial organization economists often suggest that managers strive after empire-building and capturing market power. Non-value maximizing behaviour may occur when the management's focus is primarily oriented to growth in sales or assets. Mueller (1972) has suggested, that firms are likely to merge, especially through diversification, when they are in either the mature or declining stage of their life cycle. They may then attempt to acquire new prospects for further growth and profitability in other industries. However, these firms could alternatively pay out their free cash flow to their existing shareholders. Free cash flows are cash flows in excess of those required for funding a firm's projects with positive net present values. Jensen (1986) presumes that, at least firms in declining industries that dispose of large free cash flows from their cash cows, are more likely to undertake low-benefit or even value-destroying mergers. Especially, the third merger wave was full of unrelated expansions, based on a corporate strategy which, according to Porter (1987), has mostly dissipated value instead of created shareholder value.

Donaldson (1984) puts forward, on the basis of a detailed in-depth study of twelve large Fortune 500 corporations, that managers are not driven by maximization of shareholder wealth, but rather by maximization of what he calls "corporate wealth". He defines it as (p. 3): "the aggregate purchasing power available to management for strategic purposes during any given planning period." Corporate wealth provides management with resources that it can use at its discretion to implement its own strategy, which is not necessarily in accordance with the optimal strategy from a shareholder's point of view. Payment of superfluous cash to shareholders reduces the resources controlled by managers, thereby reducing their power. Non-value maximizing behaviour is mostly aggravated by tying up compensation schemes to size or growth in size of the corporation. According to this view on management behaviour, strategic decision-making, including the appraisal of mergers and acquisitions, takes place on other grounds than is usually assumed in the theory of financial economics. As mentioned before the development of agency theory tries to cope with some of these complicating factors.

b) *Management encounters serious problems*

In this approach maximization of shareholder wealth is assumed to be the basic principle, but there are serious problems in its execution. In assessing a merger or acquisition, it will be generally rather difficult to make a proper estimation of the advantages to be expected, let alone to choose the right cost of capital to discount the relevant future cash flows. There may exist differences between the stock market on the one hand and management on the other in assessing the attractiveness and value generating power. Some years ago, Roll (1986) put forward his meanwhile well-known hubris hypothesis. Hubris refers to an animal-like spirit of arrogant pride and self-confidence. Bidders that have been infected by hubris are convinced that they cannot do wrong and have the only right opinion. They get caught up in the battle for some target and are inclined to pay eventually too much for their prey (the winner's curse). However, one may also explain the high premiums in the case of takeover battles as a consequence of severe competition between bidders for a very favourite target. Some authors (e.g. Jarrell (1987)) report that multiple bidders for one target are associated with significantly higher abnormal returns to target shareholders. Also, target shareholders themselves sometimes successfully claim for a higher premium than is originally offered. Then, target shareholders reap the benefits by virtue of the eagerness in the takeover market to acquire some specific firm at the expense of the bidder's shareholders. Nevertheless, such a high premium may in certain cases be defended, as the opportunity costs of losing the battle for a target going to a competitor, are not observable. Sometimes, a high premium may be rational in order to forestall a dreaded rival.

Finally, it might be argued that, irrespective of the intended objective of maximizing shareholder wealth, in many cases the possible benefits that are to be expected from a merger or acquisition are not fully exploited in the actual process of integration and implementation. This may be due to problems of cultural adjustment, unexpected reactions from personnel, competing firms, or something else. Then, the ex ante expectations with respect to the value-enhancing potential of some merger or acquisition are not materialized in practice.

Thus, there may be a whole bunch of reasons why the management team of a bidding firm, although in principle striving for maximum shareholder wealth, cannot actually succeed in accomplishing it.

5. Anglo-Saxon versus Continental European Takeover Markets

As stated before, mergers and acquisitions take place through the exchange of property rights between different groups of shareholders. However, specific ownership control structures and takeover barriers may restrain the actual possibilities of exchange. In some areas of the world the takeover market is more liberal than in others. Roughly speaking, in Anglo-Saxon countries, such as the United States, the United Kingdom and Canada, the takeover market is traditionally largely free. There, the role of common stock is an essential element of corporate behaviour and Stock Exchanges are highly active and well-developed. Shareholders, principally and often effectively, have the possibilities and the power to influence the way in which a corporation is controlled, by appointing or dismissing directors or executives when necessary, through a proxy contest or a contested takeover. During the last decade frequently applied practices like corporate raiding, asset stripping, crude hostile takeovers, greenmail and the creation of defensive measures (shark repellents, e.g. poison pills) have provoked critical questions with respect to the evolving nature of the takeover market. While a common notion is growing that excesses in corporate restructuring may be damaging to particular stakeholders as well as to the economy as a whole, there is still a fundamental belief in the benefits of a rather liberal regime in the market of corporate control.

Contrary to the Anglo-Saxon countries, the takeover market is much less developed in countries like Japan and on the European Continent. The corporate landscape of Japan is characterized by a multitude of cross-holdings between a number of firms constituting networks of interrelated companies (keiretsus). Remarkably, at the moment this contribution is being written, (summer 1990), the flamboyant Texan corporate raider T. Boone Pickens is conducting a crusade for shareholders' rights in an attempt to exert influence on Koito, a head-lamp factory belonging to one of the most powerful Japanese keiretsus (under the leadership of Toyota). It is rather doubtful that Pickens will be successful, as this type of action is not in keeping with Japanese corporate culture. The role of common stock as a piece of ownership and voting right is much less pronounced in Japan than in the Anglo-Saxon countries.

Figure 1 *Market Capitalisation*
(billions ECU)

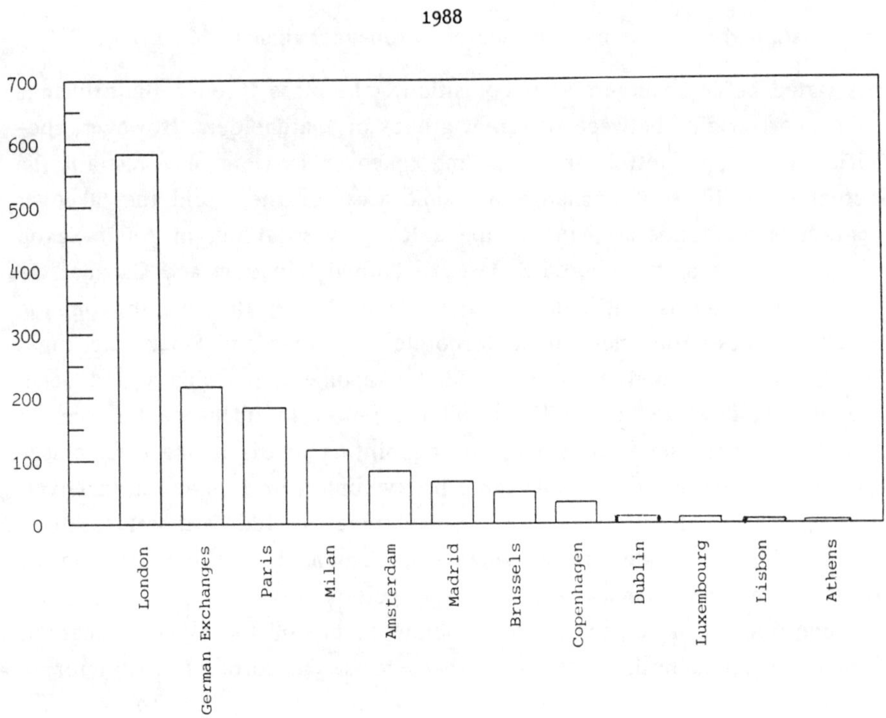

Source: European Stock Exchange Annual Statistical Report 1988, Committee of Stock Exchanges in the E.E.C.

The same is more or less true for the countries of Continental Europe, be it that structures and cultures may differ per country. Mostly, there are substantial barriers of one kind or another that may hamper or frustrate intended mergers or acquisitions. Those barriers may come from restrictions on the voting power of outside common shareholders, by preferential treatment of certain categories of shareholders such as families and management-related institutions, or by cross-holdings of equity interests between friendly corporations, just as in Japan. In principle, the role of common stock is traditionally a significant one, but the influence of outside stock owners has been gradually eroded in favour of inner circles (incumbent management, family ties, etc.). The role of Stock Exchanges is illustrated by figure 1. Clearly, the London Stock Exchange is by far the most important one. Its volume is nearly as large as that of all other Continental Stock Exchanges together (total ECU 784.8 billion).

The Gross Domestic Product of the UK (1988) is a bit smaller than that of France and of Italy, and much smaller than that of W. Germany. Therefore, it is interesting to relate the volume of a country's market capitalisation to its respective level of GDP, as is done in figure 2. Note the relatively high ranking of the Benelux-countries and the low ranking of France, Germany and Italy.

Figure 2 Market Capitalisation as % of G.D.P.

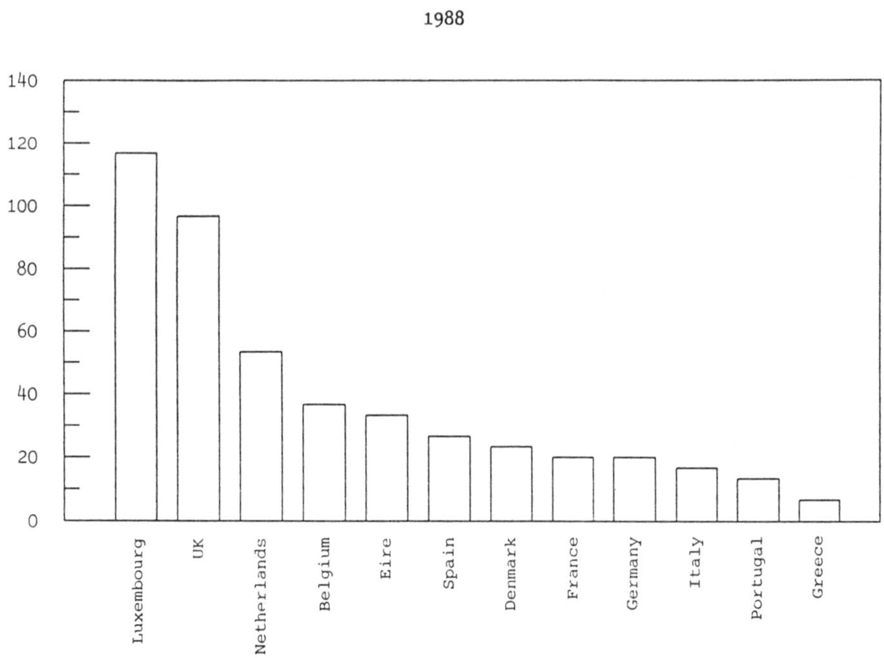

Source: European Stock Exchange Annual Statistical Report 1988, Committee of Stock Exchanges in the E.E.C.

Historically, there are great differences in corporate structure and culture between the United Kingdom and most other E.E.C.-countries. Successful contested bids are rare in all countries, except of course in the UK and to a limited extent in France. In many E.E.C.-countries (Belgium, France, W. Germany, Italy, Spain) a majority of voting shares in a great number of corporations are deposited with families or closely linked institutions. In Italy, only seven corporations have a majority of their shares in public hands, and five of these seem to be effectively controlled by family groupings. In Belgium, France and Spain, cross-shareholdings serve as major structural barriers to undesired takeovers. In the Netherlands, and to some modest degree in W. Germany, widespread share-ownership is largely prevalent. However, a number of defensive measures hampers nearly any attempt to acquire a company against the will of the incumbent management. In W. Germany as well as the Netherlands, outside shareholders have little or no influence on the composition of the Supervisory Board, while a number of limitations on their voting rights further preclude nearly any substantial interference with a company's control. In W. Germany, general banks and insurance companies have substantial equity stakes in big industry, along with positions in the Supervisory Boards. In addition, financial institutions are allowed to collect proxy rights of small shareholders ('Depotstimmrecht') and use these at their discretion in voting procedures.

Thus, in the Continental E.E.C.-countries, structural and technical barriers restrain the degree of freedom of the market for corporate control. This implies that it will be rather difficult, if not impossible, to acquire a corporation against the will of its incumbent management. The same holds for a number of other European areas (non E.E.C.-countries) like Austria, Scandinavia and Switzerland.

Does this mean that Anglo-Saxon companies on the one hand and Continental European companies on the other show different patterns of behaviour and performance? According to De Jong (1990) this is actually the case. He has recently done very interesting theoretical and empirical research with respect to growth rates, profit rates, etc. for a great number of large companies in different countries, including US, Japan, European. His conclusions are (p. 17-20): (...) "Anglo-Saxon companies are profit maximizers, whereas the Continental European companies strive for maximum sales or sales growth. Roughly speaking, the Anglo-Saxon net profit rates (...) were twice as high as those for Continental European and Japanese companies, whereas the growth rates show a reverse picture. (...)

(O)nly the British companies belonging to the European largest owe their high market values to their profitability more than to their size. The contrast with the Germans, Swiss and Italians, whose size of companies is impressive, but whose profitability is not, could not be more pronounced. The French do have highly profitable companies, though the market values are not commensurate. The other continental countries (Benelux, Spain, Sweden, Norway) occupy a middle ground position, in which the variables are better balanced, though profitability is always on a relatively lower level than market value."

It should be noticed that De Jong bases his distinction between profit maximization and growth maximization on differences in the freedom and ease of takeovers. In his view, Anglo-Saxon corporations are thus to be seen as profit maximizers. This seems to conflict with the above reviewed evidence that especially American corporations tend to pay too high takeover premiums, or at least premiums that are held to diminish ex post profitability. For this reason, pure profit or value maximization to be accomplished by agents (management) acting on behalf of principals (shareholders) seems to be illusory. However, and that is the way I am inclined to interpret De Jong's conclusions, in an Anglo-Saxon institutional environment the disciplinatory mechanisms for monitoring managerial behaviour are much stronger than in a Continental European one. In my view, the distinction between profit maximization and growth maximization does not represent a pure contrast regarding objective functions, but rather a significantly different degree to which management is allowed to diverge from value maximizing behaviour.

6. E.E.C.-Regulation for a more Liberal Takeover Market

At the moment, E.E.C.-regulation on mergers and acquisitions is developing. The proposal for the 13th Directive Company Law on Public Bids, when adopted in its present form, will significantly change takeover practice in Continental Europe. Roughly speaking, the proposed regulatory model strongly resembles the present English City Code on Takeovers. It requires an acquirer who has acquired one third of the shares of a target company to make a public bid on all issued shares of such a company. Once a bid has been announced, the target company may not issue securities carrying voting rights or engage in transactions other than current operations concluded under normal conditions without prior approval of the shareholders meeting.

As a consequence of these E.E.C.-proposals, a number of existing defensive measures, especially in W. Germany and the Netherlands, will have to go in the near future. The English are asking for a level playing field in all countries of the E.E.C., which will make takeovers as easily possible as is the case in the United Kingdom. However, besides legal and statutory defensive measures, in a number of countries there are mainly structural barriers to free takeovers, such as cross holdings, closely held ownership, and so on (e.g. France, Italy, Spain). Those barriers can of course not be quickly and easily eliminated. Technical barriers are less difficult to remove than structural barriers. Thus, the way to a fully reciprocal playing field for corporate takeovers throughout all E.E.C.-countries seems to be still rather long. Nevertheless, public policy tends to point in a more liberal direction and its implication will be that managerial entrenchment loses importance in favour of more freedom on the market for corporate control in Europe.

7. Concluding Remarks

The assessment of mergers and acquisitions differs substantially between two branches of economic science: industrial organization and financial economics. Ex ante expected gains seem to be overestimated by financial economists, since industrial organization economists generally come out with disappointing ex post changes in profitability. We have pointed at several possible explanations for this paradoxical evidence. A further integration of both branches in economics and their research methods used might pave the way to a fuller understanding on the usefulness and efficacy of mergers and acquisitions.

The degree of freedom on takeover markets differs considerably between Anglo-Saxon and Continental European countries. When technical or structural barriers to takeovers are prevalent, as is the case in many European countries, entrenching management teams seem to have much room for departures from value maximizing behaviour, i.e. more than in liberal takeover markets as present in Anglo-Saxon countries. However, in view of the approaching E.E.C. regulation on takeover bids, the working and freedom of Continental European takeover markets will be improved. This will further stimulate domestic and cross-border takeover activity. Whether this is going to lead to mainly efficacious transactions, will for the time being remain a puzzling question, as long as financial economists and industrial organization economists disagree about their methods and results.

Bibliography

Berle, A.A. and G.C. Means (1932). *The Modern Corporation and Private Property*, New York, Mc Millan.

Black, F. (1986). Noise, *The Journal of Finance*, 41, 529-543.

Du Boff, R.B. and E.S. Herman (1987). *The promotional-financial dynamic of merger movements: a historical perspective*, paper presented at the Conference of the American Economic Association, Chicago.

Browne, L.E. and E.S. Rosengren (1987). The merger boom: an overview, in Browne, L.E. and E.S. Rosengren (eds.), *The Merger Boom*, proceedings of a conference held at Melvin Village, New Hamshire, Federal Reserve Bank of Boston, Conference Series no. 31.

Caves, R.E. (1987). Effects of mergers and acquisitions on the economy: an industrial organization perspective, in Browne, L.E. and E.S. Rosengren (eds.), *The Merger Boom*, proceedings of a conference held at Melvin Village, New Hampshire, Federal Reserve Bank of Boston, Conference Series no. 31.

Committee of Stock Exchanges in the E.E.C. (1988). *European Stock Exchange Annual Statistical Report*, Brussels.

Donaldson, G. (1984). *Managing Corporate Wealth*, Praeger, New York.

Fama, E.F. (1980). Agency problems and the theory of the firm, *Journal of Political Economy*, 88, 288-307.

Fama, E.F. and M.C. Jensen (1983a). Separation of ownership and control, *Journal of Law and Economics*, 26, 301-326.

Fama, E.F. and M.C. Jensen (1983b). Agency problems and residual claims, *Journal of Law and Economics*, 26, 326-351.

Franks, J.R. and R.S. Harris (1989). Shareholder wealth effects of corporate takeovers; the U.K. experience 1955-1985, *Journal of Financial Economics*, 23, 225-249.

Jarrell, G.A. (1987). Financial innovation and corporate mergers, in Browne, L.E. and E.S. Rosengren (eds.), *The Merger Boom*, proceedings of a conference held at Melvin Village, New Hamshire, Federal Reserve Bank of Boston, Conference Series no. 31.

Jarrell, G.A. and A.B. Poulsen (1987). Shark repellents and stock prices, the effects of antitakeover amendments since 1980, *Journal of Financial Economics*, 19, 127-168.

Jensen, M.C. and W.H. Meckling (1976). Theory of the firm: managerial behavior, agency costs and ownership structure, *Journal of Financial Economics*, 3, 305-360.

Jensen, M.C. and R.S. Ruback (1983). The market for corporate control, the scientific evidence, *Journal of Financial Economics*, 11, 5-50.

Jensen, M.C. (1984). Takeovers: folklore and science, *Harvard Business Review*, 62, 109-121.

Jensen, M.C. (1986). Agency costs of free cash flow, corporate finance, and takeovers, *American Economic Review* (papers and proceedings), 76, 323-329.

Jensen, M.C. (1988). Takeovers: their causes and consequences, *Journal of Economic Perspectives*, 2, 21-48.

De Jong, H.W. (1989a). *Dynamische Markttheorie* (Dynamic Market Theory), fourth edition, Stenfert Kroese, Leiden.

De Jong, H.W. (1989b). The problem of mergers, *Northwestern Journal of International Law and Business*, 9, 605-611.

De Jong, H.W. (1990). *The takeover market in Europe; control structures and the performance of large companies compared*, paper for the International Conference on "Merger, Oligopoly and Trade, Aix-en-Provence.

Kirzner, I.M. (1973). *Competition and Entrepreneurship*, University of Chicago Press, Chicago.

Manne, H. (1965). Mergers and the market for corporate control, *Journal of Political Economy*, 73, 110-120.

Marris, R. (1963). A model of the "managerial" enterprise, *Quarterly Journal of Economics*, 77, 185-209.

Mueller, D.C. (1972). A life cycle theory of the firm, *Journal of Industrial Economics*, 21, 199-219.

Mueller, D.C. (1980). *The Determinants and Effects of Mergers; an International Comparison*, Oelgeschlager, Gunn and Hain, Cambridge.

Porter, M.E. (1987). From competitive advantage to corporate strategy, *Harvard Business Review*, 65, 43-59.

Pound, J. (1987). The effects of antitakeover amendments on takeover activity: some direct evidence, *Journal of Law and Economics*, 30, 353-367.

Pound, J. (1988). Proxy contests and the efficiency of shareholder oversight, *Journal of Financial Economics*, 20, 237-265.

Ravenscraft, D.J. and F.M. Scherer (1987). Life after takeover, *The Journal of Industrial Economics*, 36, 147-156.

Roll, R. (1986). The Hubris hypothesis of corporate takeovers, *The Journal of Business*, 59, 197-216.

Ruback, R.S. (1982). The Conoco takeover and stockholder returns, *Sloan Management Review*, 23, 13-33.

Rydqvist, K. (1986). *The Pricing of Shares with Different Voting Power and the Theory of Oceanic Games*, Dissertation Stockholm School of Economics, the Economic Research Institute.

Ryngaert, M. (1988). The effect of poison pill securities on shareholder wealth, *Journal of Financial Economics*, 20, 377-417.

Scherer, F.M. (1988). Corporate takeovers: the efficiency arguments, *Journal of Economic Perspectives*, 2, 69-82.

Schumpeter, J.A. (1934). *The Theory of Economic Development*, Harvard University Press, Cambridge.

Shleifer, A. and R.W. Vishny (1986). Greenmail, white knights, and shareholders' interest, *Rand Journal of Economics*, 17, 293-309.

Shleifer, A. and R.W. Vishny (1988). Value maximization and the acquisition process, *Journal of Economic Perspectives*, 2, 7-20.

Smith, A. (1776). *The Wealth of Nations*, Glasgow, ed. 1976.

Stulz, R.M. (1988). Managerial control of voting rights, financing policies and the market for corporate control, *Journal of Financial Economics*, 20, 25-54.

Summers, L.H. (1986). Does the stock market rationally reflect fundamental values?, *The Journal of Finance*, 41, 591-602.

Weston, J.F. en T.E. Copeland (1986). *Managerial Finance*, The Dryden Press, Chicago.

7 THE CONTRIBUTION OF ECONOMISTS TO THE ORIGINS OF UK COMPETITION POLICY

DENYS GRIBBIN

1. Introduction

This paper describes the contribution made by economists working in government during the 1939-45 world war to the first UK competition law. Their distinctive contribution was made as part of the economic planning for postwar reconstruction, and while the paper is primarily about economists in the UK, as much of the initiative for planning international reconstruction came from the United States, economists there also played a part at a crucial period, and this will be described.

Apart from the Economic Section of the War Cabinet, economists as specialists were not employed in the UK civil service during the war, but a number did become temporary civil servants. Initially the task was to create a war economy, but as early as 1940 some planning for reconstruction began, and it was inevitable that economists should have been drawn into the conflicts over what policy should be. The conflicts over competition policy began inside the Board of Trade, and in the later stages the Economic Section became involved.

The development of policy in the UK has always been the responsibility of Ministers answerable to Parliament, but they draw on the civil servants to help design policies as well as implement them. Traditionally civil servants see their role as advising on the ministerial initiatives, and ensuring that the views of those with a substantial interest are adequately represented. Policy making was, and is the result of many influences.

Competition policy was no exception, and it was shaped by others in addition to the economists who tried consciously to have a particular view accepted. It is not possible to record all those who did participate, and it will be obvious that economists were not the sole contributors. Economists did, however, make a distinctive contribution to this policy, and made it more radical than it might have been. To describe their efforts is not meant to claim that others played no part, or to downgrade their contribution. Neither does this paper suggest that where views differed sharply, those expressing a contrary opinion to the economists were necessarily less disinterested.

To appreciate the divergence of opinions which emerged in the attempts to develop policies it should be remembered that until 1932 the UK economy was based on free trade. There was no specific competition law. Trade policy was also the policy for competition. In 1932 as a response to the emergence of the "Great Depression" free trade was abandoned in the Import Duties Act. Protection and private regulation of industry thereafter became mutually supporting instruments of economic policy. Private regulation of industry existed before 1932, but the radical change afterwards gave it a powerful stimulus particulary in those basic industries which were export based, and where new international competition had developed following the 1914-1919 world war. The Import Duties Advisory Committee, set up under the Act, played a primary role in giving protection, and encouraging UK industries to form associations which regulated home markets, and make agreements on international trade with foreign competitors. Active support was also given to this development by the Board of Trade which was the department responsible for trade policy.

A perceptive analysis of these developments was made by Arthur F. Lucas in "Industrial Reconstruction and The Control of Competition " published in 1937.[1] Three points from it help to establish the immediate prewar background,

1) "Although the control of competitive activity... has progressed without fanfare and by almost imperceptible stages, it has reached the point where it encompasses nearly the entire industrial structure..." (p. 2).
2) "The development of control in British industry is essentially a depression phenomenon, and attention has been focused on its utility as a means of protecting industry against the depredations of extreme competition in a receding market" (p. 359), and
3) "the immediate issues (of government policy) are two in number. On the one hand, there is the movement to enlist governmental aid in support of the extension of control by passing a general enabling measure that will confer upon any industry the power to enforce its programme upon a recalcitrant minority. On the other hand, there is the growing necessity for erecting adequate defenses to protect the public from monopolistic abuses" (p. 371).

Quantitative support for Lucas' view that at the end of the 1930's control was extensive is provided from two contemporary sources. The first is the broadsheet "British Trade Associations" published by PEP (Political and Economic Planning) in May 1944.[2] This suggested that the number of national and regional associations increased from about 500 in 1919 to about 2400 in 1944. The majority had private regulation as their main purpose.

The second source is two studies begun inside the Board of Trade in 1944, and published in 1976 as "Survey of International Cartels and Internal Cartels".[3] The survey of UK participation in international cartels covered 125 products, and was comprehensive. It estimated that in 1935 a minimum of 28 per cent of exports were regulated by private international agreements, and these were 16 per cent of industrial output. The survey of internal cartels was also intended to be comprehensive, but because of other pressures it was reduced to a selection of industries which accounted for about 9 per cent of manufactured output in 1935. Hence, there was a known minimum of about 25 per cent of manufactured output which was regulated, but this was inevitably an underestimation.

This evidence leaves little doubt that as the UK moved into the 1939-45 war, considerable sections of manufacturing industry were subject to private regulation through trade associations. This had an important advantage when the war began, that of providing government departments with ready made organisations which could be used for converting industry to war production. In industries where trade associations did not exist they were rapidly formed, and this was accelerated in 1940 when over 200 new associations were set up to help promote exports. The change to a war economy, therefore, gave a powerful stimulus to associations, and it also brought into the machinery of government many who believed that they were the only effective form of industrial organisation whether for war or in the peace to come.

2. Planning for Postwar Reconstruction

For the purpose of this paper planning for postwar reconstruction can be divided into two periods. The first began in late 1940, and was superseded by the second in early 1943. Between 1940, and 1942 planning was centred on rebuilding, demobilisation, and the transition from a war economy. It was not given a high priority. However, following the entry of the United

States into the war, and the publication in the UK in December 1942 of the famous Beveridge Report "Social Insurance and Allied Services",[4] the goals of planning changed, and its priority was substantially upgraded.

3. Competition Issues in the First Stage of Reconstruction Planning

The issue of competition and industrial organisation emerged quite early in the work which began on reconstructing a peacetime economy. This task was not simply a matter of ceasing production of war goods. In many industries capacity had been compulsory concentrated into a smaller number of firms, there was effective price control, and supplies of inputs were rationed.

At this time the general direction and coordination of postwar planning was the responsibility of the Minister Without Portfolio, Arthur Greenwood, and economic questions were dealt with by the Internal Economic Problems Committee. The Board of Trade set up a Reconstruction Unit headed by Henry Clay.[5] Its secretary was Ruth Cohen.[6] The unit made a series of approaches to industry to discuss the transition, and these immediately brought out the concerns over how much freedom would be allowed to industry, and the role of trade associations.

Recognising that industrial structure was an important postwar issue, the Internal Economic Problems Committee asked the Board to prepare a paper on it, and this began to reveal the sharp disagreements about what policy should be. The first draft was prepared by a temporary civil servant in the Reconstruction Unit, and faithfully reflected the views which had been put by industrialists during the discussions on reconstruction.

The perspective of the draft was pessimistic. It was based on the view that after a short reconstruction boom, international economic conditions would revert to what they had been in the 1930's, and this would make it impossible for "individualism and free competition" to be re-established. Their place would be taken by trade associations. The function of government was to accept that development, and foster their constructive aspects. It was proposed that the government should make a policy statement encouraging industries to organise themselves in associations to deal with immediate, and long term postwar problems. In the long term the UK would have to create efficient industries, and this required elimination of high cost excess capacity. The government should encourage the associations to take the initiative in preparing rationalisation plans, and if necessary back them up with legislation. Industry regulation of prices and output might be accepted if such plans were to succeed, but as a counterbalance the government would have to ensure that expansionist policies were followed, and it should set up independent tribunals to exercise general oversight, or investigate allegations about excessive prices.

A strong reaction came from Ruth Cohen who disputed the basic approach of the paper. She argued that the transition problems would be temporary, and could be dealt with by government assistance rather than private regulation. For the long term, a policy of expanding the economy would make the protective posture of trade associations unnecessary, but if they were given the proposed powers the resulting control over entry would enable them to pass the high cost of private regulation to consumers. Her proposed policy was that of

> "discouraging trade associations which regulate prices and output-a policy which is usually known as preventing restraints of trade".

Henry Clay had more sympathy for some of the arguments, believing that unless industry saw prospects of profitable expansion the transition and long term adjustment problems would not be solved by private enterprise.

Soon after this draft was prepared another contribution came from a different part of the Board. The Central Committee for Export Groups was the body which directed the export promotion drive, and early in 1942 it became involved in reconstruction issues. The Committee was composed of the Business Members who had been brought in as advisors to the President, and officials among whom were Henry Clay, and G.C. Allen,[7] a temporary civil servant in the Board.

As the Business Members wished to influence the development of policy they prepared a paper entitled "The Organisation of Industry for the Immediate Postwar Period and its Future Development". They planned to send the final version to the President, Hugh Dalton[8] in the hope that it would become government policy.

This contribution was even more pessimistic than that prepared in the Reconstruction Unit, and its remedies were more drastic. The pessimism is illustrated in the opening statement,

> "The conception that the economic system works by itself is today completely discredited... left to itself the economic system results in recurrent crises of production and distribution..."

An elaborate industrial superstructure was proposed to cope with this failure, with the government in the background providing compulsory powers in support. The first layer was to be an Industrial Council for each industry based on compulsory membership of trade associations. The Councils would have ten functions whose implementation would require a high degree of regulation. The government would nominate an independent chairman, and a consumer representative, and the Board of Trade would have power to temporarily remove uncooperative members.

As a quid pro quo for compulsory membership of trade associations there would be compulsory membership of trade unions, and the unions would have representatives on the Council for their industry.

Above the Councils, and elected by them, there were to be a National Home Production Council, and a National Overseas Trade Council, with the functions of co-ordination, and representing the industry.

The reaction to this draft by the civil servants on the Committee was negative, particulary that of G.C. Allen who made his opposition clear to the Chairman. Dissent centred on the lack of clarity about the proposed regulation, for example about control of prices and output, compulsory membership, the absence of controls over anticompetitive practices, and the need to protect consumers.

This opposition resulted in the paper undergoing several revisions until it became more muted, and it was then sent to Hugh Dalton with the request that it be published as a White Paper. When he asked the civil servants for advice it was that a White Paper should not be issued, as the proposals went beyond what was acceptable, and there was a danger that if implemented the interests of the community, and consumers would be subordinated to that of industry. The advice was accepted.

The Business Members were unhappy with this, so Hugh Dalton set up a small group under a junior Minister to see if agreement could be reached. Henry Clay was a member. A compromise emerged on the basis that there would be no White Paper, only a statement by Hugh Dalton covering the transition, that the proposals on Industrial Councils be dropped in favour of trade associations discussing issues with government, but with no compulsory powers. The compromise was an illusion. The Business Members thought they had agreement for a guidance statement to be issued, and prepared a draft. This reverted to most of the ideas of the first draft, so once again Hugh Dalton was advised that it was not possible to reach agreement.

No more efforts were made to get another compromise, and the disagreement was left at that point.

In the summer of 1942 Henry Clay revised the Board of Trade paper in an attempt to reach a compromise amongst the civil servants. This draft rejected compulsion, but argued that as associations were needed for reconstruction government approval should be given to those whose functions were confined to representing the industry. However, Clay argued, while the case against price and output regulation was strong, it might be accepted for declining industries. As a counterbalance, a separate body should be established to investigate industries where regulation was permitted, and it should make public reports.

This attempt to reach agreement did not succeed. Opposition was maintained by G.C. Allen, and Ruth Cohen, and by then the direction, and priorities of reconstruction planning were changing decisively. These changes ended the attempts to give trade associations such a prominent role in determining the future structure of industry.

4. The Second Stage of Reconstruction Planning

International Reconstruction

International economic issues had not been important in reconstruction planning, but this was to change through the growing involvement of the US with the UK as the main supplier of war materials, and then following its entry to the war in December 1941.

Financing imported war materials was a major strain on the UK economy, and in late 1940 it became apparent that the UK would face economic collapse if it were required to continue to pay in currencies or other assets. The solution proposed by President Roosevelt was Lend Lease, and this was embodied in the "Act to Promote the Defense of the US" in March 1941. Immediate payments were no longer required, instead the concept of a deferred reciprocal benefit from the UK was introduced, and discussions began between the governments on what this might be.

The discussions were overtaken by the entry of the US into the war. The economic relationship was then put on a new basis, and formalised in the Agreement "Principles Applying to Mutual Aid" signed in February 1942.[9] Article VII of the Agreement dealt with the reciprocal benefit, and its resolution was a considerable act of generosity by the US. The UK was relieved of the obligation to repay war debts, and in return pledged itself to hold early meetings with US with the objective of reaching agreement on common postwar purposes. The text speaks of

> "agreed action ... directed to ... expansion of production, employment and the exchange and consumption of goods ... to the elimination of all forms of discriminatory treatment in international trade, and to the reduction of tariffs and other trade barriers."

These words might have been no more a rhetorical flourish, instead, the agreement became the foundation stone for many aspects of postwar international economic co-operation.

The discussions leading upto Article VII, and the need to prepare for further talks gave an impetus in the UK for a fundamental rethink about postwar international economic policy of which two initiatives are relevant here. The first was undertaken by Lord Keynes,[10] who because he had been closely involved in the Article VII discussions had an intimate knowledge, and understanding of US views. He was then a member of the Official Committee on Post-War External Economic Problems and Anglo-American Co-operation on which also sat Lionel Robbins),[11] R.F. Harrod,[12] and J.E. Meade.[13] The task of this committee was to prepare draft policy papers for ministers for the forthcoming discussions.

Lord Keynes' paper, "External Monetary and Economic Policy", was concerned with the restoration of international trade and monetary mechanisms. His proposals for dealing with the settlement of balance of payments, and international capital movements centred on an International Clearing Union with its own currency, Bancor. Around this would be gathered other agencies concerned with international reconstruction such as post-war relief, development, and commodity schemes. On trade policy Keynes, influenced by the immediate postwar need to re-establish the export trade, was cautious about a speedy abolition of protection. He was prepared to use trade restrictions as a support to the balance of payments.

The second major revision concerned overseas commercial policy, and came from Hugh Dalton. He suggested that the UK should take the lead in proposing a major move towards trade liberalisation. This would involve the creation of an International Commercial Union to parallel the Clearing Union. Its purpose would be to prevent the formation of economic blocs, get agreement on reducing tariffs and import quotas, abolish absolute prohibitions on imports and exports, and there would be an International Commerce Committee to resolve disputes.

Mr Dalton's ideas were quickly taken up, and a committee was established to examine solutions to the problems involved. This revealed strong divisions over postwar commercial policy which mirrored the disagreements over home economic policies. The debate polarised between those who saw an opportunity to create an expansionist international economy, and those who regarded protection as the only choice open to the UK to retain what economic power it might have when the war ended. Part of this group had a strong attachment to Imperial Preference, and were suspicious of the US motives over trade liberalisation. The division was eventually resolved by a small group of ministers, and Hugh Dalton's proposals became the UK policy.

When these, and other revisions of policy were settled in early 1943 the UK was able to suggest that the Article VII discussions should begin. The US agreed, and proposed that they be held in Washington. The monetary policy and international investment talks were to be with the US Treasury, and those on commercial policy, commodity policy, and related topics with the State Department.

Lord Keynes headed the UK group for the monetary topics. These talks began earlier than those on commercial policy, and were to lead to the Bretton Woods Agreement. The UK delegation for the commercial policy discussions was led by a Foreign Office Minister, Richard Law, and included Lionel Robbins and James Meade.

5. International Reconstruction and International Cartels

By the time the Washington talks began international cartels had become an important issue in the US. As well as their relationship to commercial policy, the greatly expanded programme of anti-trust enforcement initiated in 1940 by Mr Thurman Arnold, then head of the Anti-Trust Division of the Department of Justice revealed numerous examples where monopoly and participation in international cartels had reduced the US military and economic capability for war. At the beginning of 1943 Mr Arnold was replaced by Mr Wendell Berge, but he was equally hostile to monopoly, and cartels whether domestic or international.[14] Thus, it was not surprising that the US wished to have the subject on the agenda at the commercial policy talks. It became the concern of one of the six policy sub-committees. The chairman of the Sub-Committee on Cartel Policy was L. Edminster, Vice Chairman of the US Tariff Commission, and amongst the US officials were

Corwin D. Edwards[15] of the Anti-Trust Division, and E.S. Mason[16] of the Office of Strategic Services. UK membership fluctuated as they were a much smaller group, and had to attend the other sub-committees, but J.E. Meade, and F. Lee, a Treasury official were constant attenders, and spokesmen for the UK.

The UK officials had gone ill prepared on this subject. Prewar, membership of international cartels had been thought to be a useful supplement to tariff policy, but they had ceased to be a policy concern by 1940 when foreign trade became controlled. Also, there had been no progress in the development of a policy towards competition. Although James Meade was involved in discussions to develop a policy, this was purely informal, (see the section on "The Control of Monopoly"). Consequently, the officials had no guidance from ministers, and neither had they had time to explore the factual background. There was also a suspicion that the US might want to force a Sherman Act type of legislation on the UK. The UK stance, therefore, was to be neutral, and try to avoid a commitment to future policy.

The neutral stance changed soon after the meetings began when the initial suspicion was quickly dispelled by the US appreciation of the different historical situation of the UK, and its willingness to be flexible about solutions. The other thing which helped to produce a shift in the UK approach was the realisation of the amount of preparation which been done in the US.

A convergence of views was also helped by the pragmatic approach taken by J.E. Meade. While agreeing that restrictions on competition interfered with the aim of expansion, he distinguished between cartels, and large firms based on natural monopoly conditions, or significant economies of scale. A desire to preserve the benefits from the latter suggested that government action should be varied according to circumstances, and he outlined five possible remedies,

1) the establishment of fact finding organisations,
2) the creation of legal and institutional conditions favourable to competition,
3) breaking up monopolistic organisations,
4) public regulation, for example price control, and
5) public ownership.

The empirical foundation to the US position was illustrated by a paper written by Corwin Edwards in co-operation with the State Department. In addition to information in the Anti-Trust Division, he had access to censorship intercepts, and Grand Jury proceedings. These were a unique source of material on international cartels and multinational companies. The paper he presented was entitled "The Economic Activities of International Cartels", and a version omitting the secret material was published in 1944 as "Economic and Political Aspects of International Cartels".[17]

The US views on the relationship between international cartels and commercial policy was put forward by E.S. Mason. He illustrated the concern by describing how cartel activities such as allocation of markets, dumping, restriction of output or exports, and price maintenance would negate the aim of reducing trade barriers. His conclusion was that although nations with serious balance of payments problems might believe that membership of international cartels would help them, any gains would only be short run. Because of retaliation by other countries, and the inefficiencies which the restrictions could induce, in the long run they would have been better to have opted for greater competition.

Corwin Edwards presented the information on the security issues raised by international cartels, and gave examples of essential war materials where it was believed Germany had used US participation to severely limit its preparedness for the war. A list which included UK firms was attached to the minutes, but it is not among the UK public records.

The extent to which the UK moved closer to the US position is shown by the text of the final agreement. It restated the UK reservations, but notwithstanding these both sides agreed that an examination of international cartels, and of national and international remedial measures should form part of the further discussions on Article VII. The US position on remedies had three elements,

1) the registration of all private international agreements, including those where there was an ownership interest, and with the right of participating governments, and international bodies established to deal with commercial policy to examine the registered information,
2) an international agreement to prohibit a specified list of objectionable international cartel practices, and
3) the fostering of national and international conventions and laws on corporations, patent and trade marks, and commercial law to reduce the danger from international cartelisation.

Both groups expressed the view that it would be a matter of regret if their respective governments followed widely different commercial policies, particularly over international cartels, and the UK group undertook to recommend that its government give sympathetic consideration to the proposals for further study.

The text of this accord then became part of the final agreement between the two countries on commercial policy, commodity policy, and the coordination of international measures for the maintenance of full employment.

When the UK group returned home their experience of the greater preparedness of the US, and the importance which it attached to the issue persuaded the government that equal attention had to be given to it. An immediate result was that the Board of Trade began the studies of international and national cartels referred to above. G.C. Allen was given the task of preparing them.

6. Postwar Full Employment and Competition Policy

Perhaps the most important single policy decision which crystallised the economic planning for reconstruction was the commitment made by the wartime Coalition government to devise the means of achieving postwar full employment.

The issue of postwar full employment was brought into the arena of public debate through planning for social rather than economic reconstruction. In June 1941 an Interdepartmental Committee on Social Insurance and Allied Services was set up under the chairmanship of Sir William Beveridge who had devoted his life to the issues of unemployment, and social security.

Sir William's interpretation of the Committee's terms of reference went considerably wider than had been intended. His aim was, through economic and social policy to abolish poverty, as far as that was possible. Drawing on his own, and other studies of social conditions in the interwar years in a number of the principal towns he identified the two main causes of poverty as unemployment, and the failure to relate earnings to family size. His solution to these was government action to create and maintain a high level of employment, and to develop an extensive range of social policies, including family allowances and a comprehensive health service.

The report, published in December 1942, had a dramatic impact on public opinion, but the War Cabinet did not immediately feel able to commit itself to the proposals because of the misgivings expressed by the Treasury about the costs of implementation, and the extent to which it might pre-empt other important claims.

These reservations led to the setting up of the Ministerial Reconstruction Priorities Committee to conduct a review of the needs for financial assistance in the immediate post war period. It proposed that at that stage of the war, there could only be a simple order of priorities. International security came first, and second came the re-establishment of industry and trade, together with maintaining employment at the highest possible level. All other claims would have to wait until the outcome of the war became clearer.

Once this was decided the Cabinet felt able to commit itself to the acceptance of the three basic assumptions of the Beveridge proposals, full employment, family allowances, and a health service, even though it was not then possible to implement them. The public commitment was given in February 1943.

Of the three basic assumptions, that of full employment gave the Ministerial committee the least difficulty in accepting that it might be achieved. Earlier in February, before the commitment was given, the Economic Section was instructed by the Committee to make a study of the various measures which might be used to maintain full employment after the war.

The Economic Section's paper was ready by the middle of May. It was not intended to be a definitive document on all that was needed. Instead it set out the general principles of Keynesian thinking on demand management, and their application to the immediate postwar period, together with a discussion of obstacles to achieving full employment, and a list of topics for further detailed study.

The discussion of demand management was designed for the non economist, and the paper made it clear that there were two important assumptions on which a successful application of the policy rested. Both were about flexibility. The first was the need for effective mobility of labour between industries, and between different parts of the country.

The second laid the basis for the subsequent development of competition policy with the statement,

> "There is a second assumption qualifying the connection postulated between employment and expenditure, the assumption, namely, of the absence of monopolistic price raising and the prevalence of reasonable

> stability in the general wage level. If an increase in aggregate demand is taken out either in increased prices or in higher wages, then clearly the increase of employment may be frustrated. Similarly, if in a state of full employment, wages are pushed up faster than the rise in productivity, then costs rise, the amount of expenditure necessary to maintain full employment is increased, and there is the danger of general inflation."

Eight topics were proposed for further study of the main policy instruments, one was restrictive practices in industry and commerce.

The paper was considered at the Reconstruction Priorities Committee meeting on the 31st of May, but there was a disagreement about whether a decision should be taken then or deferred. The Chancellor of the Exchequer wished to leave decisions about full employment until after problems of the transition had been dealt with, but the Labour ministers thought this was an attempt to get out of the commitment. The disagreement went to the Cabinet, and was resolved in July with the compromise that a committee of officials be set up to begin work on the problems. It was called the Steering Committee on Post-War Employment, and its report became the basis of the White Paper "Employment Policy".[18] The Ministerial Committee selected six issues for study,

1) Location of industry,
2) Mobility of labour and structural unemployment,
3) Control and timing of public investment,
4) Control and timing of private investment,
5) Regulation of consumption, and,
6) Restrictive practices of employers and employees in industry and commerce.

The Steering Committee consisted of officials from the Reconstruction Secretariat, Treasury, Ministry of Labour, Board of Trade, and the Economic Section. Sir Arnold Overton, the Permanent Secretary (chief civil servant) represented the Board, and Lionel Robbins represented the Economic Section. The Board was asked to take responsibility for developing the policy on restrictive practices.

7. The Board of Trade, and Competition Policy

The change of priorities in reconstruction showed itself quickly in the Board of Trade. In January 1943 the Reconstruction Secretariat became the Internal Reconstruction Department. It was headed by Miss A. Kilroy,[19] with G.C. Allen as deputy, and became responsible for co-ordinating all work inside the Board as well as dealing with matters put to it by the Steering Committee. Ruth Cohen was given increased responsibilities.

One consequence was an expanded programme of interviews with industry. As in the earlier stage, contacts with industrialists brought out the issue of trade associations. The Board intended to avoid getting drawn back into the controversy, but this proved to be impossible. There were major adjustment problems for those industries which had been in decline before the war, or were overtaken by technical change, or where there had been enforced concentration of industry. These required policy decisions on how to ease the transition. Many of the industries had devised their own schemes, often asking for statutory backing to control prices, output, entry, and foreign trade. There were other examples where the reconstruction schemes were simply based on a desire to regulate for the benefit of existing producers. The manufacturers of aluminium hollowware, in return for introducing standardisation wished to control entry so that newcomers could not take advantage of the economies of scale which it brought. The Export Group in the telephone, and telephone equipment industry told the Board,

> "the system evolved by the Export Group for the avoidance of uneconomic competition among members had worked satisfactorily (and) the industry desired to see it continued after the war".

The need for a policy towards competition also began to be apparent in two other areas of the Board's work. The control of inflation in the transition had been identified as a major issue, so thought was being given to how the wartime price controls could be modified. The existing method was based on the profit margins earned in 1939. As the legislation did not permit this to be changed monopoly profits were protected during the war, and those firms which in 1939 had low profits were not able to improve them. Hugh Gaitskell[20] who had been brought into the Board in 1942 by Hugh Dalton, was the official responsible for price control.

Early in 1943 the work of the Postwar Export Trade Committee, which also required extensive contacts with industry, brought up the issue of participation by UK firms in international cartels. This had been examined in

1942 in a paper by Professor D.H. MacGregor[21] as part of the preparation for the Article VII discussions, but it had not been discussed before the talks took place. Professor MacGregor's opinion was that as international cartels had become so pervasive governments had to accept them, but should impose on their citizens minimum conditions in return for participation. The conditions were publicity for the arrangements, and the establishment of an international office with powers to approve, or amend them.

The Board's Commercial Relations and Treaty Division was also prepared to accept international cartels, but wanted more stringent conditions. These were that in the immediate postwar period there would be no participation until the UK had been able to adjust to the new situation, a competitive parity fixed for sterling, and excessive protection eliminated. Additionally, there had to be international control and supervision over prices, and that an international office be set up as a pool of information, and publicity.

A response to these ideas was prepared by G.C. Allen, and submitted in March to the Departmental Reconstruction Committee which was trying to see if a concensus was possible. He argued that if there was to be an expansion of postwar trade, acceptance of international cartels would defeat that objective, and it would be particularly detrimental to the UK which needed a substantial increase in its exports. This would not be possible if shares were solidified by private international agreements.

No concensus was reached so it was decided that the Board should neither encourage or discourage UK firms from making plans to participate, but the government must be made aware of any arrangements which they contemplated.

8. The Internal Reconstruction Department and the development of Policy

Although the Internal Reconstruction Department was the part of the Board best placed to take the initiative in developing a policy, there was an early disagreement between Miss Kilroy, and G.C. Allen as to what it should be. She accepted that there were disadvantages from private regulation, but was prepared to accept cartels, provided that they were efficient, price reducing, and subject to government regulation. G.C. Allen thought this was contradictory, and argued,

> "(an) expansionist cartel is an illusion and monopolies of all kinds are certain to follow policies contrary to the policies of expansion, full employment, and freer international trade..."

To take the initiative further Miss Kilroy asked that a paper be drafted, to be called "The Control of Monopolies in the Public Interest". It's purpose was to examine the methods, short of nationalisation, by which abuses of monopoly power could be prevented.

The draft reviewed the prewar state of industrial organisation, and the attempts made in specific industries to control or regulate the abuse of monopoly power. It concluded that these had not been effective, and neither had the common law doctrine on restraint of trade, having been substantially eroded by judicial interpretation.

Two sets of improvements to previous remedies were suggested. The first was based on publicity as an antitrust remedy. More information about individual firms could be put in the public domain if company law required greater disclosure, if there were uniform company accounts, and the position of auditors strengthened. For trade associations it was suggested that they could be required to register with a government department or authority, and file their agreements. The body would have power to obtain information, conduct enquiries, issue reports, and exercise supervision.

The second strengthening would be a requirement on individual firms or trade associations to get prior approval for certain pricing decisions, responses to competition, and mergers. Approval could be given by a Monopoly Court, which would have a general duty to deal with abuse of economic power. This paper was much less sympathetic to private regulation than had been those written earlier. Nevertheless, being based on an acceptance of it, the remedies were aimed at only a cautious concensus. The draft was taken no further, because it was soon overtaken by a more radical document prepared by a number of economists and temporary civil servants who were dissatisfied at the failure to tackle what they saw to be the real issue, the contradiction between private regulation, and the potential for postwar full employment and growth.

9. "The Control of Monopoly", and its Influence on Policy

The group dissenting to the philosophy expressed in "The Control of Monopolies in the Public Interest" comprised Hugh Gaitskell, G.C. Allen, James Meade, and Ruth Cohen, and three civil servants W.B. Hughes, Miss

G.L. Coleman, and C.K. Hobson. They had begun in mid 1943 to discuss reconstruction amongst themselves, and identified the need for an alternative policy towards competition.

Encouragement to develop other ideas was given by Hugh Dalton who was involved in competition questions through his membership of the ministerial Lord President's Committee, and the Reconstruction Priorities Committee. The Lord President's Committee were considering whether the government should intervene on behalf of ICI Ltd which was facing a US Department of Justice suit alleging monopolisation with the US firms Du Pont and Remington.

The result of the discussions in the group was a paper entitled "The Control of Monopoly".[22] Although it initially met with powerful opposition, it was to have an crucial influence on the development of policy.

The paper was in three parts. The first was written by G.C. Allen, and reviewed prewar, and wartime developments, analysed the economic problems raised by monopoly, and made the policy proposals. It made the point that a policy favouring competition was an economic instrument to help achieve the full employment pledge. The second and third parts were written by Hugh Gaitskell, and explored the feasibility of extending wartime price control as part of the control over monopoly.

The word "monopoly" was used to cover a wide range of industrial organisation from informal arrangements between firms, through cartels, financial links, common directorships, interchange of shares, and to giant firms controlling the greater part of industry output. The conflict with the full employment objective arose because monopoly was likely,

"a) to reduce the demand for labour and thus create unemployment unless wage earners are willing to accept lower wages in relation to prices...
b) to check new entrants and thus limit the field open to newcomers...
c) to raise costs, thus hampering exports and making national income smaller than it need be by:
   - enabling inefficient firms or methods to persist and preventing the transference of output from high cost to low cost producers, and
   - hindering the best distribution of resources between industries,
d) to create a biassed distribution of income between occupations by permitting some groups to exploit others."

The Policy Proposals

One set of proposals was intended to weaken market power irrespective of its base. Existing laws which favoured monopoly should be amended, with patent law identified as particularly in need of change. The paper suggested that a strong expert committee should be set up, "not overweighted on the legal side", to consider patent, and trade mark issues. Libel law needed alteration because it was easy for a seller to prevent the publication of adverse judgements on quality by experts. Company law also required amendment, because existing law made it easy for undesirable concentrations of control to be acquired, and concealed.

The remaining proposals made a distinction between cartels, and giant firms based on substantial scale economies. As cartels were founded on restrictions their undesirablity could be inferred simply from that fact. For giant firms the economies might be so great as to exclude the possibility of competition, hence the remedies had to be different.

Cartel Agreements

A drastic remedy was proposed for cartels. There should be a comprehensive prohibition of,

"1) minimum price agreements among manufacturers and traders, including agreements about distributors' margins;
2) agreements for the restriction of sales or production, or agreements calculated to have that effect, including agreements for the division of sales in certain proportions among suppliers, for territorial division of markets or for the pooling of proceeds or profits;
3) agreements to destroy or seal capacity;
d) agreements designed to reinforce agreements of the three preceding types, including agreements among suppliers concerning boycotts, exclusive dealing, tying clauses, deferred rebates and price discrimination."

It was recognised that in special circumstances limited exceptions might be necessary, for example where there was a large amount of excess capacity, and an organised contraction was the only way of dealing with it. These should only be licensed where adequate safeguards could be devised to maintain efficiency, and protect the public against abuse.

If these prohibitions were implemented then the functions of trade associations would be fundamentally altered, but to deter any tendency to revert to private regulation there should be a register of all associations with details of their functions, memorandum and articles of association, membership lists, and reports and accounts.

The policy towards international cartels was more cautious because it would depend on the post-war commercial policies of the UK and other governments, but whatever it was to be the government needed to know about them, and have powers to control. (The Washington talks had not taken place when this paper was prepared).

Giant firms

The paper recognised that the prohibitions on cartel practices might stimulate the formation of giant firms, for example by greater use of interlocking directorships, exchange of shares, and mergers as a substitute for agreements, but because these could also be mechanisms for achieving greater efficiency, there ought to be no general ban on them.

The policy towards giant firms should be based on weakening the incentives to achieve market power. This might be done in four ways,

a) the imposition of maximum price control,
b) attacking practices such as excluding new entrants, attempts to tie customers to particular suppliers through boycotts, deferred rebates, tying clauses, price discrimination, and resale price maintenance.
c) through publicity. The proposed Commission would have power to investigate costs, prices, and trade practices of firms having a "dominating position in the market", and to publish its findings.
d) if the above methods were ineffective, giant firms might be taken into public ownership.

10. The Machinery of Control

The proposed machinery of control was also more radical. Four executive tasks needed to be carried out, licensing agreements, price control, the application of other controls over giant firms, and the registration of trade associations. As these involved aspects of economic policy for which ministers would be responsible, it was suggested they be done by the departments with a sponsoring role for industry. The Board of Trade should be responsible for licensing any international agreements.

As a counterbalance to the sponsorship role, and possible political interference, there should be an independent Statutory Commission on Restrictive Practices with the powers and the staff needed to collect information, and advise on the executive tasks, and other matters affecting competition such as company and patent law.

In concluding their proposals for a more radical policy the authors made the point that there were also strong non economic grounds for an active competition policy,

> "Large industrial organisations even those completely justified on grounds of efficiency, represent a concentration of economic power in the hands of individuals. Such a concentration, if extended to numerous industries might become hard to reconcile with a democratic system... (and) ... an attack on monopoly is not to be confused with an attack on private enterprise. On the contrary, private enterprise and private monopoly are ultimately incompatible. In a democratic country the public must be the master of industry. This condition is sufficiently satisfied in trades in which free competition is maintained; but where free competition does no exist, it can only be satisfied by the introduction of adequate measures of government control or supervision over monopolies, or by actual state ownership".

11. The Short Term Impact of "The Control of Monopoly"

"The Control of Monopoly" was completed in July 1943 at the time the request for a paper on restrictive practices was made by the Steering Committee. Hugh Dalton took a direct interest in the preparation of the Board's advice, and a small group was set up to report to him. It comprised Sir Arnold Overton, G.L. Watkinson, Hugh Gaitskell, and G.C. Allen who was asked to prepare the first draft.

The draft was a shortened version of the full paper, and when circulated in the Board for comment it produced strong opposition. The arguments in favour of cartels ranged from almost uncritical support to a reluctant acceptance of them.

The supporters asserted that many cartels had increased efficiency. Other advantages from "orderly marketing by interfirm price agreement and/or market allocation" covered the claim "price competition between British exporters would only benefit the foreigner", to the argument that agreements in international trade would result in greater price and output stability. A common thread was though there had been many opportunities "to fleece the consumer", "The Control of Monopoly" had not produced evidence that this had happened.

The views of the reluctant acceptors were influenced by the immediate prewar economic history, and the belief that these conditions would soon return presenting British industry with a very difficult future.

In the drafting group the first amendments were put forward by G.L. Watkinson who, although amongst the reluctant acceptors was friendly to G.C. Allen, and probably had a keener sense of what was politically acceptable. The remedies of "The Control of Monopoly" were intended to be applied across the economy, and his suggestions, by narrowing the target reduced the potential opposition. He proposed that references to changes in other laws, and nationalisation be dropped, and instead of the more powerful Statutory Commission on Restrictive Practices, the role of investigating and making recommendations on agreements could be performed by the Industrial Commission which was being proposed separately by the Board as part of the machinery for improving the efficiency of industry.

Substantial alterations were proposed by Sir Arnold Overton. These were,

a) the scope to be limited to industry,
b) all agreements to be registered with the Board which could refer them to the Industrial Commission if it thought they might be against the public interest,
c) if the Commission found against an agreement the Board would have power to ban it, or suspend any import duties or restrictions,
d) dominant firms could be investigated by the Commission, and price control might be recommended as a remedy.

For Hugh Gaitskell, and G.C. Allen acceptance of these would have meant the abandonment of what was central to their case so no agreement was reached on the advice to be given to Hugh Dalton. Sir Arnold Overton wrote a note setting out the disagreement, (describing "The Control of Monopoly" as "the economists' paper"), and recommended that the Board should aim for a less politically contentious objective. He argued,

> "it may be unwise at this stage to throw mud at the cartel or trust...(if changes are to be made) we must be quite sure what they are, and on what evidence they are based ... if we do not do this ... we may be badly defeated and fail to get the minimum powers ... namely the power to require information about cartel and such-like arrangements".

He also advised that if Hugh Dalton accepted a complete ban on agreements, he would propose that a Royal Commission be appointed before a decision was made.

The files do not reveal Hugh Dalton's private opinion. The paper which went to the Steering Committee accepted Sir Arnold's proposals, but it was not a complete repudiation of "The Control of Monopoly". It followed the economic analysis, and accepted the weakness of existing remedies, but stressed the lack of evidence on detriment, and the possibilities of benefits. Ministers were offered a choice of remedies, those put forward as the Board's proposals, or the complete ban. They were recommended to accept the former on the grounds that a ban, while perhaps more favourable to competition and employment, would put a heavy burden on the Board, and on those trying to obtain a license, and would arouse considerable opposition from business with potential adverse effects on the war effort.

The Economic Section then submitted a paper which argued for the stronger policy. It opposed the Industrial Commission as the regulating body, preferring a separate government department, and reiterated the case for changes in company and patent law, as well as nationalisation. However, there was no serious dissent by the rest of the Committee from the Board's proposal, and it went forward as the preferred policy, including the suggestion that patent law be examined.[23] Ministers were urged to take an early decision on restrictive practices because of the attitude of the US.

Lionel Robbins did not give up easily. Attached to the Steering Committee's 65 page report, "Post-War Employment", which went in January 1944 to the ministerial Reconstruction Committee, is a four and a half page note of dissent to the recommendation on restrictive practices. He argued that it would be ineffective because placing the burden of proof of detriment on the Board, and a semi independent body would give them an impossible task, particularly as there would be hundreds of agreements. Also, as not all agreements could be challenged, those which were not would acquire status and respectability. In support of this belief he wrote,

> "The proposals which have been put forward by my colleagues bear a disturbing resemblance to the German Kartelverordnung (Cartel Decree) of 1923. I submit that it would be hard to contend that the effect of that Decree was either to check the growth of the cartel movement or to weaken its evil influence in German economic and political life".

The Reconstruction Committee, which had replaced the other ministerial committees, began in early 1944 to work through "Post-War Employment". As there was no serious disagreement over the main proposals events moved quickly. On restrictive practices the Committee approved the recommendation, and in April the President, and the Minister Without Portfolio were asked to prepare alternative proposals for legislation. In May the White Paper "Employment Policy" was published.

This document is regarded as the foundation of the postwar concensus on economic policies. Competition policy is dealt with in the section which discusses the stability of wages and prices. Paragraph 54 reads,

> "Workers must examine their trade practices and customs to ensure that they do not constitute a serious impediment to an expansionist economy and so defeat the object of a full employment programme".

Employers, too, must seek in larger output rather than higher prices the reward of enterprise and good management. There has in recent years been a growing tendency towards combines and towards agreements, both national and international, by which manufacturers have sought to control prices and output, to divide markets and to fix conditions of sale. Such agreements or combines do not necessarily operate against the public interest; but the power to do so is there. The government will therefore seek power to inform themselves of the extent and effect of restrictive agreements, and of the activities of combines; and to take appropriate action to check practices which may bring advantages to sectional producing interests but work to the detriment of the country as a whole".

In August the Reconstruction Committee approved a Statutory Commission to examine restrictive practices, rather than the Board's proposed Industrial Commission. Approval for draft legislation then followed, and in November and December a group with John Jewkes[24] as secretary prepared a Bill to establish a Restrictive Practices Commission, define the practices and monopoly, public interest criteria, procedures, and its powers.

This Bill's fate is described in Hugh Dalton's memoirs.[25] For the 1945 Parliamentary session he pressed for two Bills, one on the regional distribution of industry, and a

> "Restrictive Practices Bill. I wanted a simple Bill; a Tribunal to which the President of the Board of Trade could refer any firm or group of firms, suspected of any practice which he deemed restrictive; the Tribunal to investigate and report on the facts, and to make any recommendations it chose for remedial action in the public interest,

> including, for example, the nationalisation of the offending firm or group of firms. On this contentious subject Ministers were never in sight of agreement. Some wanted something much more complicated, and much less dangerous to monopolists and restrictive trade associations".

Only the Distribution of Industry Bill became law.

Postscript

In the first postwar elections in 1945 a Labour Government was elected, and in its earlier years were occupied with reconstruction, creating full employment and the social services, and nationalisation. By 1948 free markets were being re-established, so it was judged appropriate to introduce competition legislation. The Bill prepared in 1944 was the model, and it became the Monopolies and Restrictive Practices (Control and Inquiry) Act 1948. It did not contain powers to investigate restrictive labour practices, or for nationalisation as a remedy.

The Monopolies and Restrictive Practices Commission began to operate early in 1949. Miss Kilroy was the first Secretary. In 1951 G.C. Allen became a Member of the Commission, and remained for 12 years. Between 1949 and 1956 20 industry investigations were carried out, 18 of them into cartels. The programme began with four references from the Board of Trade, selected from the studies of international, and national cartels which had been initiated by G.C. Allen. Subsequently, a further five from the studies were referred.

The cartels fared badly on investigation, with their restrictions on competition being directly linked to substantial failures of economic performance.[26] The accumulating evidence of this link led the Board in 1952 to make a general reference of cartel practices which was published in 1955 as "Collective Discrimination: A report on Exclusive Dealing, Collective Boycotts, Aggregated Rebates, and other Discriminatory Trade Practices".[27] G.C. Allen was a Member of the group which wrote the report, and by this time W.B. Hughes was the Commission's Secretary. It concluded that the general effect of the practices was against the public interest.

Two types of remedy were discussed, and the debate was a re-run of that in "Post-War Employment". The first would require all agreements to be registered, with the possibility that after investigation they might be prohibited. This was rejected on the grounds that it would be cumbersome, slow, and unfair. Instead, a general prohibition was recommended, with the possibility of exceptions in highly special circumstances.

The Conservative Government acted quickly on the recommendation, and in 1956 the Restrictive Trade Practices Act became law. This presumed that all agreements between two or more parties where each accepted a restriction on their competitive freedom were against the public interest. Such agreements had to be placed in a public register, and if the participants wished to continue to operate the agreement, they had to persuade the newly created Restrictive Practices Court to reverse the presumption. There was a narrow specification of the economic grounds for conducting this argument.

The prohibition was effective. By the end of 1959 2240 agreements had been placed in the public register, and the overwhelming majority were quickly abandoned. By 1972 the parties to 37 agreements had attempted to persuade the Court to allow them to continue, and only 11 were successful. Subsequently, all but one have ceased to operate, (RPM on books). The Act turned out to be the most significant postwar instrument of industrial restructuring, and cartels have ceased to be part of the economic environment of the UK. The solution to them proposed by the "economists" in 1943 demonstrated its efficiency, although it had taken rather longer than they had hoped. That it contributed to creating a more efficient industrial sector is not in doubt.[28]

Competition policy remains, grappling with the more complex issue of the giant firm. The authors of "The Control of Monopoly" did not suggest that there were easy solutions.

Notes

This paper is based on material which forms part of a book in preparation. The main sources are relevant files of the wartime Board of Trade, Cabinet, and Ministerial and Official Committees available in the UK Public Records Office. These files are too numerous to list here. The paper has benefited from discussions with a number of the participants.

1. Lucas, Arthur F (1937). *Industrial Reconstruction and the Control Of Competition.*
2. British Trade Associations (1944). A broadsheet issued by Political and Economic Planning, No 221, May 12.
3. Survey of International and Internal Cartels 1944-1946 (1976), Two volumes, Board of Trade, London.

4. Social and Allied Services, Sir William Beveridge, cmnd 6404 1942, HMSO London.
5. Sir Henry Clay, 1883 to 1954. Prewar Economic Advisor to the Bank of England. Author of Economics An Introduction for the General Reader.
6. Miss Ruth Cohen CBE. 1906. Principal Newnham College, Cambridge 1954 to 1972. Author of Economics of Agriculture.
7. Professor George Cyril Allen. 1900 to 1982. Member of the Monopolies and Restrictive Practices Commission 1951 to 1963. Author of British Industries and Their Organisation, The Structure of Industry In Britain: A Study in Economic Change, Monopoly and Restrictive Practices etc.
8. The Right Honourable Hugh Dalton PC MP. 1887 to 1962. President of the Board of Trade 1942 to 1945, Chancellor of the Exchequer 1945 to 1947. Author of Inequality of Incomes in Modern Communities, Principles of Public Finance, The Fateful Years etc.
9. Agreement between the Governments of the United Kingdom and the United States of America on the Principles applying to Mutual aid in the Prosecution of the War against Aggression. Washington, February 23, 1942. Cmnd 6391, HMSO London 1942.
10. Lord John Maynard Keynes. 1883 to 1946. Advisor to His Majesty's Treasury 1940 to 1946. Author of the General Theory of Employment, Interest and Money, A Treatise on Money etc
11. Professor The Lord Lionel Robbins. 1898 to 1984. Director of Economic Section of the War Cabinet 1941 to 1945. Author of Essays on the Nature and Significance of Economic Science, The Great Depression, Autobiography, Report of the Committee on Higher Education Cmnd 2154 1963, (known as the Robbin's report), etc.
12. Sir Roy F Harrod. 1898 to 1978. Oxford University Lecturer in Economics 1929 to 1937, and 1946 to 1952. Author of International Economics, Towards A Dynamic Economy, The Life of John Maynard Keynes etc.
13. Professor James E Meade. 1907. Director Economic Section 1946 to 1947, Professor of Commerce London School of Economics 1947 to 1957. Author of National Income and Expenditure, with R Stone, Planning and the Price Mechanism, The Control of Inflation, Principles of Political Economy etc.
14. Statement of the Honorable Wendell Berge Assistant Attorney General of the United States before the Subcommittee on War Mobilisation. Committee of Military Affairs of the Senate of the United States, (Kilgore Committee). Washington October 15th, 1943.
15. Corwin D Edwards. 1901 to 1979. Chairman Policy Board Anti Trust Division, US Department of Justice 1939 to 1944, Director Bureau of Economics, US Federal Trade Commission 1948 to 1953. Author of Maintaining Competition A Cartel Policy for the United Nations, Control of Cartels and Monopolies An Internatioinal Comparison, etc
16. Professor Edward S Mason. 1899. Author of Economic Concentration and the Monopoly Problem, Ed. The Corporation in Modern Society.

17. Economic and Political Aspects of International Cartels. A study Made for the Subcommittee on War Mobilisation of the Committee on Military Affairs United States Senate. United States Government Printing Office Washington 1944.
18. Employment Policy. Cmnd 6527, May 1944, HMSO London.
19. Now Lady Alix Meynell DBE. 1903. Joined Board of Trade 1925, Secretary to the Monopolies and Restrictive Practices Commission, 1949 to 1952.
20. Right Honourable Hugh Gaitskell PC MP, 1906 to 1963. Reader in Political Economy University College London 1938. Chancellor of the Exchequer 1950 to 1951. Leader of the Labour Party
21. Professor D.H. MacGregor, 1887 to 1953. Author of Industrial Combination, Evolution of Industry.
22. After 30 years Professor Allen placed a copy in the Watson Library, University College London.
23. This suggestion was taken up and resulted in the Patent Act 1949.
24. John Jewkes CBE, 1902 to 1988. Author of The Sources of Invention, with Sawyer and Stillerman, Ordeal By Planning etc.
25. H. Dalton, The Fateful Years, Memoirs 1931-1945,
26. Elliott D.C. and J.D. Gribbin. Cartels and Structural Change in the United Kingdom, in Jacquemin A.P. and H.W. de Jong (eds.), *Welfare Aspects of Industrial Markets*.
27. Collective Discrimination. Cmnd 9504, HMSO London 1955.
28. Competition in British Industry, Swann, O'Brien, Maunder, and Howe.

8 PUBLIC OWNERSHIP VERSUS PRIVATISATION

KEN GEORGE

1. Introduction

One of the most important, and certainly the most controversial, changes in British industry over the past decade has been the privatisation of many of the corporations that were once part of the public sector. Before the privatisation programme began with the first Thatcher administration in 1979 the public sector in Britain included all the great utilities - electricity, gas, postal services, telecommunications, rail and water. Over the post-War period up to the late 1970s public ownership was widely viewed as an appropriate regulatory device for dealing with the market failure associated with the natural monopoly status of these industries. Other industries had been brought into public ownership for a mixture of motives such as national security, industrial strategy or the rescue of ailing companies in the private sector. The nationalisation of coal in 1947 was inevitable once the Labour government had swept into power in 1945. The War-time government had already assumed full control of the industry in 1942, and the Reid Committee, reporting in 1945, drew attention to serious weaknesses resulting from decades of poor management and underinvestment. The Committee called for drastic overhaul and reconstruction, and fundamental changes in organisation and control. Like coal, the steel industry was regarded by Labour as one of the "commanding heights" of the economy and was thus a key element in industrial strategy. It had also been slow to invest in new technology and suffered from major structural weaknesses. The industry was nationalised in 1949, denationalised in the mid 1950s and re-nationalised in 1967. During the 1970s several major companies were rescued from public funds and were taken wholly or in part into public ownership. They included Rolls Royce (aero-engines), British Leyland (vehicles), Ferranti (electronics), ICL (computers) and Alfred Herbert (machine tools). Much of the rescue work was the responsibility of the National Enterprise Board, set up by the Labour government in 1975 to regenerate British industry.

In 1979 the tide changed. Public support for industry did not cease but it was much diminished. The emphasis was on reducing government aid and on returning as much industrial activity as possible to the private sector. Before turning to the privatisation programme, however, section II examines some of the problems of public ownership. These problems explain, in part at least, the discontent with public sector performance and thus the support for many if not all the government's public sector asset sales

2. Problems of Public Ownership

The most important form of public ownership in Britain has been the public corporation. It has been the legal form adopted for all the major utilities. There have been two major problem areas with this form of ownership. The first has been the relationship between the board of the corporation and the responsible government minister; the second has been the setting of objectives and the putting in place of incentives and monitoring systems.

In theory, accountability and control is straightforward. Public corporations have statutory duties which are laid down by Act of Parliament. The relevant minister, who is answerable to Parliament, appoints the members of the management board. The division of responsibility between the minister and the board is that the former lays down general directions leaving the latter to get on with the day to day tasks of managing the business. One of the major difficulties in the post-War history of the nationalised industries is that the original intention of having an "arms length" relationship between the minister and the board was quickly lost sight of. Ministerial interventions in decision making have been common. They include interventions to keep wages and prices down as part of government anti-inflationary policy; at other times to push prices up so as to reduce the public sector borrowing requirement; and to influence decisions on plant location or plant closures because of government concern over regional unemployment.

Turning to objectives, the statutory duties of the public corporations, as laid down by Act of Parliament, were expressed in very broad terms and thus of little use as a guide to management. More specific objectives were contained in a series of White Papers in 1961, 1967 and 1978. In 1961 the emphasis was on setting financial targets, typically in the form of a return on capital employed. However nothing was said about pricing policy. The corporations could therefore meet their financial targets by raising prices as well as by cutting costs. There was also no guidance as to how prices should relate to costs so that there was no impediment to cross-subsidisation as a means of supporting non-commercial activities. The 1961 White Paper was also silent on methods of investment appraisal.

These weaknesses were addressed in the 1967 White Paper. The emphasis now switched to optimal pricing and investment policy, and the financial targets given to each corporation were, as far as possible, to be consistent with the pricing and investment objectives. Prices were to be set equal to long-run marginal cost, though if capacity happened to be way out of line with demand they could be adjusted to reflect short-run marginal cost. A test discount rate was introduced for investment decisions, and non-commercial activities were to be identified for the government to decide whether or not to subsidise them.

There are many well known problems associated with marginal cost pricing, but for present purposes two deserve particular attention. The first is that when there are increasing returns to scale losses are incurred and these have to be financed by government subsidy. This raises the problem of managerial incentives, for if managers know that losses are inevitable and will be met out of taxation the incentive to minimise costs may be seriously attenuated. The second is the practical problem with any form of marginal cost pricing of identifying and calculating costs and monitoring the policy. These problems are especially acute in the presence of sunk costs and multi-product supply. There is also the problem of specifying the time period over which marginal costs are to be calculated in order to produce tariff schedules. Whatever the time period that is chosen demand and cost conditions cannot be known with certainty so that a whole spectrum of out-turns is possible. This allows the managers of public enterprise to introduce elements of discretion into pricing schedules which accord with their goals and their own ideas of how the industries should be run. Similar problems exist in relation to investment appraisal. Rate of return calculations, like prices, are subject to demand and cost uncertainties so that again it is possible for a large amount of managerial discretion to be present both in investment decisions and in the reporting of outcomes. As a result of these and other problems the instructions given in the 1967 White Paper were never effectively implemented. One of the main concerns once again was the problem of managerial incentives to minimise costs. The emphasis in 1967 was on allocative efficiency, but as Sir D.H. Robertson put it as far back as 1952: "A right distribution of productive resources between employments is a "good thing" economically, but not the only good thing, even economically".

In the 1978 White Paper the focus of attention shifted once again to financial targets, and marginal cost pricing was given less prominence. Each industry was also required to produce performance indicators such as productivity and unit cost indices, so that a check could be kept on internal efficiency. The same concern for devising directives that could be more easily monitored led to the test discount rate for individual investment projects being replaced by a rate of return target for investment expenditures as a whole. The emphasis, therefore, was very much on the setting of objectives that were more amenable to effective monitoring. The judgement had been made that, in practice, there was more to be gained from greater internal efficiency, brought about by tighter financial control and more effective monitoring, than would be lost through departures from optimal price and investment policy.

A policy that gives financial targets pride of place is, of course, not without its problems. Where, as it often the case, the corporation has market power, the target may be met by monopoly pricing rather than by increased efficiency. The corporation may also impede or distort competition by engaging in price discrimination or cross-subsidisation. (See, for instance, the Monopolies and Mergers Commission reports on the London Electricity Board 1983, British Airports Authority 1985 and British Gas, 1988). The government may relate financial targets to macroeconomic objectives such as a reduction in the public sector borrowing requirement. One example of this is the price increases imposed upon the electricity supply industry throughout the 1980s, which consistently exceeded the rate of inflation and which were not justified on grounds of cost or investment needs. The external financing limits (EFLs), introduced by the government in 1979 as a further financial constraint on the public corporations, resulted in the rejection of many worthwhile investment projects.

The UK experience of public ownership certainly demonstrates that there have been important obstacles in the way of attaining allocative and internal efficiency. Arguably (see for instance Vickers and Yarrow, 1988) many of these obstacles could be removed without a change of ownership. Efficiency could be increased, for instance, by using independent bodies to scrutinise the performance of public sector bodies including their price and investment decisions. Several efficiency audits of public corporations have in fact been carried out by the Monopolies and Mergers Commission and there is no doubt that some measure of success has been achieved. In addition efficiency-enhancing effects would very likely occur if managerial rewards were more closely related to performance. More important perhaps would be the salutory effect of exposing public corporations to competition wherever that is feasible. It would also be beneficial to have a more arms length relationship between the government and the boards of public corporations for there can be little doubt that some of the problems facing these corporations have been government imposed. These include the use of the corporations to achieve macro-economic objectives, the external financing limits and restrictions on diversification. Just to give one example of the latter: while under public ownership British Gas had successfully diversified into oil and gas exploration but was forced by the government to divest itself of this activity. In the run-up to privatisation one of the advantages which the minister claimed for the change of ownership was the freedom that the new corporation would have to diversify into new areas, including oil exploration!

It is one thing, however, to argue that the government should adopt a "hands off" approach; whether in reality this can be achieved is another matter. So long as major activities are under direct government control it is hard to imagine that ministers will not make use of this for short term economic policy objectives or indeed (especially!) for political gain. The fact of the matter is that successive administrations failed to establish and operate an effective arms length regulatory mechanism with a consistent set of objectives. The difficulty in practice of achieving a durable arms length relationship between the government and public sector corporations is one of the more compelling arguments for privatisation. The question remains to be asked, however, as to how badly the nationalised industries have actually performed. Several different approaches have been used in an attempt to answer this question; none is entirely satisfactory. Some international productivity comparisons, e.g. Aylen (1980) and Pryke (1981), have indicated that UK nationalised industries perform less well than privately owned counterparts overseas. However, international comparisons show UK industry generally to perform relatively badly. The important question is whether the relatively poor performance is even worse for publicly owned firms. The specific contribution of the form of ownership per se to relative performance is not at all clear. Some studies e.g. Collins and Wharton (1984) have looked for clues in the public sector investigations of the

Monopolies and Mergers Commission. In each of the twenty seven investigations carried out by the MMC from 1979 to 1989 the MMC has found something to criticise, and often the criticism has been of a serious kind relating to failures in allocative or managerial efficiency. In particular, attention has been drawn on several occasions to inadequacies in management information flows; failure to relate prices to costs; insufficiently challenging performance targets, and the absence of effective monitoring mechanisms. However in the majority of cases the MMC has also found much to commend, and in only three cases did it judge a problem to be sufficiently serious to merit an adverse public interest finding. Moreover MMC investigations of private sector monopolies have also on many occasions been highly critical. The results of the MMC's efficiency audits of public sector bodies do not therefore form a safe basis from which to draw conclusions about relative performance.

We are on somewhat safer ground when dealing with productivity comparisons with privately owned domestic industries. These studies have proceeded on the basis of comparing *changes* in productivity which are not necessarily a good measure of relative *levels* of efficiency. Consequently the results have to be viewed with caution. The figures in Table 1 show the findings of two such studies. Both suggest that the nationalised industries have, on the whole, performed well relative to the average performance of the manufacturing sector. The striking improvement in the performance of Coal, the Post Office, British Rail and British Steel shows what can be achieved under public ownership.

Table 1 Productivity Changes (output per head)

	1960-75 (% change)		1968-78 (% per annum)	1978-85 (% per annum)
British Airways	150	British Airways	6.4	6.6
British Gas	242	British Gas	8.5	3.8
Electricity	127	Electricity	5.3	3.9
Coal	25	Coal	-0.7	4.4
Postal Services	-6	Post Office	-1.3	2.3
Telecommunications	169	British Telecom	8.2	5.8
		British Steel	-0.2	12.6
		British Rail	0.8	3.9
All Manufacturing	51	All Manufacturing	2.7	3.0

Source: NEDO (1976) Source: Molyneux & Thompson (1987)

It is on the basis of financial performance indicators that the public corporations come out badly. For instance, for all public corporations over the ten year period 1970-1979 gross trading surpluses, net of subsidies, averaged 4.3 per cent of the net capital stock at replacement value. By comparison, for all industrial and commercial companies gross trading profit as a percentage of net capital stock at replacement cost averaged 17.1 per cent. This profitability comparison can not however be taken as evidence of a high level of internal inefficiency within public corporations. Part of the difference may be due to monopoly price distortions in the private sector and government price controls in the public sector. In some cases e.g. rail transport, financial results may be depressed because public sector pricing policy is being used to correct for external diseconomies in the private sector. More generally, the use of profit as an indicator of efficiency is valid only if the price of a good or service reflects society's valuation of it relative to other commodities, and if the cost of inputs reflect the social value of those inputs. When these conditions do not hold, due for instance to monopoly or externalities, financial measures may be a poor indicator of relative performance. It is impossible to estimate the extent to which these factors explain the disparity in the financial performance of the public and private sectors in the 1970s, but it is improbable that all of it could be explained away. However, what is clear is the emphasis that came to be placed on financial performance by successive governments after 1979. This was particularly noticeable during the dispute over pit closures in the early 1980s when financial performance clearly dominated wider economic and social appraisal. (See, for instance, George et.al., 1989.) The overriding aim of government during the last decade is that "every tub should stand on its own (financial) bottom"; subsidy has become a dirty word and wider economic efficiency arguments have stood little chance when confronted with the virtues of financial rectitude. For whatever reason, the poor financial performance of public corporations proved a major handicap to those seeking to defend public ownership.

3. Privatisation

An alternative to instituting reform of the nationalised industries is to return their activities to the private sector. This policy has been pursued by a number of countries in recent years, but none so enthusiastically as the UK where several industries, including telecommunications, gas, airports, and water, have already been privatised, with others such as electricity to follow.

Ownership and efficiency

It is important to note that privatisation simply transfers a monopoly from the public to the private sector. All the resource allocation problems of monopoly thus remain. If there is a case for privatisation per se it must rest on a link between internal efficiency and the form of ownership and control. This involves inter alia the relationship between shareholder and manager or, in the case of nationalised industries, between government and managers. These belong to a more general set of problems known as *principal-agent* or *agency* relationships. A principal-agent relationship exists where one party (the agent) agrees to act in the interests of another party (the principal). Thus managers are appointed by shareholders to run companies on their behalf. Likewise the government appoints managers to run nationalised undertakings in accordance with policies laid down by Parliament. Two conditions are necessary for agency relationships to pose interesting problems. First, the agent's objectives must differ from those of the principal. Second, the principal must have access to less information than is available to the agent, e.g. on cost, market conditions and the agent's behaviour. There is in other words a problem of asymmetric information and thus a need for monitoring the agent's behaviour and performance.

Agency-type relationships exist between managers and other employees as well as between owner and manager. At the latter level, which is the one that interests us here, these relationships pose no problem in firms where there is no divorce between ownership and control e.g. the single proprietor who also manages the firm. A problem does exist, however, in large firms where, typically, there is a degree of divorce between owner and manager and where organisational complexity together with imperfections in product and capital markets allow managers to pursue objectives other than the maximisation of shareholders wealth. On the face of it the agency problem would appear to be more acute under public ownership. In large part this is due to the fact that there are more layers of responsibility and thus more opportunity for directives to be distorted, messages misunderstood and grievances left unresolved. The management board is given directives by a government minister who is answerable to Parliament, which in turn represents the owners, who are the taxpaying public. In addition there are the civil servants who advise the minister and the rest of the Cabinet who may not support him on key issues. There are more principal-agent relationships therefore than one would find in a typical large private company. The objectives of the various parties involved are also liable to display more variety, so the potential for conflict is greater. For instance, in transport, social as well as economic objectives are likely to be important to the "owners". Governments have indeed often set nationalised industries social as well as economic objectives but the trade off between the two has never been entirely clear. This reflects the fact that, given the different weights attached to these objectives by members of the public, the trade off *is* not clear. This in turn allows politicians wide discretion and ample opportunity to manipulate the weights accorded to economic and social objectives in decision making for maximum political advantage. The setting of several, possibly conflicting, goals also increases the scope for managers to exercise discretion.

It would seem therefore that there is an *a priori* case in favour of privatisation on the grounds that it imposes more binding constraints on management, and is thus likely to increase efficiency. More specifically, the following arguments can be advanced. They are deliberately put rather strongly in order to emphasise the main points at issue.

1) The profit motive provides incentives, to employees generally but to management in particular, which are largely absent in state-owned corporations. Generally, rewards are more closely linked to performance.
2) Privately owned firms have a clearly defined objective - the maximisation of profits - which is easy to monitor. This aids the coordination of effort within the firm. State owned firms, however, have to pursue a mixture of economic and social goals which results in inefficiency in day to day operations and ambiguities in pricing and investment decisions.
3) Private companies are more responsive to market conditions and will more readily take advantage of new opportunities such as diversification into new growth areas. This is aided by the fact that privately owned firms have greater freedom in raising capital.
4) Private companies are not plagued by government intervention when making decisions on prices, wages, investment, location etc., whereas such intervention is common in the public sector.

5) Private companies are more accountable to their owners who are better able to monitor performance and organise a revolt against inefficient management.
6) Efficiency is encouraged in privately owned companies not only by the profit motive and clearly defined objectives but also by the threat and occurrence of take-over.

Points 1 - 4 involve matters which, as mentioned earlier, could in principle be dealt with without change of ownership. Greater incentives could be introduced into publicly owned corporation as an inducement to greater efficiency. Where social objectives are important these could be identified and the efficiency with which socially desirable activities are supplied could be monitored; otherwise the corporation could be instructed to behave commercially. Public corporations could be given greater freedom to raise capital and to diversify, and with sufficient will the government could adopt an arms length approach to day to day operations. In addition it should not be supposed that the advantages claimed for private ownership are always realised especially when considering large firms, which is the appropriate comparison to make. Managerial incentives may be severely attenuated in large firms; there may be an asymmetry in managerial rewards - failure being punished more harshly than success is rewarded - which tends towards excessive caution in decision making; and because of the vested interests of different groups within the firm clearly defined overall objectives may be just as elusive in large private companies as in public corporations. Of particular concern is the charge that the private sector has failed to generate adequate funds for investment on a long term basis. Spokesmen for the financial sector tend to argue that there is no evidence of any shortage of funds for profitable investment projects. However this defence has to be heavily discounted if the financial markets themselves take a short view in investment appraisal.

On point 5) there are several reasons to doubt the effectiveness of shareholder monitoring, especially when shares are highly dispersed. Take, for instance, the case where shares are higly dispersed amongst individuals. An individual will typically find it difficult and costly to get detailed information on company performance. If he feels sufficiently discontented it will not be easy to organise a revolt and any attempt to do so may be thwarted by management's use of the proxy vote. Further, the incentive to upstage management is severely attenuated by the free-rider problem. If a small number of shareholders succeed in removing management and improving performance the consequent rewards will be enjoyed by the whole body of shareholders, and the "activists" will gain but a small proportion of the benefits. The position should be better where institutional shareholders are important. Again, however, there is the problem of obtaining access to the detailed information needed to judge performance. The institutions are liable to make judgements on the basis of readily available indicators such as earnings per share which say nothing directly about efficiency. Institutions also typically hold a small percentage of shares in a single company so the free-rider problem is still present. Finally, the alternative to getting involved is getting out. In the UK the choice which institutions have between active supervision and passive portfolio adjustment has generally been exercised in favour of the latter.

This brings us to the argument that privatisation will result in efficiency gains because private sector firms are exposed to the discipline of the take-over bid. It would seem reasonable to suppose that the threat of takeover would have a beneficial effect on efficiency. One way of modelling this effect is to adapt an approach applied by Leibenstein (1979) to product market competition. The essence of the argument presented here is that the threat of takeover is directly related to managerial or internal efficiency, as measured by long-run average costs, and that the latter is a function of managerial effort. We assume that it is long-run costs that are important, i.e. that the threat of takeover will be high if outsiders see large unexploited opportunities for increasing efficiency, including long-term programmes of modernisation, rationalisation, R&D effort, labour force training and so on. The emphasis on long-run efficiency and the effort required to achieve long-run improvements as opposed to short-run cost cutting, which may imply *less* effort, is crucial.

In Figure 1 curve A shows that as effort increases average cost falls. The degree of effort is in turn a function of cost, because if costs increase as a result of inefficiency the firm will be more exposed to takeover. The higher costs are the more pressure there is to increase effort in order to avoid takeover.

Figure 1

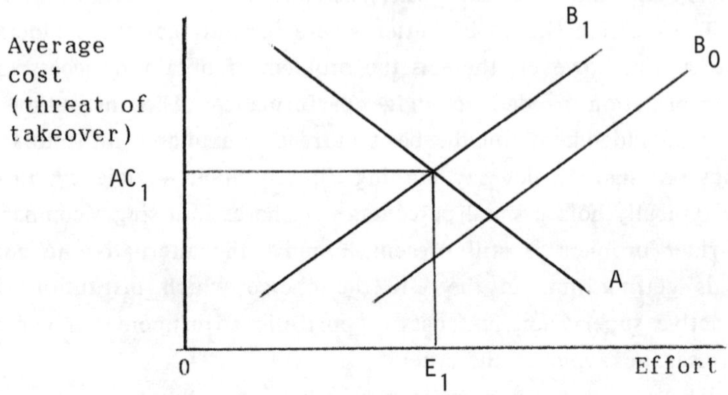

This relationship is shown in curve B_1. The optimum amount of effort is E_1 with average costs AC_1. There is a family of B curves, each representing a state of the environment i.e. the perceived takeover threat. The more protected the firm the lower the pressure to minimise costs and thus the less effort there will be at any given level of average cost, and vice versa. If the takeover threat increases the relevant B curve will be positioned to the right of B_1 e.g. at B_0; managerial effort will be higher and costs lower. This result depends on the assumption that takeovers are motivated only by long-run cost and profit considerations and that the potential for cost improvements is known equally well to both incumbent managers and raiders. However there are several reasons for doubting the reasonableness of this assumption. Where cost conditions are not well known by outsiders there may be a large random element in takeover activity. Takeovers may also be motivated by considerations such as empire building, which are not closely related to costs. When costs are important the emphasis may be on opportunities for short-run gains rather than on longer term efficiency considerations. In these circumstances the effect of a more hostile environment, in the form of increased probability of takeover, might be the opposite to that suggested above. The incumbent management might judge the extra effort needed to improve long-run competitiveness to have no noticeable effect on the chance of being taken over and may decide to reduce effort. Indeed in certain circumstances a reduction in effort will be clearly indicated. For instance, a firm's costs may be temporarily high, and profits and share prices temporarily depressed, because it is in the middle of a modernisation or rationalisation programme, and predators may see this as an opportunity for launching a takeover bid. Some examples of this possible outcome, taken from investigations of the Monopolies and Mergers Commission, are given in George (1989). Where the threat of takeover is high one possible effect, therefore, is that firms eschew longer term investments and concentrate on the less arduous cost-cutting exercises needed to boost short-run profits even though this may have adverse consequences on long run competitiveness.

There are other reasons why too much emphasis should not be placed on the efficiency - enhancing effects of takeovers, especially in the case of the large utilities. First, although it seems that even very large companies are not immune from the threat of takeover there is still a general tendency for the incidence of takeover to be negatively related to size. Certainly the size of the major utilities gives them a substantial measure of protection and their strategic importance suggests that they are unlikely to be exposed to the full rigours of capital market competition. Second, studies of the effects of mergers such as Singh (1971), Meeks (1977) and Kumar (1984) do not yield very reassuring conclusions. One specific aspect which is particularly relevant in the present context, and which ties up with the earlier analysis, is the suggestion that a high level of takeover activity may lead to short termism in managerial decision making. To the extent that this tendency exists it is serious because by the very nature of their activities the utilities need to take a long view.

Competition

During the course of the privatisation debates ministers have often argued that one advantage of the policy is that it exposes the firm to more competition in product markets. However, as already emphasised, privatisation per se does nothing to change the structure of an industry. If there is anything in the competition argument it must be related either to the threat of new entry or to the actual existence of competitors. Potential competition has received a great deal of attention in recent years especially in its most extreme form - the perfectly contestable market. The assumptions that underpin the theory of contestability however give it little relevance in the anlaysis of firm behaviour and industrial performance. Though the threat of entry in general can have important efficiency-enhancing effects what matters most, especially for large firms, is actual competition. In this connection it is important to distinguish between two groups of firms that have been privatised in the UK - those that were already operating in more or less competitive industries, and the utilities with very substantial monopoly power.

a) Privatisation of firms in competitive markets

The majority of firms that have been privatised to date were operating in markets which might loosely be described as "competitive". Seven of them are shown in Table 2. Other major asset sales include British Petroleum (1979), Amersham International (1982), Enterprise Oil (1984), Rolls Royce (1987) and the Rover Group (1988). Product market competition is clearly severely attenuated in some cases. For instance, airline regulation means that British Airways operates in a market that falls far short of being fully competitive. Nevertheless BA has to compete against several major firms which is not true of companies such as British Telecom or British Gas.

Table 2 *Profitability performance of privatised firms operating in competitive markets*

OPERATING PROFIT AS % OF NET ASSETS				COMPANY						
Year ending	B Ae	C&W	NFC		B.Oil	ABP		Jr		BA
1979	15.4	27.3	--		--	17.2		--		--
1980	13.4	24.4	--		--	9.4		--		--
1981	10.5 *	19.2 *	--		--	-3.0		--		-8.5
1982	10.6	18.2	12.8 *		57.1 *	8.4		9.1		1.3
1983	8.9	23.8	18.8		51.9	9.6 *		46.6		19.4
1984	11.1	23.6	18.3		48.6	-4.5	-4.9	50.3 *		26.0
1985	12.5	23.2	19.5		46.4	11.9	11.8	46.1	45.0	30.3
1986	12.3	22.8	21.4	21.9	8.7	15.3	16.5	34.3	10.2	21.4
1987	10.9	23.8	22.4	24.1	20.8	19.5	17.4	25.6	5.3	18.4 *
1988	8.8	23.7		23.9	14.7		15.3		-34.0	14.4

* = Year of first share issue
B Ae = British Aerospace; C&W = Cable and Wireless
NFC = National Freight Corporation; B.Oil = Britoil
ABP = Associated British Ports; Jr = Jaguar
BA = British Airways

Source: Yarrow (1989) and Company accounts

Yarrow (1989) examined the post-privatisation performance of the companies in Table 2, and identified, largely on the basis of profit performance, three "clear success stories" - Cable and Wireless, the National Freight Corporation and Associated British Ports. Three out of seven would not appear to be a particularly impressive record. Furthermore, the results cannot be accepted as evidence of the beneficial effects of privatisation per se without qualification.

First, there are the well known problems of using profit performance as a measure of improved efficiency. However, since the companies concerned were operating with considerable autonomy before privatisation it may be reasonable to assume that most of any improved performance is due to efficiency gains rather than increased use of monopoly power. Second, the period after 1981 was one during which the profitability of UK companies in general displayed a marked upward trend. Between 1981 and 1987 the average rate of return on capital at current replacement cost for the UK industrial and commercial sector (excluding North Sea Oil) doubled from 4.8 per cent to 9.6 per cent. When the profit performance of privatised companies is "normalised" to take account of this the apparent benefits of privatisation become much less impresive. Third there are special features associated with each of the three success stories in Table 2. Cable and Wireless' profits are derived largely from overseas and are thus sensitive to exchange rate movements. This helps to explain the dip in profit performance in 1981 and 1982. However, the company was operating profitably before privatisation occurred. Indeed, operating profit as a percentage of net assets was higher in 1979 and 1980 than in any post-privatisation year up to 1988. In the case of Associated British Ports most, if not all, the improved profit performance has come from its ownership of property in dockland areas which, during the 1980s, has seen a great boom in housing and office development. National Freight is the clearest success story. This case is unusual in that the company was acquired by the employees. The corporation is in effect a conglomeration of small units in which there is a clear relationship between individual and overall performance. Incentives to be efficient are consequently high.

Yarrow asks why the other four corporations in his sample did not perform particularly well after privatisation. Why, for instance, did Jaguar which operates in a more competitive product market than Associated British Ports perform badly after privatisation? He suggests that one possible answer is that the management of Britoil, Jaguar, British Aerospace and British Airways were given protection against takeover by means of "golden share" arrangements or limits on the size of individual shareholdings, and that the discretion so afforded to management relaxed the pressure to increase efficiency. Though protection from takeover may be a factor which, in general, weakens efficiency incentives it does not appear to be an entirely plausible explanation of the relative performance of the firms under discussion. For instance, the National Freight Corporation's success up to 1988 was achieved with complete immunity from hostile takeover threats. It may also be noted that though the government has a golden share in British Steel, in the first full financial year, 1989-90, since it was privatised in December 1988, the Company declared a 24 per cent increase in pre-tax profits. Jaguar's failure was more likely the result of sub-optimal size, resulting in fundamental weaknesses in production, marketing and R&D, than the result of insufficient exposure to capital market discipline. Jaguar was in fact acquired by the Ford Motor Company in 1989.

More generally it is a mistake to assume that exposing a company to more competitive pressure is sufficient to bring about improved performance. Though the discipline imposed by product market and capital market competition is important that discipline works rather imperfectly. It can also kill as well as cure and may fail to give birth to profitable activities. This certainly seems to be the experience of the UK. For instance, some successful companies now operating in the private sector (e.g. Enterprise Oil, Britoil which is now part of BP, and Amersham International) would not have existed but for initiatives taken in the public sector. (Interestingly, Enterprise Oil is now 25 per cent owned by Elf-Aquitaine a publicly owned French company. Elf-Aquitaine is reportedly interested in a full takeover which if it occurred would create an interesting case of a privatised UK firm re-entering the public sector of another country.) There are many examples of large private companies which failed to adjust to changing market conditions and the post-War experience of the UK industrial sector in general is hardly a shining example of efficiency. Several of the bankrupt companies (e.g. British Leyland and later the Rover Group - now part of British Aerospace, Ferranti - now part of GEC and Rolls Royce now part of Vickers) were rescued out of public funds.

b) Privatisation of monopolies

The public asset sales that have attracted most attention have been those, and in particular the major utilities, where the firm has considerable market power. The first such privatisation was that of British Telecom (BT) in 1984. This was followed by British Gas (1986), the British Airports Authority (1987) and the regional water authorities (1989). Electricity will be privatised in 1991. In these cases the degree of market power enjoyed by the monopoly incumbents is such that there would be general agreement that some exposure to competition would have a beneficial impact on both allocative and internal efficiency. There is a problem, however, in that the opportunity for introducing competition without losing some of the benefits of scale may be limited by natural monopoly elements in industry structure.

The monopoly problem was recognised in the deregulation legislation of the early 1980s. The Telecommunications Act 1981 and the Oil and Gas (Enterprise) Act 1982 heralded the introduction of more competitive markets. In some areas of telecommunications, such as the retailing of customer apparatus and certain value-added network services, a substantial increase in competition has occurred with noticeable benefits to consumers. In BT's core network operations, however, the government has deliberately restricted competition. Mercury was licensed as a new network operator in 1982, its aim being to take a small percentage of the lucrative business market. The privatisation of BT in 1984 was seen by some commentators as an ideal opportunity for creating a more competitive industry structure along the lines of the AT&T divestiture in the US. However, the government announced that no new licenses for network operation would be issued before 1990. Thus the market structure was left with a dominant supplier facing limited competition from the much smaller Mercury Communications Co. (now part of Cable and Wireless) and a local network company operated by Hull City Council. In the case of gas, the Gas Act 1986, which privatised the British Gas Corporation, gave the privatised company a monopoly in the supply of tariff (mainly domestic) customers but, in line with the 1982 legislation, allowed new entrants into the contract business (generally large industrial and commercial users). Any new entrant would of course have to use British Gas (BG) pipeline systems and would have to negotiate terms including matters relating to safety of supply. In the event deregulation failed to induce any new entry.

BG also has very substantial vertical market power. It has been a monopoly purchaser of gas from UK gas fields, a monopoly which, a recent MMC report recommended, should be ended (see below). Another MMC report in 1980, on the supply of domestic gas appliances, was highly critical of the Corporation's conduct as a dominant buyer, and concluded that its retailing monopoly was against the public interest. The MMC offered two possible solutions. Either the Corporation should withdraw from the retailing of gas appliances, or a number of restrictive practices should be adandoned which would have the effect of reducing its power as a retailer. In July 1981 the Minister of State for Consumer Affairs announced that the Corporation would be required to cease selling domestic appliances and dispose of its showrooms over a five-year period. However in October 1981 the Secretary of State for Energy announced that the sale of gas showrooms would be delayed until complex safety legislation had been debated in Parliament, but that the Government remained fully committed to breaking up the monopoly as soon as possible. The management of the British Gas Corporation argued vigorously against enforced division and four years later the government announced its intention to privatise the corporation intact!

The government also set its face against restructuring in the case of the British Airports Authority (BAA). BAA owns and operates seven airports in Britain - Heathrow, Gatwick and Stansted near London, and Prestwick, Glasgow, Edinburgh and Aberdeen in Scotland. Competition between airports is bound to be blunted by the inevitable government involvement in this sector. In view of the sensitive environmental issues, and other externalities, it would be naive to imagine that airports could be allowed to engage in unfettered competition. Even so a beneficial increase in competitive pressure by, for instance, privatising the three London airports as separate companies, could have been achieved without jeopardising the government's legitimate concern with wider issues. The possible benefits, which are examined in detail by Starkie and Thompson (1985) include more competition for off-peak business thus making better use of capacity, and more information to the regulatory authority which would be beneficial in the setting of regulatory standards. However the government argued that any benefit from a more competitively structured industry would be very limited and would be more than offset by efficiency losses. Doubtless, the government was also concerned with the proceeds of the asset sale. In addition, and as in the case of British Gas, the management of BAA campaigned vigorously against enforced division of the company.

In the case of telecommunications, gas, and airports, therefore, the government decided against restructuring. A heavy burden was thus placed on the regulatory agencies to curb monopoly abuse. The magnitude of the problem is seen clearly in the case of British Gas. In 1988, just two years after privatisation, BG's contract business was referred to the MMC following complaints about abuse of monopoly power. The MMC criticised BG for, amongst other things, extensive discrimination in the pricing and supply of gas, and for failing to provide adequate information on the costs of common carriage. The Commission was of the view that BG's behaviour served to deter new entrants and to inhibit the development of competition. The MMC recommended that BG should be required to end its discriminatory practices, to publish price schedules, and to provide more information on common carriage terms. It also recommended that BG should not be allowed to contract for more than 90 per cent of gas supplies from any new UK gas field.

For telecommunications, gas and airports it would appear that a more competitive industry structure could have been achieved without loss of efficiency. In view of the MMC's highly critical 1980 report on the sale of gas appliances more effective measures would have been justified at that end of the market. The area gas boards could also have been privatised as separate companies - a policy which is to be adopted in the case of the electricity supply industry. The same can be said of BT and the privatisation of local networks as separate companies, and also of the division of BAA into two or more separate entities. In all three cases reducing the size of the company would have reduced the scope for anti-competitive behaviour. Decision making would have been spread more widely and the existence of a number of separate companies would have allowed performance comparisons to be made which would have facilitated the setting of standards for regulatory purposes.

To what extent, however, if at all, would this restructuring be achieved at the expense of economies of scale or of scope? Relatively little is known about the nature of cost conditions within the newly privatised utilities. A long-held presumption is that they exhibit natural monopoly features and that these should be kept intact, whether in public or private ownership. Some recent work in this area has yielded interesting results. For telecommunications, Hunt and Lynk (1990a, 1990b) have estimated logarithmic, multi-product cost functions, using time-series data for the period 1950/51 to 1980/81. The aim of their study was to examine the case for the divestiture of British Telecom along the lines advocated by Beesley and Littlechild (1986) and Vickers and Yarrow (1988). The former suggested the separation of domestic (local and trunk) from international voice telephony services as a means of introducing an element of competition. The latter advocated the separation of local from long distance (trunk and international) services along the lines of the AT&T divestiture in the US. Hunt and Lynk find cost complementarities, and thus economies of scope, between internal and external services, but not between local and long distance. The implication of their results is that the divestiture of local services would not result in efficiency losses. This finding is perhaps not surprising. After all, the US, Japan and Denmark operate local, regional services, and the Hull Telephone Co. also operates a profitable local telephone service.

It is still rather early to judge the performance of the privatised monopoly firms, but what evidence there is does not come as much of a surprise. The profitability of BT, British Gas and BAA has remained high, which can be expected given their strong monopoly positions. Attention has already been drawn to the MMC's strictures concerning British Gas' abuse of monopoly power. In April 1990 attention was drawn to BT's extremely high profit margins - nearly 60 per cent on average - on international calls. BAA is able to make very high profits on its commercial activities (see MMC report on the British Airports Authority, 1985). Moreover, there is very little evidence to suggest that privatisation has been followed by a marked improvement in productivity performance. For BT, Bishop and Kay (1988) estimated that total factor productivity increased at an average rate of 2.0 per cent per annum between 1979 and 1983 and at 2.5 per cent per annum between 1983 and 1988. However, the improved performance in the latter period is due in large part to the faster growth in demand for BT services. And BT's performance falls well below that of British Rail and British Steel in which, over the period 1978-85, total factor productivity increased at an average annual rate of 2.8 per cent and 2.9 per cent respectively (Molyneux and Thompson, 1987).

4. Concluding Comments

The privatisation programme in the UK was launched as part of a strategy for strengthening the supply side of the economy. Agency theory suggests that there should be some reason to expect internal efficiency to be higher in privately owned firms than in public corporations. However, there is no clear evidence that privatisation per se has had a significant effect. In fact, performance of public sector corporations comes out well in comparison with that of the private sector. It has been suggested that the improved productivity performance of many public sector companies in the 1980s may have been the indirect consequence of the privatisation programme. Certainly, in firms that have been privatised, there have often been very substantial productivity gains in the years leading up to privatisation, which suggests that privatisation had a substantial indirect effect. However, it is difficult to argue that the prospect of privatisation had much to do with the improved productivity performance of British Rail, British Coal, the Post Office or even British Steel where labour productivity doubled between 1977 and 1984 - well before privatisation was placed on the agenda. The explanation for the improved performance is more likely to be the straightforward one of greater management and government resolve to increase efficiency.

Where firms have been privatised into competitive markets the post-privatisation performance has been mixed. In general there is no clear evidence that the privatised firms have performed better than they would have done had they remained in public ownership. If, in these cases, privatisation exposed the firms to more competitive pressures that too was not sufficient in all cases to improve performance. Exposing firms to the full rigour of product and capital market competition is not a certain recipy for success. A high level of contested takeover bids may, for instance, diminish incentives to take a long view when making investment decisions and so reduce long term efficiency and competitiveness. It is also interesting to note that British Steel's remarkable change in fortune was achieved under the protective regulatory umbrella of the European Coal and Steel Community (see Baber and Mainwaring, 1988). A general point that emerges from this is the importance of striking the right balance between market power and competitive pressure. The point is well understood in the analysis of franchising where it is accepted that too much competition (in the form of a high probability of failing to have a franchise renewed) will tend to result in underinvestment and underperformance generally.

In the case of the privatised monopolies - BT, British Gas and BAA - the balance has been tilted decidedly too much in favour of market power. In these cases the government, at the time of privatisation, missed an opportunity to improve the balance by restructuring the industries along more competitive lines. The evidence suggests that this restructuring could have been achieved without loss of internal efficiency. Finally, what light does the UK experience throw on the role played by privatisation in improving business performance. Was it either necessary of sufficient? There can be little doubt that it was not sufficient. Whether it was necessary is more open to argument.

Bibliography

Aylen, J. (1980). Britain's Steelyard Blues, *New Scientist* (26 June).

Baber, C. and L. Mainwaring, L. (1988). "Steel", in George, K.D. and L. Mainwaring (eds), *The Welsh Economy*, Cardiff: University of Wales Press.

Beesley, M. and S. Littlechild (1986). "Privatisation: Principles, Problems and Priorities", in Kay, J., C. Mayer and D. Thompson (eds), *Privatisation and Regulation - the UK Experience*, Oxford: Clarendon Press.

Bishop, M. and J.A. Kay (1988). *Does Privatisation Work? - Lessons from the UK*, London Business School.

George, K.D., L. Mainwaring, J.S. Shorey and D.R. Thomas (1988). "Coal", in George, K.D. and L. Mainwaring (eds), *The Welsh Economy*, Cardiff: University of Wales Press.

George, K.D. (1989). "Do we Need a Merger Policy?" in Fairburn, J.A. and J.A. Kay (eds), *Mergers and Merger Policy*, Oxford: Oxford University Press.

Hunt, L.C. and E.L. Lynk (1990a). "Telecommunications Industry Divestiture in the UK: A Time Series Analysis", *Oxford Bulletin of Economics and Statistics*.

Hunt, L.C. and E.L. Lynk (1990b). "Telecommunications Divestiture in the UK: A Crossed Line?", *Applied Economics*, (forthcoming).

HM Treasury (1961). *Financial and Economic Obligations of the Nationalised Industries*, Cmnd 1337, London: HMSO.

HM Treasury (1967). *Nationalised Industries: A Review of Economic and Financial Objectives*, Cmnd 3437, London: HMSO.

HM Treasury (1978). *The Nationalised Industries*, Cmnd 7131, London: HMSO.

Kumar, M.S. (1984). *Growth, Acquisitions and Investment*, Cambridge: Cambridge University Press.

Leibenstein, H. (1979). "A Branch of Economics is Missing: Micro-Micro Theory", *Journal of Economic Literature*, Vol.17.

Meeks, G. (1977). *Disappointing Marriage : A Study of the Gains from Merger*, Cambridge: Cambridge University Press.

Molyneux, R. and D. Thompson (1987). "Nationalised Industry Performance: Still Third Rate?", *Fiscal Studies*.

Monopolies and Mergers Commission (1980). *Domestic Gas Appliances: A Report on the Supply of Certain Domestic Gas Appliances in the United Kingdom*, HC 703, London: HMSO.

Monopolies and Mergers Commission (1983). *London Electricity Board: A Report on the Direction and Management by the London Electricity Board of its Business of Retailing Domestic Electric Goods*, Spare Parts and Ancillary Goods, Cmnd 8812, London: HMSO.

Monopolies and Mergers Commission (1985). *British Airports Authority: A Report on the Efficiency and Costs of, and the Service Provided by the British Airports Authority in its Commercial Activities*, Cmnd 9644, London: HMSO.

Monopolies and Mergers Commission (1988). *Gas: A Report on the Matter of the Existence of or Possible Existence of a Monopoly Situation in Relation to the Supply in Great Britain of Gas through Pipes to Persons other than Tariff Customers*, Cmnd 500, London: HMSO.

National Economic Development Office (1976). *A Study of UK Nationalised Industries*, London: HMSO.

Pryke, R. (1981). *The Nationalised Industries: Policies and Performance Since 1968*, Oxford: Martin Robertson.

Reid, Sir Charles (1945). Chairman of Parliamentary report: *The Coal Mining Report of the Technical Advisory Committee*, Cmnd. 6610, London: HMSO.

Robertson, Sir D.H. (1956). *Lecture in Economic Principles*, Volume 1, p. 168, London: Staples Press.

Singh, A. (1971). *Takeovers: Their Relevance to the Stock Market and the Theory of the Firm*, Cambridge: Cambridge University Press.

Starkie, D. and D. Thompson (1985). "Stansted: A Viable Investment?" *Fiscal Studies*.

Vickers, J.S. and G.K. Yarrow (1988). *Privatisation: An Economic Analysis*, Cambridge Massachusetts: The MIT Press.

Yarrow, G.K. (1989). *Privatization and Economic Performance in Britain*, Carnegie-Rochester Conference Series on Public Policy 31, North Holland.

9 SOCIOPOLITICAL COMPETITION OR HARMONIZATION IN THE EUROPEAN COMMUNITY?

Some Fundamental Reflections

PETER OBERENDER

1. Introduction and Problem Presentation

The answer to the topic of this paper gains political importance in the wake of the termination of the EC-Common Market in 1992. Trade union representatives in particular have been emphatically demanding again and again the passing of a "social charter" that sets forth certain basic social rights. In December 1988, the EC-heads of state and government promised that 1989 would become "the year of social course setting". In the meantime, the year 1990 has begun without the passing of concrete proposals by the EC-Commission for a common social policy. This fact is not surprising by itself because, since the beginning of the European unification, a fundamental question has been repeatedly in the center of disagreement. "Is harmonization or competition the adequate solution to an adjustment of the different conditions within the European Community?" (Meyer and Willgerodt, 1956; Liefmann-Keil, 1961, pp. 366-372.)

Especially in the area of social policy, the different opinions clash strongly with each other, due to the fact that the legal bases of a European social policy are being interpreted in different ways. The EEC-Treaty of 1957 contains approaches to an EC-social policy. The freedom of manpower is materially created by Article 51 of the EEC-Treaty which guarantees social security. This regulation ensures "the addition of all the different periods of time that had to be considered according to the various intrastate legal regulations for the aquisition and preservation of the entitlement to benefits as well as the calculation of services to emigrating and immigrating employees" (Article 51 (a) EEC-Treaty). Title III ("Social policy") as well as Title V ("Economic and social cohesion") constitute its basis. In general, it concerns letters of intent if "a close cooperation among member states in the area of social questions, relating especially to employment, labor law and working conditions, job-related formation and advanced training, social security, prevention of job-related accidents and diseases, health protection during work, right of association and collective negotiations" (Article 118 EEC-Treaty) is demanded. The goal of European integration is the creation of a common market in which all tariff and non-tariff barriers for the trade of goods and services are gradually abolished as well as obstacles to cross-frontier movements of the productive factors labor, capital and technological know-how. With regard to this goal, the answers to the following questions are of prime importance:

- What does the initial situation in the area of social policy in the EC look like?
- Which objectives exist in the EC and which measures have been taken in the EC thus far in order to unify social policy? How are they to be evaluated?
- Does the European integration require a unified social policy at all, i.e. is harmonization the prerequisite for integration?
  Which reasons for a harmonization are brought forward and how are they to be evaluated?
  Can harmonization be theoretically justified at all?
  Which problems arise in the process of harmonizing the national social policy?
- What is the adequate way towards a European social policy and how can this way be (theoretically) justified?

2. Initial Situation in the EEC

2.1 Diverging Social Policy

The member states of the EEC differ in various ways. Particularly in the area of social policy, which is as diverse and different as the people and landscapes of the EEC. The wages and the social level in particular are the center of current political disscussion. German employers often maintain that the international competitiveness of the location Federal Republic of Germany would be threatened by high wages and incidental wage costs which are primarily caused by the high level of social security. Indeed, the money-wage level in the EEC varies considerably (Figure 1). The average gross income from dependent employment per dependent employee in the FRG in 1987, evaluated in ECU, was 22% above the EC-average and 377% (!) above the average money-wage in Portugal (Vogler-Ludwig, 1989, pp. 13-16). It is, however, not the money-wage but the relation between money-wage and labor productivity, i.e. the unit labor costs, that is relevant. These costs, however, have only been 3 % above EC-average and 20% above the average money-wage in Portugal. In comparison with national money-wages, the unit labor costs in the EC vary less (Figure 1).

Figure 1   Wages and Productivity

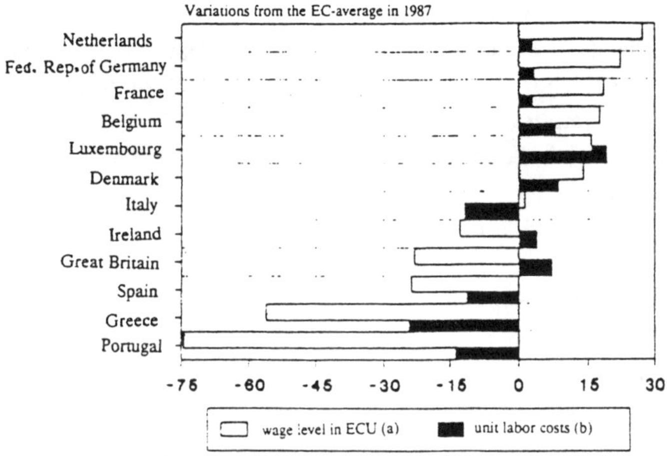

a) gross income from dependent employment per dependent employee
b) gross income from dependent employment per 1000 ECU GDP at market prices

Figure 1a   Wages and Exchange Rates

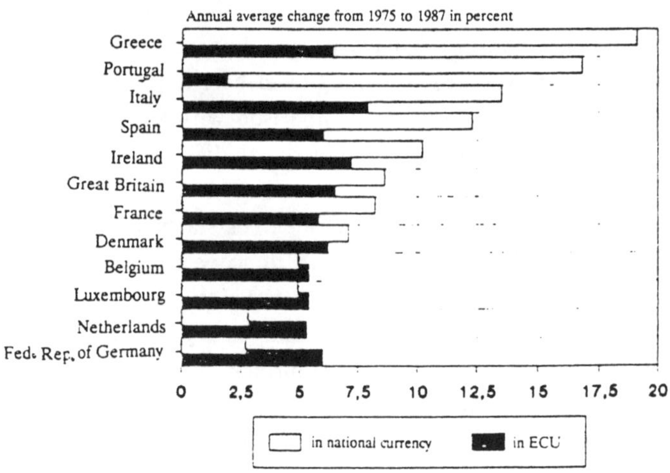

Source: Eurostat, EC-Commission
IFO-Institute

Source: Vogler-Ludwig, 1989

The different levels of competitiveness among member states has, to an extent, been levelled out by developments in the exchange rate system. Concentration in the period between 1975 and 1987 depicts that the great changes in unit labor costs in national currency are greatly compensated by changes in the exchange rate. Therefore, the increase in unit labor costs has been reduced considerably by devaluation in countries with a great increase in unit labor costs (Greece, Portugal).

But countries (FRG, Netherlands) lost the advantages of a relatively small increase in unit labor costs by undergoing revaluation of their national currencies. This implies that money-wages by themselves do not yet reveal very much about the unit labor costs and, consequently, about national competitiveness.

There are considerable differences in the wage-level, the social security benefits and the working hours of the individual member states. For example, the Federal Republic of Germany has the shortest working hours by collective agreement, the second highest wage level as well as the third highest social security benefits per capita in the EEC. If these components are evaluated with scores, the FRG reaches the highest score with 100 points for the working hours, i.e. the shortest working hours by collective agreement are valid, 77 points for wages, i.e. 77% of the highest wage level (Luxembourg) in the EEC, and 91 points for the social security benefits. If working hours, wages and social security benefits are combined to form an indicator for "social level", it is revealed that the FRG takes the second place with 268 points within the EEC behind Luxembourg with 271 points (Table 1). While the differences in social level between the countries in the center of the EEC are moderate, the comparison with Southern and Western countries of the EEC reveals remarkable social differences. Portugal holds the last position with a score of 88 points.

The social security systems of the EC-member states vary in many ways. There are considerable differences relating to scope (disease, age, accident, unemployment), validity range (whole population, all wage and salary earners, only a certain group of wage and salary earners, only certain population groups), the financing (contributions, state grants), the volume of benefits (money, real benefits, continuation of benefits, waiting days) as well as the form of organization (state institution or compulsory insurance) (Institut der Deutschen Wirtschaft, 1989).

Table 1 Social-level in the EC 1987

Country	Social-level (Scores)
Luxembourg	271
FGR	268
Netherlands	260
Denmark	254
Belgium	244
France	239
Great Britain	221
Italy	218
Greece	177
Ireland	170
Spain	161
Portugal	88

Total maximum possible scores 300.
Maximum score 100 each for highest wage, highest social security benefits and lowest hours of work.

Source: Author's own computations on the basis of empirical data, in Medikannt & Meinung 11/1989 (15-11-1989)

The individual social security systems are systems that have grown over decades and that are based on very divergent concepts and ideologies. The individual national systems have come into being during the last 100 years at different points in time, for different reasons and with rather different concepts. Next to the classical social insurance (Bismarck), sheer supply systems (Beveridge) have existed in some countries. In the course of time, distinctions among the individual concepts have become blurred, but they are still governed by diverging objectives. There are, for example, systems that place a stronger emphasis on self-responsibility and proper provisional means of the individual than other systems. Furthermore, supply systems often constitute wage-related systems, while classical social insurance systems often grant minimum benefits or protect the individual policy-holder by means of social security benefits.

2.2 Example: Health Insurance in the EEC

The variety of European social security systems can be depicted by using the example of health insurance. In all EC-countries, precautions have been taken so that the sick can be treated without taking their economic situation into account. Furthermore, wage and salary earners generally have the claim for continued wage payments in case of sickness. Despite these common characteristics, considerable differences are existing between the concrete national forms.

Concerning the form of organization, there are two basic forms: a National Health Service (Great Britain since 1948, Ireland since 1971, Denmark since 1973, Portugal since 1979, Italy since 1980, Greece since 1983 and Spain since 1986) that has increasingly adopted throughout the EEC, and a health insurance system (FRG, France, Netherlands and Luxembourg). It is characteristic for the National Health Service that medical services are provided for free, that financing is generally taken care of by budget funds (only a small part being provided by dues) and that medical doctors are state employees.

The health insurance system is marked by the fact that the services are completely, or at least predominantly financed by dues; the payments to medical doctors, as well as the collection of dues, are undertaken by different kinds of health insurances.

Medical doctors are generally free lance professionals. The health insurances work according to the performances-in-kind principle (FRG, Netherlands) and/or according to the refund of costs principle (France, Belgium, Luxembourg; in certain areas, e.g. dentures, also in the FRG). With the exception of four countries (FRG, Great Britain, Greece, Spain), there exists a deduction for the patient on the doctor's and hospital care costs. With the exception of the Federal Republic and the Netherlands, there is also a general deduction on medication.

A right to wage payment continuation exists for employees in all EC-countries, but it is regulated in very different ways. In the Federal Republic of Germany, Belgium, Italy (for nonmanual employees), Luxembourg and Denmark, the employers are required by law to continue wage or salary payments at least for a certain time. The health insurance or the National Health Service take over these payments later. In Portugal, Spain and Italy (for workers) as well as, with certain modifications, in Great Britain and Ireland, the social security takes over wage or salary payments in the beginning of a disease.

Greater differences also arise with regard to the regulation of waiting days. Except for the Federal Republic of Germany, the obligation to pay a sickness benefit does not start on the first day, but only after one to three waiting days. Differences exist also in the amount and duration of the sickness benefit payment.

2.3 Example: Old Age Protection in the EEC

At present, there are two basic types of state old age protection (Institut der Deutschen Wirtschaft, 1989 b, pp.4-5; Berié, 1989):

In Denmark, Ireland, Great Britain and in the Netherlands, there is an *old age pension for all inhabitants* that generally covers the minimum subsistence level at old age. In Great Britain and Denmark additional systems have been established in addition to this basic protection which are financed by dues and certain benefits depending on the income.

In the Federal Republic of Germany, Belgium, France, Greece, Spain, Italy, Luxembourg and Portugal, however, *pension insurance funds* are preponderent. There exists a financing of the benefits which are closely linked to the paid dues.

With regard to financing, there are great differences within the EEC. While the old age pension for all inhabitants is financed by taxes up to 100 % in Denmark and up to 90 % in Great Britain, taxpayers, employers and employees have to bear the costs in Ireland. In most of the other countries, except for the FRG where employers and employees share the dues, the employer pays the dues while state limits herself to contributions. However, one must not overlook the fact that, in this case, a part of the wage or salary is concerned which is merely kept by the employer and paid over like a wage tax.

The nationally unified pension for single persons annually amounts to DM 9.500 in Denmark (DM 11.800 for married people), DM 7.800 in Ireland (DM 12.200), DM 8.060 in Great Britain (DM 12.740), DM 12.480 in the Netherlands (DM 18.000) per year. In all these countries, the old age pension is adjusted, but the referential basis is different. While the income of the working employees is the key factor in the Federal Republic of Germany and the Netherlands, the alignment is oriented towards the price index in the other EC-member states.

In nearly all countries of the EEC, pensionable age is 65 years for men and 60 years for women. In Denmark, however, it lies at the age of 67 for both men and women, while women in Italy can receive their old age pension from the age of 55 onwards. There are also considerable differences with regard to the waiting periods. In the FRG the waiting period amounts to five years, in Italy to 20 years, in Spain to 15 years and in Portugal to 10 years. In Greece, the person in question has to have 4.050 work days and 156 weeks of dues in order to be eligible for an old age pension.

In view of these basic differences, efforts are being made in the EEC to align the national security systems to each other by way of harmonization (Myrdal, 1956, p. 128). The Portuguese socialist deputy Gomes, for example, has demanded that "the social framework conditions are not to be left to the decisions of the market" (Schavoir-Ysselstein, 1989, p. 5).

3. Sociopolitical Objectives of the EEC and Previous Measures

Next to the already mentioned Article 51 of the EEC-Treaty, the Articles 117 to 122 (Title III "Social Policy") and the Articles 130 a to 130 e (Title V "Economic and Social Cohesion") of the EEC-Treaty are of prime importance for the European social policy. Title III was supplemented by the Uniform European File (UEF), while Title V was inserted into the EEC-Treaty by the Uniform European File according to Article 23 UEF. The UEF came into force on July 1, 1987 in order to "contribute to concrete progress on the way to a European Union" (Article 1 UEF). The UEF pursues three principal goals:

- realization of the European Market by the end of 1992 (time plan)
- substitution of the Principle of Unanimity by the Principle of the Qualified Majority (law instrument) in selected areas
- strengthening of the Environment Protection and Structural Fund (strengthening of economic cohesion).

3.1 Relaxation of the Principle of Unanimity

In view of the various difficulties in finding unanimity for different regulations, the EC-Commission decided to introduce the Principle of the Qualified Majority. This qualified majority has so far explicitly referred only to minimum standards in the area of work and health protection at the work place (Article 118 a EEC-Treaty). In other social areas, the Principle of Unanimity continues to be valid, i.e. also with regard to the regulations on labor mobility and rights of the employees in the EEC. Therefore the EC-Council releases guidelines at the EC-Commission's proposal which define the minimum regulations of work and health protection.

Beyond these minimum requirements, the individual member states can release further protection rules. According to Article 100 a, Paragraph 4, Sentence 2 EEC-Treaty, this higher level of work protection may not, however, be suitable for limiting the trade among member states or hindering it in concealed ways.

3.2 Structural Fund

According to the resolution of the EC-Council of Ministers, the EC-Structural Fund is supposed to be increased from ECU 3.1 billion (1987) to ECU 14.5 billion, from 1993 on. It is the main objective of this fund to reduce the economic and social differences among the individual EC-regions by means of assistance in the areas of social policy, as well as agriculture. It remains to be seen how far this objective can be reached through the help of the Structural Fund.

3.3 Social Dialogue

Article 118 b of the EEC-Treaty intends to encourage an intensified dialogue concerning social matters among corporate economic partners on the European level. Therefore, a new aspect is introduced into European social policy. The President of the Commission, Jacques Delors, advocates a strengthened linking of the employee representatives to the construction of a European social order. Collective and frame-work agreements should also be created by means of dialogue between labor and management. In this context, Delors values the German model to be of prime importance (Delors, 1988, p. 5).

This model sets the following premises: a large and functioning market; autonomy of the corporate economic partners; participation of employees in the form of codetermination; adoption of macroeconomic responsibility of the State and the Central Bank. At present, this German model has a good chance of be converted into a European model, especially because eleven out of twelve member states (Great Britain is the exception) have reacted in a positive way to this idea (Delors, 1988, p. 5).

3.4 Social Charter

At the end of May 1989, the EC-Commission presented a preliminary draft for a "Community Charter of Social Basic Rights" which is supposed to effectively reduce the differences in sociopolitical regulations of the individual EC-countries, and thereby create uniform competition regulations.

It is intended to provide the citizens, and particularly the community employees, with the guarantee of labor mobility, fair payment, free choice and exercise of profession, improvement of living and working conditions (i.e. right to paid annual vacation), appropriate social protection, right to freedom of coalition and to salary negotiations, right to freedom of association and wage negotiations, right to exercise an occupation, of equal treatment of men and women, of information, hearing and participation, namely in companies and multinational firms with plants in several member states (Birk, 1989). Up to now, these basic rights have been formulated in a very general way, but the tendency is evident that it is at last a matter of harmonizing ex-ante the social basic rights in the EEC.

At the end of November, the EC-Commission published a memorandum on their program of action which aimed at applying the Community Charter of Basic Social Rights in order to accelerate the harmonization in the area of social policy (EC-Commission, 1989).

On December 8 and 9, 1989 the European Council in Straßburg which deals primarily with recommendations, discussed the social charter without passing a concrete resolution. One has to wait to see how the Social Charter, which has been proposed by the EC-Commission, will develop further. The realization of most of the proposals will probably fail, because of the British government's veto in a situation that requires an unanimous decision.

4. Harmonization of Social Policy: A Precondition for EC-Integration?

4.1 Problems of Harmonization: Minimum versus Maximum Principle

A harmonization of social policy is often supported by the argument that a "wage dumping", "social dumping" or "capital dumping" of the EC-countries with an underdeveloped social policy would be left to those EC-countries with elaborate welfare systems. In this context, it is interesting to consider that, especially in the U.S.A., the protection of national work from the lower foreign "trash wages" (Meyer and Willgerodt, 1956, p. 27) is demanded in the form of protectionist measures (Isaacs, 1948; ITC, 1977).

Even if the "semantically wrong grasp" (Paqué, 1989, p. 117) of the word "Dumping" is neglected because there exists no price in the exporting country below its costs of production (Haberler, 1933, p. 103, pp. 183-204), the search for the referential basis for everything that is to be considered socially appropriate and generally valid has remained. Such a basis is necessary in order to have a generally binding guideline for harmonization. Such an absolute ethical measure does, however, not exist for a "correct" social policy.

Even more so, the national social policies show rather diverging traditions and national identities that have developed in the course of history. For example, the U.S.A., Switzerland and the Southern European countries of Greece, Spain and Portugal in comparison to the FRG, Denmark or the Netherlands have only a very limited social system which lays great emphasis on private self-provision and self-responsibility, more than is the case in the Middle and West European countries. It also has to be taken into consideration that different preferences exist with regard to the scope and nature of social policy so that an ex-ante harmonization is forbidden from this perspective as well.

Based on their high political relevance, the problems of harmonization according to the maximum and minimum principle are to be considered despite the refusal to harmonize social policies in the EEC.

The minimum principle exists in two different versions. On the one hand, mandatory minimum regulations that have to be strictly adhered to can be created for all EC-member states. On the other hand, it can be a matter of minimum regulations that there is a certain level below which the standards may not drop, but that may be surpassed in the upward direction in the individual countries. In general, the second possibility is dealt with when a harmonization minimum is discussed. This concept foresees the stipulation of social standards and social norms at a minimum level with the help of such harmonization: countries with a high sociopolitical level can continue their social policy while countries with a low level are forced to increase their sociopolitical efforts, at least until they have reached the stipulated minimum level. However, this implies rising labor costs for these countries, if not compensated by a corresponding progress in productivity increase.

In the end, the labor factor becomes more expensive which, as it has already been mentioned above, creates the danger of labor displacement. This could only be avoided if the work force was willing to accept respective wage reductions equal to the additional social costs. Such a measure might, however, encounter little or no acceptance in view of the already relatively low wages in these countries. Unemployment would be the final consequence of that measure. This would strike the already poor countries in a very serious way.

This negative effect is even intensified if harmonization is pursued according to the maximum principle. In this case, a harmonization at the highest social level takes place which results, among other things, in an even greater increase of unemployment in the poor countries than with the minimum principle. Further demands for state help, e.g. in the framework of the European Social Fund, would be the consequence for these countries. In this way, an intervention spiral could come into being, leading to new political conflicts which might result, among other things, in a further delay of the European integration.

As an interim result, the statement can be made that every ex-ante harmonization of social policy, no matter what nature it might have, is arbitrary with regard to the level and scope of such an alignment. The poorer EC-countries would be especially affected by such a harmonization because the additional incidental wage costs could, as a result from lower labor productivity and the corresponding lower wages, only be financed by means of a rising sum of socially subsidized wages and consequently by a higher factor price. Hence it follows that the interregional wage structure would grow closer together, but that the structure of unemployment would become more heterogeneous as well. Consequently, unemployment levels from central Europe towards the peripherial regions (Greece, Southern Italy, Southern Spain, Southern Portugal and Ireland) would increase and would, therefore, support the demands for state, regional and sociopolitical measures. For example, the wealthier EC-countries would be confronted with demands for higher transfers and an extension of the structural fund in order to support the poorer EC-countries. Furthermore, it is not to be overlooked that the unemployed of these countries would increasingly migrate to the richer EC-regions. This would imply not only an increase of the regional agglomeration in the EEC, but also a creation of further problems (e.g. on the housing market, on the transportation sector, in the training and educational system).

In view of this situation, it is to be depicted and explained in the following lines why competition as a search and discovery technique serves as the adequate way to adjust social policy within the EEC.

4.2 Necessity of Harmonization of Social Policy?

The sum of all location factors, like e.g. infrastructure, raw material availability, factor endowment (quality and quantity) and factor prices, explains the advantages and disadvantages as a producer of international goods and services (Oberender, 1988). Each region "makes up a package of conditions that has to assert itself in the border crossing, respectively in the interregional competition" (Paqué, 1989, p. 115-116, translated by the author). In so far, the social policy of a country constitutes in the end as nothing else but a location factor. In this context, it is pointless to argue that, in opposition to the so-called natural location factors, this case is concerned with factors that have been created by human actions. Consequently, harmonization of the different natural location factors would also have to be demanded in this case, if harmonization is supported at all. But especially the heterogenity of space is the decisive component for the achieving of international division of labor if freedom of trade and free movement of labor is given (Oberender, 1988).

National social policy constitutes a determining factor of the international competitive position of a country. A common market guaranteeing an unlimited free movement of labor finally subjects the individual states and their social policies to an optimum efficiency test (Paqué, 1989).

This leads to the conclusion that no harmonization of social policy in the EEC is required. Consequently, such an alignment does not constitute a precondition (a means) of European integration, but can, if at all, only be the result of such a process. Does this imply that there are no harmonizing measures required in the EEC at all?

4.3 Necessary Harmonizations

An ex-ante harmonization could be required if negative or positive external effects come up. Such a situation is given, for example, if environmental pollution takes place in one country, harming the environment of other countries as well. An analogous situation exists if the workers ruin their health because of insufficient labor protection devices and later migrate to another country in order to take part in the better social security there because, based on the equal treatment principle, i.e. that EC-foreigners have to be treated as residents, an adoption into the social security system of the respective country has to take place.

In such a case, however, the citizens of the country to which the sick people migrate, have to pay for the negative externalities of the other country. Therefore, it is necessary to define exceptional areas by uniform regulations (ex-ante harmonization) so that the externalities are internalized and the country that harms the environment will also be charged with the arising costs.

In this context, it also has to be taken into consideration that, even with the same system of social policy in the EEC, different burdens could develop for individual branches as well as individual companies because very different possibilities of passing along exist (Liefmann-Keil, 1961, p. 377).

5. Competition as the Adequate Way of Adjustment

Each ex-ante harmonization in the area of social policy signifies a regulation and reglementation. It not only leads to a reduction of national sovereignty of the individual EC-member states, but also to a limitation of individual citizens' freedom of opinion because they, no matter whether they are employees, employers or consumers, have to subject themselves to norms that do not correspond to their needs. Therefore, it has to be warned of the dangers of an unnecessary centralization and bureaucratic harmonization in the EC. At last, this also implies that it is not necessary to transfer further economic and sociopolitical authority to the EC in order to realize the EC-Common Market. Even more so, it is relevant to use the manifold advantages of a decentralized decision making. A correctly organized decentralized social policy is people-oriented and it facilitates an effective control of bureaucracy (Frankfurter Institut, 1989, p. 2).

Competition as a search and discovery technique is always superior to all other methods if complex systems have to be coordinated. Social policy deals with such a situation. Since competition processes also require certain rules, it is to be worked out first which framework conditions are necessary for them in the EEC. Conformity of objectives and conformity of order of competition as the means to adjust the national social policies in the EEC, are discussed.

5.1 Framework Conditions

The freedom of establishment as well as the freedom of labor movement on behalf of the employees have to be absolutely guaranteed, so that entrepreneur and employee have the chance to establish themselves in the EC-member state which offers the best location advantage. In this context, it is irrelevant whether this opportunity is also taken, but it only matters whether this freedom of decision exists and is guaranteed. Now, both freedoms are already assured in the EEC-Treaty and the UEF, but individual coordination measures (Lell, 1966, p. 33) are required which facilitate job location movements to another country for the employees. In this way, obstacles to the employees' freedom of labor movement are avoided.

Similar to the country of origin principle for goods and services which acknowledges the legal regulations, norms and standards of the other member countries (Giersch, 1988, p. 12), claims and duties in the EC-countries also have to be mutually acknowledged in the area of social security in order to protect the freedom of labor movement in the socio-political field (Schuler, 1986, p. 63).

In this context, the principle of equal treatment, the principle of addition as well as the principle of performance export are of special importance. In the ordinances 1408/71 and 574/72 for a coordination of the national systems that have been passed according to Article 51 EEC-Treaty, these principles are already applied. Furthermore, it has to be avoided that individual persons remain unprotected (Schuler, 1986, p. 64) and that double benefits (Domsch, 1973, p. 167) are obtained. This is either regulated by ordinances or the member states are given the opportunity to pass anticumulation rules (Wanders, 1986, p. 87) which results in a certain social protection. At the same time, the granting of benefits that exceed these regulations is avoided (Wanders, 1986, p. 85). Therefore, general establishments of the right to social security that have been demanded in the Social Charter (Brok, 1989, p. 14; Commission of the EC, 1989) are superfluous because social security exists already in all member states, even if it is of a very different nature, and the EC-regulations are applied when collision problems arise with migrant workers.

In conclusion it can be stated that direct interference by the EC-authorities in the framework of social policy with regard to the Common Market is not required and also does not make sense. Individual coordination regulations in the way they have already been existing have to be applied, in order to prevent a unilateral exploitation of a social security system that is caused by a cumulation of individual citizen's claims.

5.2 Conformity of Objectives

The Common Market is to be seen as the means of reaching the economic and social objectives of the community. The realization of the Common Market is not hindered if the sociopolitical differences continue to exist. Even more so, competition in the area of social policy can make a contribution to an adequate realization of these objectives by taking the individual citizen's interests and preferences into consideration.

The Common Market, in which the five freedoms are guaranteed, will provide intense competition in which the companies of the individual countries can only assert themselves if they show the flexibility required to adapt to the changing needs of the market (Günther, 1963, p. 201). Flexibility is only necessary if the companies have enough room for decision making and if the exercise of their sovereignty is not restricted by a variety of regulations and reglementations in the framework of an ex-ante harmonization of social policy (Frickhöffer, 1989, p. 14). In this case, the companies can use their location as a competitive advantage and can react in a flexible way to the changing needs of the citizens.

Instead of delaying an international division of labor which would be the case with an ex-ante harmonization (Lell, 1966, p. 132), competition is not supposed to prevent changes of location, but to encourage increased division of labor. Intense competition leads to efforts on the part of the companies to improve their proper productive performance (Böhm, 1937, p. 32). It can be expected that an appropriate economic growth with simultaneous price stability will be the result (Europäisches Gewerkschaftsinstitut, 1988, p.10). Intense competition of locations is the prerequisite for high income and social improvements (Frankfurter Institut, Nr. 23, 1989, p. 4). At the same time, an improvement of the standard of living is promoted and the level of employment is influenced in a positive way (Bundesministerium für Wirtschaft, 1988, p.4).

The individual member states can use their respective locational advantages in their competitive strategies. These exist in the lesser developed countries and regions particularly because of the low wage level and social regulations which incur fewer costs (author unknown, Die soziale Dimension des Binnenmarktes, 1988, p. 39). These cost advantages constitute the prerequisite for a capital flow into these regions and an arising development of these countries in the economic and social "catching up" (Bundesministerium für Wirtschaft, 1988, p. 6).

As a conclusion it can be stated that competition in the area of social policy within the EEC is a suitable means of reaching the objectives set for integration. Therefore, conformity of objectives exists.

5.3 Conformity of Order

Competition is the essence of every free market order. Therefore, the liberal concept which also foresees competition in the area of social policy, is conformal to order. Basically, no interferences on the community level are to be made in the area of social security. General rules are to be applied only when necessary - e.g. for the social protection of migrant workers - for the coordination of the different systems. Consequently, they are merely a general framework, but they do not interfere directly with the market process. Everything else has to be left to the operation of the Common Market.

This sociopolitical abstinence on the EC-level has an overall positive effect on efficiency. Readiness to adapt on the part of the entrepreneurs and willingness to work on the part of the employees cannot be ordered, however the application of the liberal concept can create a sociopolitical environment which renders a positive economic development possible. Hindrances, which would make innovations and achievements more difficult or would prevent them, are removed or even not created in the first place (Frankfurter Institut, 1989, p. 2).

As long as different systems exist in the EEC, both employers and employees have options which give the employers as much freedom for economic activities as possible. In addition, the employees have the opportunity to decide for a better social security or a higher available income and perhaps a personal supplementary insurance. This implies that every individual can decide for himself how to divide up the whole pay into payment by results and into socially subsidized wage. The extension of the individual's freedom of decision increases economic performance and therefore also promotes social progress (Kleinhenz, 1986, pp. 19-20).

If priority is given to competition, and freedom of establishment as well as the employees' freedom of labor movement are guaranteed, the individual social system can enter into competition. This makes it possible to overcome old and encrusted structures because the increasing mobility on the Common Market results in locational changes of the productive factors labor and capital. It is to be expected that continuous venturing and following of individual regions take place in the competitive process (Rüter, 1987). These changes of location and the resulting modifications of competitiveness of a location are not only determined by the social policy, but they depend, as already mentioned above, on a variety of factors. Therefore, all framework conditions play an important role in the competition of locations. In this context, it always matters how much is offered in comparison with the taxes and dues that have to be paid at a location. Therefore, a "populistic redistribution policy" is not to be feared (Giersch, 1988, p. 11). In this way, high benefits and generous subsidies can be an incentive for entrepreneurs and employers, but already the danger of an increased tax which has to be levied for a financing of these "charities" will deter employees and employers who are willing to migrate (Giersch, 1988, p. 19).

This is the reason why a "competition of conservation measures" is not to be expected in a free EC-market (Stegemann, 1966, p.100). Consequently, there is the possibility that, during the competition of systems, it will be the best and most productive system rather than the superficially most suitable which will assert itself. So competition fulfills its function as a search and discovery technique (von Hayek, 1968). It is to be expected that a certain adjustment of the social policy in the EEC will take place. Where differences in social policy reflect differences in productivity, however, the differentiation will remain.

In a Europe of great variety, a total alignment is neither to be expected nor to be desired because, on the one hand, the needs and abilities of the individual citizens as well as institutions are rather different, implying continuously new venturing modifications of social policy and, on the other hand, because only a great variety can take the different desires of the people into adequate consideration.

In conclusion it can be stated that competition in the area of social policy as opposed to an ex-ante harmonization is in both order and objective conformative with a free market order.

6. Resumé

One can conclude as a result that the ex-ante harmonization of the national social policy is no precondition for the integration of the EC, but, even more so, it is a result of the integration process.

"The elimination of differences in taxation systems and social security provisions, while often considered a condition of economic union, is also likely to be a consequence of it. The greater mobility of labour would put pressure on governments to emulate the social security provisions of neighbouring countries; the greater mobility of capital would provide incentive for tax reform and an intra-European coordination of tax systems." (Scitovsky, 1958, pp. 22-23).

A precondition is, however, that the five basic freedoms which are laid down in the EEC-Treaty are guaranteed: free merchandise movements (Article 9-37, EEC-Treaty), employees' freedom of labor movement (Article 48-51, EEC-Treaty), freedom of establishment (Article 52-58, EEC-Treaty), free service of transactions (Article 59-66, EEC-Treaty) as well as free capital movement (Article 67-73, EEC-Treaty). The necessity for common regulations exists wherever negative effects arise. Basically, the country of origin principle should also be valid in the area of the social dimension, which means that, for example, professional qualifications and certificates are also acknowledged in other EC-member states.

Bibliography

Anonymous (1988). Die soziale Dimension des Binnenmarktes, *Europäische Wirtschaft*, Nr. 38 (November), 39.

Berié, Hermann (1989). Europäischer Sozialraum, Soziale Zukunft oder Fata Morgana? *Kompaß*, 409-415.

Birk, Ralf (1989). Die soziale Sicherung im Binnenmarkt, *Mitteilungen der LVA Oberfranken und Mittelfranken*, 31. Jg., 455-466.

Böhm, Franz (1937). *Die Ordnung der Wirtschaft als geschichtliche Aufgabe und rechtsschöpferische Leistung*, Stuttgart - Berlin.

Brock, E. (1989). Die soziale Dimension des Europäischen Binnenmarktes, *Frankfurter Allgemeine Zeitung*, Nr. 22 (21.02.1989), 14.

Bundesministerium für Wirtschaft (1988). *Soziale Dimension der Europäischen Gemeinschaft*, o.O.

Deutscher Bundestag (1989). *Bundestagsdrucksache* 11/4699 (06.06.1989).

Domsch, Alexander (1973). *Harmonisierung der sozialen Sicherungen in der EWG*, Köln.

Engels, Wolfram et al. (1989). Europäische Sozialcharta: Ein sozialpolitischer Regulierungsfahrplan für den Binnenmarkt? In Frankfurter Institut (ed.), *Argumente zur Europapolitik*, Nr. 1 (Dezember), 2-5.

Europäische Kommission (1988). Die soziale Dimension des Binnenmarktes. Arbeitsdokument der Kommission vom 14.09.1988 (SEC (1988) 1148 endg.). Abgedruckt in *Bundestagsdrucksache* 11/4645 (31.05.1989).

Europäisches Gewerkschaftsinstitut (1988). *Die soziale Dimension des Binnenmarktes. Teil 1: Beschäftigung*, Info 25, Brüssel.

Frankfurter Institut (ed.) (1989). Europa morgen und übermorgen - Die Weichen werden heute gestellt, *Argumente zur Wirtschaftspolitik*, Nr. 23 (Februar), 1-6.

Frickhöffer, Wolfgang (1989). Sozialraum Europa - Bewährungsprobe der Gewerkschaften, *Frankfurter Allgemeine Zeitung*, Nr. 45 (22.02.1989), 14.

Giersch, Herbert (1988). Der Europäische Binnenmarkt als Chance und Risiko, *Kieler Diskussionsbeiträge*, Nr. 147, Kiel.

Günther, Eberhard (1963). Die ordnungspolitischen Grundlagen des EWG-Vertrages, *Wirtschaft und Wettbewerb*, 13 Jg., 191-202.

Haberler, Gottfried (1933). *Der internationale Handel*, Berlin.

Hayek, Friedrich A. von (1968). *Der Wettbewerb als Entdeckungsverfahren*, Kieler Vorträge N.F. 56, Tübingen.

Institut der Deutschen Wirtschaft (ed.) (1989). *Sozialraum Europa* (IW-Dossier Nr. 7). Köln.

Idem (ed.) (1989a). Sozialraum Europa (2): Schutz bei Krankheit, *Informationsdienst*, 15 Jg., Nr. 23, 4-5.

Idem (ed.) (1989b). Sozialraum Europa (4): Probleme mit der Überalterung, *Informationsdienst*, 15 Jg., Nr. 32, 4-5.

Isaacs, Asher (1948). *International Trade - Tariffs and comercial policies*, Chicago.

Klang, Klaus A. (1986). *Soziale Sicherheit und die Freizügigkeit im EWG-Vertrag*, Baden-Baden.

Kleinhenz, Gerhard (1986). Die Stellung der Sozialpolitik im politischen Gefüge der EG, in Hagen Lichtenberg (ed.), *Sozialpolitik in der EG*, Baden-Baden.

Kommission der Europäischen Gemeinschaften (1988). *Soziales Europa. Die soziale Dimension des Binnenmarktes*, Luxemburg.

Kommission der Europäischen Gemeinschaften (1989). Mitteilung der Kommission über ihr Aktionsprogramm zur Anwendung der Gemeinschaftscharta der sozialen Grundrechte, *Kommissionsdrucksache* (1989), 568 endg.

Lell, Hans-Joachim (1966). *Die soziale Harmonisierung in der europäischen Wirtschaftsgemeinschaft und ihre wirtschaftlichen Auswirkungen*, Berlin.

Liefmann-Keil, Elisabeth (1961). *Ökonomische Theorien der Sozialpolitik*, Berlin - Göttingen - Heidelberg.

Meyer, Fritz W. und Hans Willgerodt (1956). Der wirtschaftspolitische Aussagewert internationaler Lohnvergleiche, *Bundesministerium für wirtschaftliche Zusammenarbeit* (ed.): *Internationale Lohngefälle:*

Wirtschaftspolitische Folgerungen und statistische Problematik, Bonn, 9-78.

Myrdal, Gunnar (1956). *An International Economy*. New York.

Oberender, Peter (1988). *Marktdynamik und internationaler Handel*, Tübingen.

Paqué, Karl-Heinz (1989). Die soziale Dimension des EG-Binnenmarktes - Theorie, Bestandsaufnahme und Kritik, *Die Weltwirtschaft*. Heft 1, 112-123.

Pompe, Peter (1989). EG-Sozialraum 1993: Was kommt in der Sozialversicherung auf uns zu? *Soziale Sicherheit in der Landwirtschaft*, Heft 3.

Rüter, Georg (1987), *Regionalpolitik im Umbruch*, Bayreuth.

Schavoir-Ysselstein, Renate (1989). Bericht aus Brüssel zur sozialen Dimension des Binnenmarktes, *Informationsdienst der Gesellschaft für Versicherungswissenschaft und -gestaltung*, Nr. 213, Köln.

Schuler, Rolf (1986). Strukturen und Methoden zwischen staatlicher und gemeinschafts-rechtlicher Sozialrechtsbeziehungen, in Hagen Lichtenberg (ed.), *Sozialpolitik in der EG*. Baden-Baden, 51-80.

Scitovsky, Tibor (1958). *Economic Theory and Western European Integration*, London.

Stegemann, Klaus (1966). *Wettbewerb und Harmonisierung im gemeinsamen Markt*, Köln.

Tumulir, Jan (1983). Strong and weak element of the concept of European integration, in Machlup, Fritz, Gerhard Fels, Hubertus Müller-Groeling (eds.), *Reflections on a Troubled World Economy*, London.

US House of Representatives, Committee on ways and means, US International Trade Commission (1977). *Report on watches and parts therefore* (Investigation No. 332/80), Undersection 332 of the tariff act of 1930. Washington D.C.

Vogler-Ludwig, Kurt (1989). *Soziale Aspekte des Europäischen Binnenmarktes*, ifo-Schnelldienst 25/89, 8-17.

Wanders, Wilhelm (1986). Freizügigkeit statt Sozialunion - Zur Kompetenz der Sozialrechtsintegration in der Gemeinschaft, in Hagen Lichtenberg (ed.), *Sozialpolitik in der EG*, Baden-Baden, 81-93.

10 COOPERATION IN RESEARCH & DEVELOPMENT AND EUROPEAN COMPETITION POLICY

ALEXIS JACQUEMIN

1. Introduction

During the last few years, the workings of national and international economies have been perceived as depending on strategic relationships, the main actors being firms which are endowed with varying powers and which position themselves, physically and psychologically, so as to discourage or dictate the actions and responses of their current and potential competitors. The name of the game is to co-operate with one's competitors over common components, yet maintain keen competition at the final product stage; to erect credible barriers against players likely to enter the market; to control the range of products and services likely to act as substitutes for one's own activity; to modify one's bargaining power vis-à-vis suppliers or purchasers by means of long-term contracts or control of upstream operations; to influence the balance of forces by making strategic moves and anticipating change.

In this context, competition is not based on a series of simultaneous interactions between passive agents which view comparative advantages, the structures of markets and the behavior of others as given. It is a sequential game in which the application of new forms of organization, the opening up of new markets and the introduction of new products and production methods continually undermine the possible equilibria and modify the rules of the game.

In this perspective, technology is one of the most decisive factors for industrial competitiveness, and corporations can improve their relative advantages in this domain through various forms of cooperative behavior as well as through independent actions.

From the private interests point of view, such cooperations can lead to important benefits especially in rapidly globalizing markets and industries with important technological opportunities but lead also to non-negligeable costs.

From the point of view of public interest, the question is also difficult. "Often the trade-off between competition and efficiency is a multidimensional problem: certainly it is a more complex issue than is implied in the way it is presented in static models" (H.W. de Jong and A. Jacquemin, 1977, p. XIV).

The purpose of this policy paper is to suggest that too little collusion can occur in activities where socially desirable outcomes might arise from cooperation, R&D being a case in point. In the first part, we discuss the public view of collusion in light of European competition policy which, contrary to the US approach, provides an "efficiency defence" for some collusive actions. In the second part of the paper, we consider cooperative agreements in R&D. A discussion of the private costs and benefits of joint R&D (section 1) leads to the conclusion that specific characteristics of R&D, mainly the difficulty of appropriating the results of the joint efforts, tend to impede and destabilize many agreements in this domain. A brief public cost benefit analysis (section 2) suggests in other respects that cooperative R&D can sometimes improve efficiency. This provides support for the 1985 permissive European regulation allowing cooperative research whereby members' firms agree to share the costs and the fruits of a research project.

2. Collusion and European Competition Policy

Article 85 of the Treaty of Rome contains a broad prohibition of explicit and tacit collusion where it is likely to affect trade between Member States and has as its purpose or result the prevention, restriction, or distortion of competition within the Common Market. Such collusive agreements are void unless EC Commission is notified of them and grants an exemption.

A priori, such a broad prohibition could be based on one or several goals which are traditionally at the core of competition policy. One eventual goal is the *diffusion of private economic power*, the protection of individual freedom and individual rights. The use of cartels can then be seen as a radical departure from such an individualism.[1] This aspect, which was originally basic to antitrust legislation, still occupies an important place, although perhaps more at the level of public opinion than at policy level.

A second eventual goal of competition policy may be to *protect the economic freedom of market competitors*. Here the protection of competitors takes precedence over the defence of the competitive process as such.

Attention will be directed towards abusive practices such as coercion, discrimination, refusal to sell, boycotts, and cartels through which powerful firms might endanger the existence of weaker competitors. This type of approach is particularly in evidence in European countries in the national laws of "unfair competition".[2]

A distinction is then usually made between competition policy concerning efficiency and market injury, and competition law concerning unfair conduct and private injury to one or a few firms. In most instances, like the law on boycott, fairness and efficiency require the same outcome, but there are situations where a conflict could arise. An especially important one in the domain of cartels concerns exclusive dealing agreements. The basic principle expressed in the Beguelin/G.L. Import Export case (Judgment of the Court, 25/II/71, in the Court of Justice of the European Communities, Reports of Cases Before the Court, 1971, Part II, pp. 949-972) is that an exclusive dealing agreement is liable to affect trade between Member States, and may have the effect of impeding competition if, owing to the combined effects of the agreement and of the national legislation on unfair competition, the dealer is able to prevent parallel imports from other Member States from entering the territory covered by the agreement. On this occasion, the Court of Justice clearly confirmed that the European rules of competition were not formulated to give protection to individual competitors on the basis of fair practices.

If there is a conflict between a national law on unfair competition and the European competition rules, the latter predominates.[3]

The third type of goal of competition policy is dear to the hearts of economists. Competition policy is one of the main instruments to assure consumer welfare through both allocative and productive efficiency. The neatest affirmation of a purely efficiency-directed competition policy has been made by Bork (1976). According to his view, antitrust law must challenge inefficient conducts. A necessary (but not sufficient) attribute of inefficiency is a restriction of output beyond levels which would prevail under competitive conditions. Conduct not so identified must be presumed to enhance efficiency, and should not be the subject of legal sanction.[4] On the contrary price-quantity cartels create inefficiency which can be measured by the well-known formula for deadweight loss D

$$D = 1/2 \sum_i \Delta q^i \Delta p^i$$

where p^i and q^i are price and quantities in the ith sector, the symbol Δ representing a change due to monopoly pricing.[5]

However, in recent years new research in industrial organization has shown that simple formulas for efficiency appear to be deceptive and misleading.

An important example in the domain of collusive behavior is the sharing of information by oligopolists. It has been shown that the incentives for information-sharing and its welfare consequences depend crucially on the type of competition, the nature of the goods, and the degree of product differenciation. Clarke (1983) demonstrates that with Cournot competition and homogeneous products, there are never mutual incentives for firms in the industry to share information unless they plan to collude. But Vives (1984) finds that in Bertrand competition or if the goods are not close substitutes the results are reversed.[6] More generally, "free competition" can lead to too much or to too little information, product variety, R&D, entry, etc.[7] according to the characteristics of the game.

The main implication is that once the neoclassical paradigm is abandoned, there is no longer the kind of general theorem about the Pareto optimality of the methods of strategic competition that we have for perfect competition. The results are at best ambiguous. Furthermore, with the various types of non-price competition, consumer welfare becomes more multi-dimensional and includes aspects such as the quality of the product, the speed and security of the supply and so on. Most of these aspects are not measurable. Value judgments are necessary to determine, for example, whether allocating a greater amount of resources to activities which result in technological change or product variation than would be allocated under a more "classical" form of competition contributes enough to consumer welfare to outweigh the possible losses resulting from static inefficiencies. On the whole, a precise definition of the "efficiency" criterion is more apparent than real and most of the time requires a delicate appreciation of complex trade-offs.

In contrast to the U.S. tradition,[8] such trade-offs are explicitly accepted by the Treaty of Rome in Article 85 para. 3, according to which some collusive behavior restricting competition in a non minor way may be exempted because of sufficient beneficial effects. Four conditions are required:

a) the agreement must contribute to the improvement of the production or distribution of goods or promote technical or economic progress;
b) it must allow ultimate buyers a fair share of the resulting benefits;
c) the restriction must be necessary for the attainment of the objective;

d) the firms concerned must be unable to eliminate competition in respect to a substantial part of the product in question.

What Williamson (1968) calls a "naive trade-off model" is a good way of illustrating these conditions. This model tells that in order to appreciate whether the cartel can benefit from the "efficiency defence", it is sufficient to compare the surface corresponding to the "deadweight loss", i.e. the loss of consumer welfare which is not otherwise compensated, and the surface corresponding to the savings in resources which become available for alternative use.

This "naive" static partial equilibrium model, with its cost-benefit analysis limited to two-dimensional terms requires a number of qualifications which strongly reduce its operationality. These qualifications include matters of timing, non-price competition, X-inefficiency, response of firms non-participating to the cartel, income distribution effects, second-best considerations, as well as the inference and enforcement expenses needed to prove the existence of economies.[9] What is in fact suggested by such a model is the difficulty of identifying precisely the efficiency consequences of a business conduct and of advocating fine-tuned optimal antitrust roles. The conditions of article 85 para. 3 cannot rely on a strict welfare analysis and will often require political compromise between conflicting and incommensurable values.

These dangers can be reduced in two ways. The first one would be to rely more on the use of a reasonable test in applying Article 85 para 1.[10] On the basis of the general presumption that an antitrust policy augmenting competitive forces is needed to enhance efficiency, a pragmatic interpretation of Article 85 para. 1 could broaden the number of cases where economic behavior can be said to comply with Article 85 without having to resort to the criteria and procedures of paragraph 3. For example, this interpretation might allow some type of vertical agreements which could appear to represent a restriction of competition, but which actually do not impose an unreasonable restraint on competition or even increase it in the relevant dynamic and uncertain framework. Given the previously mentioned theoretical works of the "new industrial organization", it is evident that this approach will not eliminate the ambiguities nor offer strong legal security to businessmen. Nevertheless, this interpretation is less demanding than the trade-off system of Article 85 para. 3, which requires notifying and disclosing all doubtful matters to the Commission in order to obtain an exemption.[11]

A pragmatic application of Article 85 para.1 could reduce information and transaction costs[12] and allow the Commission to use its limited resources to formulate general policies and prosecute important cases.

The second way which has effectively been used to reduce the burden of the trade-off is to implement Article 85 para.3, not so much on a case by case basis, but by granting group (or block) exemptions dealing with important types of agreements for which there exists a presumption that a situation of market failure can occur.

This system of exempting certain classes of agreements from the notification requirement avoids the necessity of a detailed analysis of each conduct. It creates codes of conduct that can increase the credibility of the policy and limit the discretionary power involved in the Article. At the same time, it preserves the Article's valuable message that antitrust policy must be sensitive to economies and that in some circumstances cooperative behavior can restrict competition in a non-negligible way and still produce socially desirable results.[13]

A clear illustration is the block exemption Regulation of R&D agreements, which came into force in March 1985. This new regulation leaves intact the 1968 Notice on cooperation between enterprises, which states that cooperation agreements relating only to R&D normally do not fall under Article 85 para.1. But it extends this favourable treatment to R&D agreements which also provide for joint exploitation of the results. To appreciate its content, it is necessary to examine in some depth the role of cooperative R&D.

3. Cooperative Agreements in R&D

In this second part, we shall first identify the main private advantages and disadvantages of R&D cooperation, then their main public costs and benefits. The paradox that will emerge is that there are more obstacles to cooperative R&D than to collusion in other areas, in spite of the positive social welfare effect often associated with such cooperation. The Policy option taken by the European Commission in its Regulation 418/85 will then be discussed.

Section 1 Private cost-benefit analysis of cooperative R&D[14]

Three types of private potential benefits of cooperative R&D can be identified. First, cooperative agreements are *an alternative to either pure market transactions or integration within the firm* under a single administrative structure. Its choice could, therefore, indicate that it is perceived as a compromise between commitment and flexibility.

On the one hand, in-house developments or mergers tend to create very rigid structures without easy mechanism for switching research capability, strategy and partners over time. This can call into question a company's ability to innovate or respond to innovation, and impede access to know-how which it cannot develop internally or can acquire only with irreductible delays in developing and testing products in-house.

On the other hand, arms'-length transactions do not allow for long-term relationships, which are generally crucial in technology. Frequent switching is costly and inefficient because the process of R&D, as well as technology transfer, require prolonged interaction and experience between partners to exploit or develop complementaries which affect the costs and benefits of innovations. Furthermore, market transactions are expected to be affected by moral hazard and adverse selection. Indeed the domain of R&D and innovation is a typical case where the agent's action is not directly observable by the principal and the outcome is a random variable whose distribution depends on the action taken. A cooperative research arrangement can then reduce the problems of asymmetric information and opportunism, as well as the vagueness of monitoring by relying on easily measured R&D inputs.

A second potential advantage of cooperative R&D is *to accelerate the speed of invention and innovation with less risk*. On the one hand, what often matters is the speed at which firms can deploy the necessary resources and enter into new markets, first mover advantage depending upon an ability to do it more quickly than rivals; on the other hand the absence of a complete and perfect set of contingency markets makes useful joint actions which permit risk-spreading, i.e. sharing the benefits and costs of a project among a number of firms, and risk-pooling, i.e. pursuing more technological avenues and (relatively) independent projects.

Finally, the pooling of various complementary resources in R&D can *provide financial capital* at better conditions if capital markets are imperfect, *spread the high fixed costs* of technology development, and *produce synergetic effects* by the combination of research information, teams of scientists, technological and marketing know-how, etc.

Despite the previous arguments, cooperative agreements in R&D are not very frequent. When they exist, empirical evidence shows that they are fragile and unstable arrangements confronted with various difficulties, which generally lead to early break-ups, buy-outs or mergers. This situation is aggravated within Europe where the majority of R&D arrangements are multicountry and where divergent objectives, strategies, domestic regulations, and institutions often combine with socio-psychological factors such as nationalistic feelings, fear of a loss of identity, and clash of corporate cultures.

Arrangements relating only to R&D have a number of important handicaps. At a first stage, *partner selection and the possibility of defining well-balanced contributions* is an important barrier. The fear is that one partner will be strengthened by the technological cooperation in such a way that it will become a dangerous competitor at the level of the product market. This situation is of course more probable for horizontal agreements than for vertical ones. In the latter case, complementarities allow the benefits to be distributed according to the respective activities and products. In the case of cooperation between competitors geographical partition is the most obvious way of trying to solve the problem but it has a side-effect on existing competition. The compromise between collaboration and independence is reflected in the organizational structure of the arrangement, which is often ambiguous, complex and implying heavy transaction costs of negotiation.

At a second stage, *the management of existing cooperative agreements and the sharing of the benefits* are also difficult. First, in the absence of an efficient system of management, the transaction costs of coordination and cooperation may outweigh the benefits, especially when a large number of actors is involved. Second, even with lengthy contracts containing explicit clauses concerning confidentiality and transmission of information, patent licenses, trademark, and copyright, there are fundamental limits on the ability to protect intellectual property, given that scientific knowledge has many aspects of a public good, that its results are not easily incorporated and that the speed of incorporation will vary from one firm to another. In fact, there are often close connections between the effectiveness of basic research, conventional R&D resources, and marketing and manufacturing resources. Von Hippel (1982) and Flaherty (1980) have shown the multiple interactions of technological advantages with conventional business resources in various fields. Their analyses imply that the full exploitation of the results of cooperative research very often requires concerted marketing to sell products which embody these results. Successful achievement of first-mover advantages in research depends upon an ability to bring quickly new products and techniques to the market where the greatest potential strategic pay-offs are encountered.

Limiting cooperation to pure R&D or to the so-called "precompetitive level" will then exercise a strong deterrent effect on the emergence of such cooperative arrangements.[15]

Section 2 Public Cost-Benefit Analysis of Cooperative R&D and the European Regulation.

The main argument in favor of socially beneficial effects of cooperative research is based on a problem of market failure, bound to the appropriability of returns.[16] The starting point is that the amount of research made by private firms and the diffusion of the knowledge generated by them may be socially inefficient over a broad range of market structures including competition. Two situations can be distinguished.

Assume first that there are *no spillovers* or externalities so that each firm's R&D influences only its own costs. Nevertheless, as long as firms in the pre-innovation market would not expect a perfect discriminating monopoly in the post-innovation market, appropriation of the entire social value from innovation will not be expected. Even the pre-innovation monopolist would not generally invest the socially optimal amount in R&D.

A fortiori when price in the post-innovation market intensifies as the number of R&D competitors in the pre-innovation market increases, it is more likely that the value of the surplus of total R&D revenues above post-innovations costs will fall short of the social value. Moreover, the knowledge generated by the R&D of the individual firm will be priced incorrectly. Given the existing degree of appropriability, diffusion of this knowledge will not be priced at the marginal cost of its dissemination (which is often close to zero), but at higher prices. This may lead competing firms to wasteful duplication of research.

Now suppose that there are substantial R&D externalities or *spillovers*: the benefits of each firm's R&D flow without payment to other firms. This leads to underinvestment in R&D relative to the social optium and to a structure of knowledge supply which is determined by the different degrees of appropriability of the various types. Incentives to innovate will also be reduced as the potential innovator knows that competitors will be freely strengthened by its own R&D investments.

It can then be argued that cooperative R&D can improve both situations and alleviate the trade-off identified by Spence (1984).

According to this trade-off, the incentives of a firm to do R&D requires a sufficient degree of appropriability of the benefits, and thus a limited diffusion of knowledge; but on the other hand a near-perfect appropriability (whether created by circumstances or policy) impedes spillovers of the results of R&D to other firms, at no-cost, and hence does not allow a sufficient decrease in aggregate R&D costs for achieving a given level of cost reduction.

Cooperative R&D can then be viewed as a means of simultaneously internalizing the externalities created by significant R&D spillovers - hence improving the incentive problem and limiting wasteful duplication - and providing a more efficient sharing of information among firms.[17]

Katz (1986) has rigourously established the conditions under which a cooperative agreement could raise welfare through its effects on the equilibrium level of R&D and on the costs of achieving a given R&D level.

- "cooperative R&D is most likely to have beneficial incentive effects in markets that have strong spillovers in the absence of cooperation;
- when firms have flexibility in their choices of both R&D cost-sharing and R&D output-sharing rates, cooperative R&D arrangements are most likely to have beneficial effects in markets where a high rate of between-member spillover or R&D sharing is feasible, such as in basic research" (p. 542).

This leads us to mention briefly a second argument for permitting or encouraging cooperative R&D.

In certain high-technology industries, such as the next generation of mainframe computers, firms are producing, under increasing returns of scale, differentiated products on which basic research can lead to production of a higher quality product. In such industries, equilibrium is characterized by the presence of a limited number of firms, each of which makes positive profits (net of any fixed costs). In this case the neo-classical competitive paradigm does not apply, as "natural" oligopolies are dictated by the exogeneous conditions of supply and demand. If certain potential entrants in such markets enjoy an advantage as a result of a cooperative agreement, this may then favour equilibrium outcomes in which the cooperating firms are able to enter while certain of their independent rivals decide otherwise.

By promoting R&D cooperation between European firms, the European authorities could then succeed in giving these firms a better base for oligopolistic competition against foreign rivals and in getting a larger share of high-return industries.

Contrasting with these potential advantages of cooperative R&D, effects leading to a *harmful reduction of competition* must also be considered. This question could be explored on the basis of a model having the standard two-stage form, with R&D expenditures in period one affecting the parameters of the second period output/price game. Solving the latter yields profit functions (gross of R&D costs) that are dependent upon the earlier R&D choices. The shapes of these functions depend, among other things, on the nature of competition: for instance non-cooperation in R&D and in output, cooperation in R&D and in output, cooperation in R&D and non-cooperation in output, non-cooperation in R&D and cooperation in output.

Using this framework d'Aspremont and Jacquemin (1989) have computed and compared the corresponding subgame perfect equilibria. Defining x^{**}, x^{*}, $\hat{x}$, and $\tilde{x}$, as the equilibrium levels of R&D obtained in the case of, respectively, the maximization of social welfare (consumer surplus + producer surplus), the fully non-cooperative game, the cooperation limited to R&D, and the cooperation occuring in both R&D and output, they obtain the following classification

$$x^{**} > \tilde{x} > \hat{x} > x^{*}$$

for large spillovers. For the total quantity produced, Q, the classification is the following

$$Q^{**} > \hat{Q} > Q^{*} > \tilde{Q}$$

One clear conclusion is that cooperation in R&D increases both R&D and quantities of production with respect to the non-cooperative solution, and that this behaviour is superior from a social welfare point of view.

In the absence of a more global model reflecting the complete picture, let us simply distinguish between two situations.

First, let us assume that it is feasible to limit the extent of the agreement solely to aspects of R&D and to exclude coordination at the level of the final product (*pre-competitive level*). The dangers of anticompetitive consequences are then strongly reduced. Still, one danger is that cooperative R&D could be a way for a dominant firm to avoid competition through innovation, by co-opting potentially very innovative rivals and by controlling and slowing down the innovation race (Reinganum, 1983). Coordinating the R&D process so as to avoid duplication can reduce initiative and lead to inflexibility and to waste in dead-end research, when multiple, not perfectly correlated, research strategies could have been feasible. At the other extreme, incumbent firms with market power can, through concerted pre-emptive operations, excessively accelerate their programmes of R&D and innovation in order to exercise a dissuasive impact on potential entrants (Gilbert and Newbery, 1982). In the situation of integrated firms, cooperative agreement for the purpose of knowledge exchange could also lead to barriers to entry downstream and foreclose firms who are not members of the agreement from some segment of the market. Firms being at the frontier of technological change could for example jointly determine standards for future products and processes, making new entry more difficult.

A second situation involves an extended collusion between partners, resulting from their action in R&D and creating common policies at the product stage (**competitive level**). Discussions about R&D can for example spill over into illegal discussions of pricing policy. Cooperative R&D can also provide a ready mechanism for side payments in the event that it is useful for cartel members to redistribute the revenues earned by the firms as a result of product market division. What makes these dangers probable is again the difficulty of appropriating technological breakthroughs. As discussed in section I of Part III, partners who have achieved inventions want to control the processes and products which embody the results of their collaboration, in order to recuperate jointly, and as quickly as possible, their R&D investments. If the firms are prevented from such a joint exploitation and if the benefits of cooperative R&D are expected to be very quickly dissipated through intense product market competition, firms will be tempted either to avoid R&D cooperation and to maintain wasteful competition in the pre-innovation market or to use their cooperation to limit unduly their R&D. If this is true, *a regulation of R&D cooperation excluding any cooperation at the level of the final markets could discourage or destabilize many valuable agreements. However, allowing an extension of cooperation from R&D to manufacturing and distribution encourages collu-*

sive behavior which impedes competition. This is precisely the dilemma faced by the European Antitrust Authorities.

The text of the regulation 418/85 expresses the compromise that has been adopted. It covers joint research and development of products or processes and *joint exploitation of the results of that R&D.*

Art. 1(2)(d) specifies that "exploitation of the results" means the manufacture of the joint venture product or the licensing of intellectual property rights to third parties. But joint marketing is not covered.

Among various conditions, the exemption applies if:

a) the work is carried out within the framework of a defined programme;
b) all the parties have access to the result;
c) where there is no joint exploitation, each party is free to exploit the results independently;
d) the know-how and the patents which result from the research contribute substantially to technical and economic progress and are indispensable for the manufacture of the joint venture product.

By imposing conditions concerning the duration of the venture and market shares, the regulation also aims to prevent agreements that might result in the elimination of competition in the relevant market. If the joint venture is of the conglomeral or vertical type, i.e. if the participants do not compete on the relevant product market, the exemption applies for five years, regardless of market share. If the joint venture is of the horizontal type, the exemption also applies for five years, but only if the parties' combined share of the relevant product market does not exceed 20%.

A comprehensive list of permissible clauses (the so-called white list) and prohibited clauses (the so-called black list) is also included.

The main aspect of the Regulation is that the European authorities, confronted with the dilemma mentioned above, consider that cooperation in R&D, in many cases, cannot be limited to the sole level of pure R&D, and that it will generally lead to joint exploitation of the results in order to stabilize the agreements and to solve the appropriability problem. Moreover the Regulation gives priority to basic research and tends to secure an efficient sharing of information. Finally it rejects arrangements able to monopolize the market.

However, several problems remain. From the businessmen's point of view, the Regulation is complex; it is necessary to overcome its opacity by issuing new guidelines. The 20% threshold market share for horizontal joint ventures is disputable, especially in high technology. The exclusion of joint selling and marketing is an important limitation, given the close interconnections between the various phases of the activities.[18] From the point of view of public interest, the Regulation might have the unwanted side-effect of exempting many production joint ventures from notification, especially given the broadness of some concepts and criteria used in the text. The drafters of joint venture contracts could indeed be tempted to include an R&D element in their agreements in order to fall within the scope of the block exemption. In this context, the Commission must be conscious of the dangers of any further relaxation of its antitrust policy, which until now has been a powerful instrument for the survival of a competitive common market.

Finally, one wonders whether modifications to the competition rules are the crucial tool needed to prod industry into forming new R&D joint ventures. As long as antitrust rules in the field of R&D cooperation reflect a form of industrial policy to foster innovations and improve international competitiveness, more positive incentives would seem appropriate. One of them could be specific tax deductions and/or subsidies like those provided by the Esprit programme. A complementary one would be transnational legal structures, such as the recently adopted **European Interest Grouping**, which provides firms with flexible instruments for pooling some business functions, while retaining their economic and legal independence.

4. Conclusion

This paper has shown that in some areas where innovative activities and R&D are central and create large spillovers, cooperative behaviour can be dialectically linked with the competitive moves and lead to socially desirable outcomes.

Such a message, well received by the European authorities, is an illustration of some of the main traits that H.W. de Jong (1986) has identified as characterizing the European approach to the study of markets. According to De Jong (see also De Jong 1985):

"- *Competition* between firms in markets is seen as the central organizing principle, from which associations among firms and concentration by firms are clearly distinguished, but not as aberrations or deviations. Associations or concentration are considered to be organization principles in their own right, having their specific merits. Only, they are regulated by the all pervasive competitive principle, inherent in any market economy.

- This is considered to be the case, because markets and their structures are not conceived statically, but *dynamically*, that is incorporating the time element. In other words, one could not speak of a market, save in an evolutionary way, in which the roles of demand and of the entrepreneur receive a more prominent position than in the Anglo-Saxon tradition.

- The idea that governments are involved in the market process, not as an exogeneous, correcting influence, but as one amongst the various participants - be it with its distinguishing traits - has been prominent. In this sense, European industrial organization economics has always been *policy-oriented* and remains so today with the discussions about how to promote innovation, and how to use industrial, commercial and similar policies besides competition policy". (pp. 71-72).

In his own contributions, H.W. de Jong has played a major international role in the diffusion of such views and has helped us to avoid the temptation of greater scientific precision at the cost of relevance.

Bibliography

d'Aspremont, Cl. and A. Jacquemin (1989). Cooperative and Non-Cooperative R&D in Duopoly, *American Economic Review* (December).

Berg, S., J. Duncan and Ph. Friedman (1982). *Joint Venture, Strategies and Corporate Innovation*, Oelgeschlager, Gunn & Hain, Cambridge, Mass.

Bork, R. (1976). The Goals of Antitrust Policy, *American Economic Review* (May).

Clarke, R. (1983). Collusion and the Incentives for Information Sharing, *Bell Journal of Economics*, 14.

Dasgupta, P. and J. Stiglitz (1980). Industrial Structure and the Nature of Innovative Activity, *Economic Journal*, 90.

Ergas, H. (1986). *Does Technology Policy Matter?* CEPS papers, no. 29.

Flaherty, M.T. (1980). *Business and Technology History of Sillicon Wafers for Integrated Circuits*, Mimeo.

Forrester, I. and Ch. Norrall (1984). The Laicization of Community Law - Self Help and the Rule of Reason: How Competition Law is and could be Applied, *Common Market Law Review*.

Gilbert, F. and D. Newbery (1982). Preemptive Patenting and the Persistence of Monopoly, *American Economic Review* (June).

Hilferding, R. (1910). *Das Finanzkapital*, Vienne.

De Jong, H.W. and A. Jacquemin (eds.) (1977). *Welfare Aspects of Industrial Markets*, Nijhoff, Leiden.

De Jong, H.W. (1985). *Dynamische marktheorie*, Stenfert Kroese, Leiden.

De Jong, H.W. (1986). European Industrial Organization: Entrepreneurial Economics in an Organizational Setting, in De Jong, H.W. and W. Shepherd (eds.), *Mainstreams in Industrial Organization*, Book I, Kluwer, Dordrecht.

Katz, M. (1986). An Analysis of Cooperative Research and Development, *Rand Journal of Economics*, Winter.

Jacquemin, A. (1987). *The New Industrial Organization*, MIT Press, and Oxford University Press, Cambridge Mass, and London.

Jacquemin, A., M. Lammerant and B. Spinoit (1985). *Compétition européenne et coopération en matière de recherche - développement. Commission des Communautés Européennes, Evolution de la Concentration et de la Concurrence*, Collection "Document de Travail", no. 80. IV/761/85.

Jacquemin, A. and M. Slade (1989). Cartels, Collusion and Horizontal Mergers, in Schmalensee, R. and R. Willig (eds.), *Handbook of Industrial Organization*, North-Holland, Amsterdam.

Kaufmann, P.J. (1986). *Passing off and Misappropriation, An Economic and Legal Analysis of the Law of the Unfair Competition*, Max Planck Institute, CVH, Munich.

Mestmacker, E. (1980). Competition Policy and Antitrust. Some Comparative Observations, *Zeitschrift für die gesamte Staatswissenschaft*, Heft 3 (September).

Ordover, J. and R. Willing (1985). Antitrust for High-Technology Industries. Assessiong Research Joint Venture and Mergers, *Journal of Law and Economics*, 2 (May).

Perry, M. (1984). Scale Economies, Imperfect Competition and Public Policy, *Journal of Industrial Economics*, 32.

Reinganum, J. (1983). Uncertain Innovation and the Persistence of Monopoly, *American Economic Review* (September).

Spence, M. (1984). Cost Reduction, Competition and Industry Performance, *Econometrica*, 52.

Stiglitz, J. and F. Matthewson (eds). (1986). *New Development in the Analysis of Market Structure*, M.I.T. Press.

Vives, X. (1984). Duopoly Information Equilibrium, Cournot and Bertrand, *Journal of Economic Theory*, 34.

Hippel, E. von (1982). Appropriability of Innovation Benefits as a Predictor of the Source of Innovation, *Research policy*, no. 2 (April).

Weizsäcker, C. von (1980). *Barriers to Entry*, Springer Verlag, Berlin.

Williamson, O. (1968). Economies as an Antitrust Defence: The Welfare Tradeoffs, *American Economic Review*, 58.

Williamson, O. (1977). Economies as an Antitrust Defence Revisited, in Jacquemin, A. and H.W. de Jong (eds). *Welfare Aspects of Industrial Markets*, Nijhoff, Leiden.

Notes

1. It is in the light of these "non-economic values" that Mestmacker (1980) has characterized the attitude adopted by German authorities with respect to cartels before World War II. "The Nazis", he wrote, "had shown how to transform highly concentrated and cartelized economy into a central plan system... Boycotts and collective discriminations were applied against outsiders in order to discipline them in the public interest. If the more traditional measures of economic coercion proved insufficient for the purpose, even the formal transformation of private cartels into compulsory cartels was provided for after 1933" (p. 388). Mestmacker adds that acceptance of cartels was not limited to conservatives who cherished them as safeguards against the anarchy of free competition. Marxists also looked upon cartels (and concentration) as forerunners of rational socialist planning. He quotes Hilferding, who interpreted this development as tending towards "a universal cartel, that is a rationally regulated society"!
2. According to the Paris Convention of 1883, unfair competition is "any act of competition contrary to honest practices in industrial or commercial matters". The corresponding laws are intended to ensure that the competitors fight in a fair way, and carry out their social functions according to an ethical code of conduct. The standard of business ethics plays an important role in developing such a code of honest trade practices, but it is ultimately ascertained through the common sense of the courts.
3. According to the Advocate-General, "the rule of national law on the subject of unfair competition should not be... used for purposes which conflict with the general objectives of the Common Market, and this places a corresponding limit of restriction on the exercise of the rights to which in this field, national rules give rise" (op. cit. p. 970). The distinction between antitrust law and laws governing unfair competition has been strongly attacked, especially in the Federal Republic of Germany. There is an increasing tendency today to consider that the "unfairness" of the individual competitor in his struggle with the other competitor(s) is mainly determined by his impact on the functioning of the market. Such a view has been defended in Germany by various members of the Max Planck Institute. For a recent analysis, see Kaufmann from the Erasmus University Rotterdam (1986).
4. This has been the typical position of the so-called "Chicago School".
5. For a general criticism of this measure, see Jacquemin and Slade (1989).
6. A relatively general result in oligopoly models is that opposite results are obtained as firms achieve equilibrium in output (Cournot) or in price (Bertrand) levels. The basic explanation is that a firm faces a very different firm-specific demand in the two cases: when the price of the rival is taken as given, the firm's perceived elasticity of

demand is larger than when the quantity of the rival is taken as given. Thus in Bertrand equilibrium, firms quote lower prices than in Cournot equilibrium. The case of information pooling is an application of this general idea. When the goods are substitutes, in Cournot competition, pooling of information has two effects. First, it reduces the variance of the errors about the random intercept of the (linear) demand function and increases expected profits. Second, it correlates the strategies that the firms choose. This decreases the firm's expected profits, given that in the case of substitutable goods the optimal choice to do for one firm is to produce a high output when the other firm is expected to produce a low one. The second effect dominates. On the contrary, in Bertrand competition with substitutes, correlation of strategies increases expected profits.

7. See for example, Von Weizsäcker (1980), Dasgupta and Stiglitz (1980), Perry (1984).
8. According to the Report of the Attorney General's National Committee to Study the Antitrust Law (1955), the standard adopted in the Standard Oil of New Jersey case (1911) "makes obsolete once prevalent arguments, such as, whether monopoly arrangements would be socially preferable to competition in a particular industry, because for example of high fixed costs, or the risk of cutthroat competition or other similar unusual conditions". See also Procter & Gamble (1967). In the 1984 revisions of its merger guidelines however, the Justice Department chose to enact as administrative policy what the US Congress has refused to enact as law: mergers that are illegal under section 7 of the Clayton Act would be found legal if they bring about a sufficient increase in efficiency.
9. Williamson (1977) provides himself a stimulating discussion of several qualifications of his model.
10. Forrester and Norral (1984) have argued that in determining whether there was a restriction of competition within the meaning of Article 85 para. 1, the economic nature and consequences of the conduct involved have to be examined.
11. There is no duty to notify, but the possibility of exemption can be one important incentive; freedom from fines is another. There are certain agreements listed in Article 4 of Regulation 17 that are exempted from notification. Furthermore, notifications are not required where there is no appreciable effect on trade between Member States. However, this "de minimis" concept is not very reliable.
12. As noticed by Forrester and Norall (1984), businessmen "wish to discern the path to sanctity or absolution without passing through the burdensome process of confession" (p. 308, note 2).
13. The European Commission elaborated a general project proposing a definition and a typology of joint ventures setting out a framework of competition policy within which constructive joint ventures can flourish. The Commission intends to provide general practical guidance for enterprises in the form of a Notice ultimately to be

published in the Official Journal. This kind of "policy announcement" could reduce the difficulty of unpredictable enforcement of the competition rules in everyday business life.

14. The following arguments are partly based on empirical studies and interviews. For the U.S. see e.g. Berg, Duncan & Friedman (1982), and for the EEC, Jacquemin, Lammerant and Spinoit (1985).
15. The characteristics of the industry play also an important role in the propensity to cooperate. In a case such as biotechnology which is in an early and highly competitive stage, in which patentable processes and know-how are of great importance, even basic research can lead to commercial concepts that companies can quickly connect to final products. There is then a limited interest in cooperative activity, non cooperative strategies being often more rewarding. On the contrary, in a more mature sector like semiconductor industry, cooperative efforts are frequent.
16. This is an essential distinction between R&D and capital, suggesting the danger of modelling R&D expenditures like investment in capital.
17. Compared with the *patent system*, cooperative R&D leads to a large diffusion of knowledge. Industry-wide cooperative research laboratories (especially important in Scandinavia) and industry-university cooperation are especially useful as they allow the results of individual development projects from firm to firm to be generalized and transferred, "thus providing a degree of economies of scope to innovation programmes across an industry or activity as a whole", Ergas (1986). Relying on *subsidies* meets several limits: it does not solve the diffusion problem, it can introduce new distortions and it is not easy to control.
18. But, an exemption could still be obtained on the basis of Art. 85 para. 3, following a notification.

11 ANTITRUST TREATMENT OF COOPERATIVE RESEARCH: HOW REASONABLE IS THE RULE OF REASON?

WILLIAM JAMES ADAMS

1. Salutation

I was never a student of Henk de Jong; but the Dutch incarnation of me surely would have been. From the day I first met him, when I was a young graduate student and he was an established figure in the profession, Henk was doing the three things that all young scholars cherish: listening to my exuberant naïvetés with great apparent interest and respect, asking ME questions, and using the telephone to open the doors behind which lay the empirical victuals needed to complete my dissertation.

One of these telephone calls went to the archival division of the Amsterdam-Rotterdam Bank. Buried there were annual reports new and old of all major companies quoted in the Netherlands. I had already gathered such reports for the United Kingdom and Sweden, and I was heading next for the linguistically and culturally familiar territory of Belgium, France, and Italy. As the clerk graciously offered me annual report upon annual report, I felt embarrassed by my inability to establish rapport or express gratitude in Dutch. Finally, I simply said (in English), "You really have a gold-mine here!" For a moment, the man seemed perplexed; but then, with a triumphant smile, he produced the current annual report of Consolidated Gold Fields. Thus did I begin to understand what it means to be an empirical economist.

I followed Henk from Leiden to Nijenrode to Amsterdam; and he followed me from Harvard to Michigan. Shortly after my arrival in Ann Arbor, Henk invited me to a first and then a second conference in the Netherlands. Apart from offering me the opportunity to disseminate some ideas from my dissertation, these conferences exposed me to European specialists in industrial organization. The diversity of views expressed was new and stimulating to the young American bred on microcurrents from the stream of neoclassical thought. It obliged me to rethink many of the tenets taken for granted by those of my contemporaries who strategically anchored themselves stateside. It also involved me in friendships more durable than a dominant position.

Henk de Jong's contribution to my professional development extended well beyond a quasi-mentor's courtesies. At a time when market structure ruled the field of industrial organization, in the sense that it was supposed to determine market conduct and market performance, without being much affected by them, Henk was already Schumpeterian in his emphasis on the dynamics of economic progress. Many of the ideas he was advancing, in conversation and in print, have been reinvented by today's proponents of metastatics. Given its importance in Schumpeterian thought, I shall focus this dedicated paper on invention and innovation.

2. Introduction

At the time I met Henk de Jong, invention was a hot topic in Europe. It owed its heat to an alleged gap in technological expertise between Europe and the United States. Shaped by Galbraith's *New Industrial State* and Servan-Schreiber's *Défi Américain* as well as by Schumpeter's *Capitalism, Socialism, and Democracy*, the conventional wisdom imputed Europe's supposed disadvantage to the paltry absolute sizes and market shares of its leading firms. Whether explicitly or implicitly, these popular beliefs usually boiled down to two propositions: that economies of scale are not quickly exhausted in inventive activity, and high levels of seller-concentration spare risk-averse sellers the humdrum vagaries of a competitive market and hence permit them to employ their dainty doses of risk-taking on invention. Both arguments seemed to justify industrial policies designed to encourage mergers of already prominent firms. The French government's fifth plan of economic and social development (1966-1970) embodied clearly this view of the world.[1]

As academic research failed to uncover strong empirical linkages between market structure ex ante and the volume of inventive activity ex post, and as the business press stripped the epaulettes of technological dominance from the uniforms of American enterprises, interest in technological change abated. Although corporate marriage partners continued to justify their nuptials in research terms, the attention of policymakers had turned away from the relationship between market structure and technological change.

Inventive activity is now back in fashion, especially in the United States, where fears abound that today's gaps in technology disfavor the United States rather than Europe or Japan. As a result, the pleas once heard in Europe for modification of those public policies which impede, or could better promote, technological change are now finding a remarkably high-fidelity echo in the United States (Jorde and Teece, 1990). Some of these proposals, such as greater funding for academic research, or greater cooperation between universities and business enterprises, have little to do with now dusty debates on the sources of invention. Others, however, seem to take up where Schumpeter, Galbraith, and Servan-Schreiber left off: In particular, they advocate relaxation of the antitrust laws - not, this time, vis-à-vis mergers but rather in the context of cooperation among otherwise independent enterprises. In this view, however noxious is cooperative *marketing* (e.g., in the form of horizontal price-fixing), cooperative *research*, and perhaps even cooperative *production*, should not be prohibited per se under the Sherman Act. To do so would put U.S. firms at a disadvantage, without good cause, when they joust with foreign rivals.

Although it would be difficult to argue that U.S. antitrust law deals harshly with with cooperative research,[2] a quick glance at foreign treatments of cooperation might seem to confirm the relative tolerance of foreign policies.[3] For example, the European Communities provide five paths along which cooperative research and development can escape the reach of competition policy.

1) In the opinion of the Commission, cooperation in research unaccompanied by so-called ancillary restraints[4] does not restrict competition in a manner prohibited by Article 85(1) of the Treaty of Rome.[5]
2) In the opinion of the Commission, cooperation in research accompanied by ancillary restraints in production and distribution does not restrict competition if the cooperators combine for annual sales of less than 50 million units of account and less than five percent of the relevant market within the EC.[6]
3) Secondary legislation of the Community[7] grants automatic legality to cooperative research agreements that restrict competition in certain specified ways. To qualify for this (block) exemption from the prohibitions of Article 85(1), an agreement must satisfy certain conditions,[8] all of its restraints of trade must appear on the list of expressly tolerated conduct (the white list), and, in consequence, none of its restraints can appear on the list of expressly intolerable conduct (the black list).
4) The block exemption just described contains a second, but non-automatic, path to legality. An agreement which contains no restraints from the black list but does include restraints not found on the white list may qualify for acceptance under the so-called opposition procedure:[9]

The cooperators notify the agreement to the Commission and request exemption from application of Article 85(1) under Regulation 418/85. If the Commission does not oppose this request within six months, the agreement is immune from antitrust attack.

5) Cooperative research agreements which do not qualify for immunity under the *block* exemption may still be granted an *individual* exemption from the prohibitions of Article 85(1). To qualify, the cooperators must notify the agreement to the Commission and request an exemption under Council Regulation No 17/62. Decisions to grant such an exemption are based on cost/benefit criteria contained in Article 85(3) of the Treaty of Rome: If the agreement improves production or promotes technical progress, *and* if it accords a fair share of its benefits to consumers, *and* if its terms are indispensable to achieving its benefits, *and* if it does not eliminate too much competition, then it may be immunized from antitrust challenge even if it restricts competition in the common market.[10]

In response, perhaps, to the perceived tolerance abroad of cooperative research, the United States adopted the National Cooperative Research Act of 1984 (NCRA).[11] The Act provides that qualifying agreements

- will be evaluated in antitrust proceedings (at the state as well as the national level) using a rule of reason rather than a per se prohibition,
- will, upon being found in violation of the antitrust laws, create liability for single rather than the usual treble damages, and
- will, upon exoneration in a frivolous or unreasonable antitrust proceeding, permit collection from claimant of the cost of defense.

To qualify for this special treatment, the cooperation cannot extend beyond research to production and marketing, and it must be notified to the Justice Department and the Federal Trade Commission.

Prior to passage of the NCRA, did U.S. antitrust law really hamstring U.S. companies engaged in global competition? Does it continue to do so? Should the recent tolerance of cooperative research be extended forward to cooperative production of jointly developed products and processes? Should potential cooperators with individually and collectively small shares of economically meaningful markets be allowed to cooperate as they please? In this chapter I shall review the recent theoretical, empirical, and legal evidence bearing on these questions. I shall suggest

- that the theoretical literature on cooperative research has ignored an important dimension of the issue - one which is likely to militate against tolerance,
- that increasingly rich sources of data, outside as well as inside the United States, do not reveal major effects on the stock of knowledge from tolerance of cooperative research, and
- that a socially desirable rule of reason is very difficult to frame in this area.

Traditional antitrust law is imperfect - more so, perhaps, in this area than in others. But the case for tolerance of certain forms of collusion involving currently or probably major enterprises is far from compelling.

3. Cooperative Research in Theory

Several recent papers compare admirably the welfare implications of individualistic versus cooperative research. In this section, I shall first summarize the stockpiles of arguments for and against public tolerance and then describe an important family of omissions from the latter.

Many of the incentives to cooperate in research are socially benign. The most important among these are:

1) The stock of knowledge is a public good. As a result, once available, knowledge should be freely available to all. If research is undertaken individually, however, those who invent will attempt to charge for their ideas. When successful, they ration excessively the use thereof. To the extent that cooperative research entails free dissemination of results among cooperators, it promotes socially desirable diffusion of knowledge.

2) Inventors are not always able to charge for use of their contributions to knowledge. Rarely, if ever, do patents or attempted secrecy protect the inventor perfectly from unauthorized emulation. Inventors poorly suited to personal use of their ideas face an additional problem. Before they can license or sell their knowledge, they may have to reveal so many of their findings as to jeopardize their ability to collect from the prospective user. Given the difficulty of establishing and then exploiting property rights in knowledge, economic actors may have little incentive to engage individually in inventive activity. Rather, each will attempt

to pirate the relevant inventions of others. Cooperative research mitigates this problem by allowing cooperators to commit themselves to multilateral expenditure on both research and enforcement of resulting property rights. In curbing the predisposition to pirate, cooperation can promote socially desirable expenditure on research.

3) Individual inventive activity can entail wasteful duplication. Such may be the case, for example, when each inventor performs exactly the same experiments with exactly the same results.[12] Cooperative exploration, whether it takes the form of coordination of separate efforts or concentration of effort in a single joint venture, can eliminate the waste. A given discovery might require fewer resources, and a given expenditure of resources might generate more or faster contributions to knowledge.

4) Individual companies, like individual inventors, bring different strengths and weaknesses to their research programs. To the extent that invention requires a variety of skills, cooperative research might facilitate the combination of complementary and otherwise underutilized resources, reducing the cost or accelerating the speed of invention.

5) The minimum efficient scale of research may be very large. If companies dislike risk, they may be unwilling to undertake individually research characterized by large investment, positive expected return, but uncertain outcome. Even risk-neutral firms might not undertake lumpy research unilaterally despite a positive expected social payoff. Such will be true, for example, if the research leads to large-scale production, and the profitability of large-scale production would evaporate if rivals also succeed in such research. Cooperation can mitigate both of these problems by reducing the technological and the market risk associated with research.

To this point, I have described the benign incentives to cooperate in research. Contrasting with such incentives are others which operate against the public interest. As described in the literature, the most important of these are:

1) Cooperation in research might retard the pace of invention. A major incentive to innovate quickly is the expected period of temporary monopoly before any rival can match or better one's idea. To the extent

that cooperation obliges a firm to share all knowledge with all rivals, that period may disappear altogether, eliminating the incentive for anyone to invest in research. On the other hand, where the inventor is not obliged to share all free of charge with fellow rivals, cooperation may facilitate bribery of research leaders by the laggards to retard the pace of change. The incentive to offer such bribes occurs because research that creates cost or product advantages for firm i usually reduce the expected profit of rival j (Katz, 1985).

2) Cooperation in research might restrict output artificially in the product market. This could occur if cooperation in research facilitates (i.e., lowers the cost of effective) cooperation in marketing, leading to increases in price-cost margins. It could also occur without explicit cooperation in the product market. Suppose, for example, that each participant in a scheme of cooperative research undertakes a mutually agreed research agenda. Successful researchers obtain individual patents but license other participants. Royalties are based on the licensee's output. In this scheme, royalty payments constitute a marginal cost of production; hence they restrict output.

3) Cooperation in research may not be the best way to deal with the threat of piracy. Even certain and instantaneous piracy by one's actual rivals may not prevent individual expenditure on socially desirable research. Suppose that a member of industry A expects a particular research program to result in a discovery which lowers unit production cost in industry B as well as in industry A. Suppose further that if the inventor fails to cooperate with any rivals, then those in A, but not those in B, will hear immediately of the discovery and pirate it.[13] On the other hand, if the the potential explorer cooperates in research with rivals in A, then agreement in research would foster enough cooperation in marketing to raise price above unit production cost.

In this setting, exclusive focus on industry A produces a social dilemma: Cooperation promotes desirably low production cost[14] but inefficiently high price-cost margins. Upon broadening the focus to include industry B, however, the dilemma might disappear. Integration by the prospective inventor into industry B may generate enough profit (given the tardy response of rivals in B) to defray the cost of solo discovery. If so, society's desire to induce performance of the relevant research does not require it to tolerate horizontal price-fixing.

The existing literature on cooperative research has certainly identified many features of technological change that affect society's choice among treatments of cooperative research. Insightful as it is, however, this literature neglects certain private incentives which bear critically on the (social) desirability of cooperation. These incentives appear clearly in a different segment of the literature on invention, namely, the papers on preemptive patenting (Dasgupta and Stiglitz, 1980; Gilbert and Newbery, 1982; Dasgupta, 1986; Gilbert, 1990). Although the preemption literature focuses on an incumbent monopolist threatened with entry, it also applies with interesting modifications to oligopolistic situations.

Preemptive invention and innovation derive their profitability from socially inefficient deterrence of new competition. In other words, behavior which deters new competition does not necessarily contravene the public interest: The introduction of new products or processes by one firm can easily enhance social surplus even if it jeopardizes the ability of rival firms to compete. The essence of preemption as defined in the literature is the incentive to engage in an activity which reduces social surplus. Preemptive invention can reduce social welfare in many ways:

1) The incentive to preempt competition can result in a socially inefficient pace of invention. In the standard model of research, invention occurs with certainty at a time determined by the volume of research expenditure: The greater the expenditure, the sooner the invention. Dasgupta and Stiglitz (1980) and Gilbert and Newbery (1982) show that the incentive to preempt can result in normatively premature invention. In effect, the cost of hastening invention exceeds the social, but not the private, benefit, so that excessive resources are devoted to research activity.[15] In an oligopolistic setting, preemption of this sort might not occur without cooperation: To the extent that preemption is a public good among incumbents, each oligopolist might otherwise attempt to free-ride on preemptive activities of ts rivals.

2) The incentive to preempt competition can induce firms to explore products and processes which they never intend to exploit commercially.[16] The discovery of such products and processes probably serves no public purpose.[17] If not, but it uses scarce resources, it should not

be undertaken. And yet, to the extent that it removes the threat of entry, it might be privately desirable indeed.

Suppose, for example, that established sellers produce their product at (constant) unit cost c_1. Suppose further that research could uncover a second technology entailing a (constant) unit cost of c_2 such that $c_2 > c_1$. From a social perspective, the new technology is strictly inferior to the old; if it is costly to discover, it should be left undiscovered. From the perspective of incumbent sellers, however, the potential new technology is viewed differently. Suppose incumbents cooperate in marketing and charge the monopoly price (P_m). Suppose further that $P_m > c_2$. If a potential competitor is able to discover and patent the new technology, he can credibly threaten to enter the business unless incumbents cease charging more than c_2. In so doing, the potential competitor can induce incumbents to buy his patent for an amount just less than the difference between profit earned at a price of P_m and profit earned at a price of c_2. If that difference exceeds the cost of discovering the new technology, the incumbents might prefer to invent and patent the novelty themselves - before storing it permanently on a back shelf.

Cooperation in research may facilitate this preemptive strategy. Although each incumbent might have an incentive to preempt the potential rival, it also has an incentive to free-ride on the explorations of actual rivals. Given its lack of intrinsic value, the new technology might not be developed by incumbents without explicit cooperation.

3) The incentive to preempt competition can induce firms to explore and introduce novelties which prevent the appearance of socially preferable alternatives. Consider, for example, a set of oligopolists currently using technology T_1. Individually or collectively, they can explore two potential technologies, T_2 or T_3. All three technologies entail U-shaped average cost curves, with c_i representing the minimum value of average cost (i = 1, 2, 3) and q_i representing the scale at which c_i is attained (i = 1, 2, 3). Now suppose that $q_2 < q_1 < q_3$, $c_2 < c_3 < c_1$. Suppose further that q_3 alone is large in relation to market demand. Finally, suppose that the cost of developing T_2 is identical to the cost of developing T_3. From a social perspective, technology 3 is strictly inferior to technology 2; it should never be explored. From a private perspective, however, technology 3 may have a desirable feature. Its large value of q may create a natural oligopoly, shielding the incumbents

from entry. This shield may protect the incumbents not simply from entry using T_3 or T_1 but even from entry using T_2. In other words, strategic behavior may distort durably the direction of invention.[18]
Note the interplay in this example between preemptive research and preemptive investment in productive capacity.[19] Note also the strategic role in this context of cooperation. Without it, each oligopolist might pursue the socially desirable T_2 rather than the collectively desirable T_3, hoping to benefit simultaneously from the low value of his own c and the high value of a rival's q. Such behavior is especially likely where the cost disadvantage of T_3 is small.

In conclusion, the theoretical literature on preemptive patenting suggests the danger of implementing a public policy toward cooperative research, especially one predisposed to tolerate or promote cooperation, before strategic inventive behavior has been studied adequately. The existing literature on preemption suffices to show that, as a result of strategic calculation, cooperative research can result in undesirably rapid (and hence undesirably costly) invention. It can also result in the intentional exploration of socially undesirable technologies - whether or not with the aim of employing them. This incentive to shape an industry's technology in a manner inconsistent with the public interest may be the greatest potential vice of cooperative research. Yet current theoretical models of research agreements are incapable of analyzing the direction of invention.

The literature on preemptive patenting suggests a second conclusion as well. Preemption can occur even if the potential rivals of incumbents are numerous and face no disadvantages in research. As a result, cooperation should not be allowed in research merely because many independent sources of potential invention appear to remain.[20]

4. Cooperative Research in Practice

The theoretical arguments discussed above cut sometimes for and sometimes against public tolerance of cooperative research and its accompanying ancillary restraints. Should one therefore embrace a rule-of-reason approach to cooperative research? Perhaps, but not before examining the determinants of actual cooperative research.[21] To the extent that most actual cooperation has been and will be of a sort that enhances social welfare, then the nontrivial costs of enforcing rules of reason might indicate the desirability - at least provisionally - of presumptions close to per se legality. On the other hand, if most actual cooperation detracts from social welfare, then enforcement costs might justify (provisional) presumptions bordering on per se prohibition. In other words, it is difficult to reach policy conclusions without examination of real-world practice.

Given the diversity of both potential motives and technological contexts, it is hardly surprising to find that cooperative research can take many forms. "Cooperation" could extend from creation of a joint venture and renunciation of independent action to exchange of information on uncoordinated activities. "Research" could range from experimentation seemingly devoid of commercial application up to the frontiers of marketing. This heterogeneity makes it difficult to define cooperative research.[22] It also impedes development of systematic information on the types of cooperation in existence. In a different vein, the incomplete legal tolerance of cooperative research undoubtedly prevents the appearance of many agreements that would exist in an unregulated environment.

The best extensive sources of information on actual cooperative research derive from notifications made to U.S. authorities under the National Cooperative Research Act of 1984 and to EC authorities under Council Regulation (EEC) No 17/62 or Commission Regulation (EEC) No 418/85.

An exhaustive list of the U.S. notifications is maintained by the Department of Justice. It includes the name(s) of the notifier(s) and the *Federal Register* location of the description of each agreement. The description contained in the *Register* contains the names and addresses of the participants and a brief description of the goals of the cooperation.[23] As of July 9, 1990, there had been 386 notifications under the 1984 Act. Many of these involved corrections to or modifications of previously notified ventures.

It is important to recognize, of course, that cooperative research conducted in the United States is not always notified to the Department of Justice. Some agreements might be so obviously immune from antitrust challenge that their participants dispense with notification. Others might be so probably illegal that their participants avoid the publicity resulting from notification. Most importantly, several might contain ancillary restraints that prevent entitlement to the Act's plums. Accordingly, the list of notifications should not be considered either exhaustive or representative of cooperative research in the United States.

In contrast with its American counterpart, the European information on cooperative research is not well suited to quantitative analysis. Pure research agreements need not be notified to the Commission. To my knowledge, not even the notified research agreements are compiled exhaustively for semi-public diffusion. References in the Commission's annual report on competition policy to the number of agreements notified under the opposition procedure of Regulation 418/85 do not always describe the agreements or identify the parties sufficiently to permit statistical analysis of the determinants of cooperative research.

On the other hand, the European record does lend itself admirably to qualitative analysis.[24] It contains several Commission decisions granting individual antitrust exemptions to particular cooperative schemes.[25] Since these exemptions are granted for finite periods of time, the record also contains some Commission decisions on renewal.

Examination of the evidence on cooperative research has left me with two impressions: that the impact of cooperation on the *rate* of invention may be exaggerated, and that the impact of cooperation on the *direction* of invention is a legitimate source of social concern.

Impact of Cooperation on the Rate of Invention

With respect to the rate of invention, my impression is based on several pieces of evidence - Japanese and European as well as American.

1) Japan is frequently cited as the home of numerous important examples of successful cooperative research. To evaluate this claim, Saxonhouse (1985) gathered financial information on companies participating in each of twenty major cooperative projects sponsored by the Japanese government between 1966 and 1981. Using standard event-study techniques, he explored the degree to which announcement of a joint project altered the securities-market valuation of participating firms. In each of the twenty cases, he failed to reject the null hypothesis of no effect.[26]

   Seven of Saxonhouse's twenty projects were susceptible to product-market analysis as well. "For these seven projects there appears to be very little relationship between participation in the government-sponsored project and change in market shares in the industries most closely related to the projects undertaken. For four of the seven projects, firms participating in the projects did not increase their market share relative to the firms that did not participate. Of forty separate instances of firm participation in only sixteen did firm market share increase!"[27] (Saxonhouse, 1985, p. 8) Thus both the product-market evidence and the financial-market evidence suggest that cooperative research impinges only slightly on its participants.

2) Europe, like Japan, is considered hospitable to cooperative research. Symbolic of this hospitality is the block exemption from antitrust liability contained in Commission Regulation (EEC) No 418/85. Although it establishes an automatic exemption for agreements devoid of noxious ancillary restraints, Regulation 418/85 also recognizes that most real-world agreements are likely to contain provisions which, although not fatal to acceptability, cannot be considered legal per se. Given the need for a rule of reason in such situations, the regulation attempts to streamline antitrust and minimize business uncertainty through creation of the opposition procedure:[28] Unless the Commission challenges a qualifying research agreement within six months of notification, it is exempted from the prohibitions of Article 85(1).

In reality, however, the opposition procedure has been used quite infrequently. Between March 1, 1985, when Regulation 418/85 took effect, and the end of 1988, the Commission received only five requests for exemption by opposition.[29] During 1988 - the period covered by the Commission's most recent annual report on competition policy - zero requests had been received for exemption by opposition.[30] This means *either* that cooperators can get by with only those ancillary restraints that appear on the white list of Regulation 418/85 *or* that they depend on ancillary restraints appearing on the Regulation's black list. To the extent that the latter is the case, as I suspect it is, the European experience suggests that moderately kindly antitrust treatment of cooperative research may not suffice to stimulate research appreciably.

The European setting contains other clues regarding the impact of deregulating cooperative research. One clue: Individual exemptions, like block exemptions, are granted for finite periods of time. Moreover, changes in the situations of the parties, or in the terms of their agreement, permit the Commission to reconsider their exemption. If cooperative research were productive, one would expect requests for renewal or modification to include evidence that the agreement has already borne inventive fruit. And yet, such evidence does not appear frequently in Commission decisions. I have seen only one such reference to the results of cooperative research, and that occurred in an initial request for exemption.[31] The Commission's second consideration of this agreement made no mention of further progress.[32]

A second clue: Most cooperative research in Europe involves coordination between the parties (usually just two in number) of their separate research programs rather than creation of a joint facility to undertake the research of both. Coordination of this sort can certainly reduce wasteful duplication and promote specialization based on comparative advantage; but it hardly permits realization of such economies of scale as might exist in research. Interchange between administrators of laboratories is not the same thing as daily conversation between scientists over chemicals or coffee.[33]

A final clue: In its discussion of whether cooperation is indispensable to attainment of its alleged benefits, the Commission often comes close to admitting - even where cooperation is approved - that the parties are capable of performing the research independently.[34]

3) As for the United States, Scott (1988) has undertaken a detailed examination of the 61 agreements notified to U.S. antitrust authorities between January 1985 and June 1986 under the NCRA. Scott divided the Federal Trade Commission's 261 four-digit industries into two groups: the 81 in which cooperative research agreements had been notified and the 180 in which they had not. He then regressed a series of industry-level variables on a dummy variable taking the value of one if the industry hosted, or was likely to benefit directly from, one or more of the notified cooperative schemes. Scott found that industries in which notified research had occured could be characterized as
   - not experiencing unusual difficulty in appropriating the commercial benefits associated with their inventions,[35]
   - containing relatively diversified enterprises, and
   - experiencing relatively rapid growth of productivity.

Scott also established that many cooperative ventures include all or most of the very largest firms in their industries. To Scott, then, characteristics of both the relevant industries and the relevant enterprises mitigate the risk that the benefits of invention cannot not be captured without cooperation. He concludes that relaxation of the antitrust laws has not stimulated research where such stimulation might be needed most, i.e., among absolutely and relatively small enterprises, where enterprises experience great difficulty appropriating the commercial fruits of their inventions, and where industries perform relatively poorly in terms of productivity growth.

Although the number of notifications has grown considerably, I shall not attempt to update Scott's findings.[36] Rather, I shall simply point out two features of the list of 386 notifications received by U.S. antitrust authorities through July 5, 1990. First, the notifications are concentrated in a very small number of cooperative ventures (table 1). Ranked by number of notifications, the five leading consortia accounted for 36, and the ten leading consortia for 54, percent of the total. Groups notifying at least five times accounted for fully 68 percent of the total. It would seem, therefore, that NCRA has affected research in a small number of industries at most. The careful study of Katz and Ordover (1990, p. 170) supports this view.

Table 1 *National Cooperative Research Act of 1984, Number of Notifications by Notifying Party*[*]

43	Bell Communications Research
28	Portland Cement Association
27	Southwest Research Institute
22	Petroleum Environmental Research Forum
18	Corporation for Open Systems International
17	Motor Vehicle Manufacturers Association
15	Semiconductor Research Corporation
14	Microelectronics and Computer Technology Corporation
14	National Association of Homebuilders
10	National Center for Manufacturing Sciences
9	OSI/Network Management Forum
8	Open Software Foundation
8	Software Productivity Consortium
8	CAD Framework Initiative
6	West Argo
5	PDES
5	Unix International
5	CAM-International

* The table includes only those parties who notified five or more times through July 5, 1990. The table includes 262 of the 386 notifications made during the sample period. Notifications include modifications and corrections to, as well as brand new, agreements.

Source: Unpublished list furnished by the United States Department of Justice.

The second interesting feature of the list is the importance of very large enterprises. Bellcore alone accounts for eleven percent of the total. The leading producers of automobiles and refiners of petroleum also appear near the top of the frequency list. These are unlikely to be the companies most in need of cooperation in order to undertake research.[37] The Portland Cement Associations of the industrial landscape are exceptional members of notification's family portrait. It is not obvious, therefore, that the so-called safe-harbors approach to deregulation, which would facilitate cooperation among smaller firms, will have much effect on inventive activity.

The evidence just discussed permits only impressions not conclusions. It demonstrates neither the unimportance nor the undesirability of cooperative research. It should, however, give pause to those who presume that recent or further deregulation of cooperative research will accelerate appreciably and broadly the pace of innovation. No wonder the Congressional Budget Office (1990, p. 113) concludes that "The evidence on antitrust legislation [as an impediment to the appearance of R&D consortia] is weak and more asserted than proven."

Impact of Cooperation on the Direction of Invention

Economic welfare depends at least as much on the direction as on the pace of invention. Evidence on the relationship between cooperation in and direction of research is anything but definitive. It does, however, suggest that the fear of strategic research behavior - of the use of technology by powerful enterprises to preempt markets in socially undesirable ways - is not unfounded.

1) In his study of NCRA notifications, Scott found a positive correlation between cooperative research and seller-concentration (in the relevant product market).[38] Using examples rather than statistical analysis, he also showed that cooperation often involves a concentrated industry's leaders rather than its fringe.[39] For both reasons, the risk of product-market power among cooperative researchers is large. While strategic research behavior depends on the state of rivalry in research as well as in product markets, Scott (1988, p. 184) clearly believes the power existed there as well.[40]

2) In Europe, a good example of potential preemption involved the conduct of Philips in the context of video cassette recorders.[41] In 1975,

Philips and Sony were the only producers of video cassette recorders designed to be used along with European television sets,[42] Philips employing the VCR technology and Sony its U-MATIC counterpart. According to the Commission, Philips enjoyed a "pre-eminent" position in the market. At the initiative of Philips, five European manufacturers of consumer electronics agreed

- to produce and market only those cassettes and recorders that employ VCR technology,
- not to change the VCR standard except with the consent of all,
- to grant royalty-free access to each other's patents relating to cassettes and recorders,
- to maintain royalty-free access by erstwhile cooperators to relevant technologies it controls should the signatory withdraw from the agreement,
- to sacrifice access to the relevant technologies of erstwhile cooperators upon withdrawal from the agreement, and
- to allow third parties to join on the same terms.

The Commission viewed this as an attempt to establish an industry standard for the purpose of restricting competition. After discussing the matter informally with Philips (and attempting, I assume, to secure modification of the agreement), the Commission was obliged to issue a formal statement of objections to the scheme. Philips terminated the agreement rather testily; but, given the importance of the issue and the unwillingness of Philips to admit violation of the Treaty of Rome, the Commission issued a formal decision finding the agreement unentitled to individual exemption from the prohibitions of Article 85(1).

3) In the United States, the most interesting example of antitrust challenge to cooperative research involved a claim by the Department of Justice that members of the Motor Vehicle Manufacturers Association had conspired "to eliminate competition in the research, development, manufacture, and installation of motor vehicle air pollution control equipment, and in the purchase from others of patents and patent rights, covering such equipment."[43] Specifically, Justice argued that cross-licensing and pooling of patents controlled by the parties, and joint evaluation of patents offered to one participant by a third party, prevented any member of the group from gaining a technological advantage over the rest.

On first impression, the principal vice of this agreement might seem to be its effect on the pace of invention: If no party can gain a technological advantage over the rest, none will have an incentive to engage in research, and the pace of technological change will slacken. On reflection, however, there may be more to this invention story than mere retardation.

Why, exactly, did the parties want to go slow on pollution-control? The usual explanation, supported easily by statements of industry executives at the time, ran as follows: The sooner is the technological feasibility of pollution-control established, the sooner will governmental bodies - local, state, and national - regulate the exhaust of motor vehicles. Inevitably, such regulation will increase the cost of producing an automobile. Although the social benefits of regulation might exceed this cost, manufacturers are unlikely to be able to recoup it because only a tiny fraction of the social benefits associated with reduction of a given vehicle's pollution are realized by the vehicle's owner. As a result, manufacturers will suffer lower price-cost margins, lower sales, or both. In any event, profits will fall.

Plausible as it may sound, this is not the only way to explain the desire to slow the accumulation of knowledge on pollution-control. The product-market power of an established enterprise depends partly on the ratio of minimum efficient scale in production to market size. The larger the ratio, the greater the natural tendancy of its industry toward oligopoly or monopoly. Suppose that the internal combustion engine constitutes an important source of scale economies in automotive production.[44] To the extent that

- invention of pollution control devices would lead to strict regulation of engine exhaust, and
- strict regulation of engine exhaust would reduce the cost advantage of internal combustion engines over other forms of motive power, and
- other forms of motive power are characterized by relatively few scale economies in production, rapid technological change in the area of pollution-control might reduce the minimum efficient scale of operation in the automobile industry, increasing thereby the vulnerability of established producers to entry. More generally, one might expect the automobile companies to shape the direction of

pollution-control technology so as to reduce the likelihood that ecology would become the ally of competition.

4) An important feature of the automotive pollution story is the interplay between government regulation and market competition. It serves to remind us that strategic behavior can take the form of attempting to manipulate public policy so as to facilitate collusion with or exclusion of competitors. The Congressional Budget Office (1990, p. 113) recognizes that cooperative research, like cooperation in general, might have such an object or effect: "consortia have the potential...to influence public policy in ways that may protect the domestic industry and restrain competition through government intervention."

5. Cooperative Research at Law

Having considered the theory and the practice of cooperative research, I want finally to examine its treatment at law. Considerable if incomplete reading of the record, especially the European record, leads me to believe that the European Communities do not tolerate any and all cooperative research, and that compelling application of a case-by-case rule of reason is very difficult in this area.

EC Tolerance of Cooperative Research

Unquestionably, the EC has authorized cooperative research in situations where the resulting threat to competition was hardly trivial.

In the first place, the Commission is willing to tolerate cooperation even when it links large and important firms. For example, in one of its earliest decisions on the subject, the Commission granted an individual exemption to an agreement between Henkel and Colgate to conduct coordinated research on laundry soaps and detergents.[45] Henkel was the second- and Colgate the fourth-largest seller of such products in the common market, where the four-firm seller-concentration ratio at the time was 80 percent. More recently, the Commission exempted an agreement between Michelin and Continental, the first and second largest producers accounting collectively for 46 percent of production in the highly-concentrated European tire industry, to introduce a new type of radial tire.[46]

In the second place, the Commission is willing to tolerate cooperation even when it includes major ancillary restraints in production and distribution. For example, in *VW/MAN*,[47] two manufacturers of commercial vehicles decided to cooperate in the development, production, and distribution of trucks with gross weight in the range of 6 to 9 tons. At the time, Volkswagen produced trucks of less than 6 tons, while MAN produced trucks of more than 9 tons. Each company took responsibility for developing a different set of components for the joint range of trucks. Each would then assemble the components into trucks using, where relevant, components produced by the other. MAN alone would then take responsibility for the marketing of both VW and MAN trucks in this weight range.

Despite the impression left by *Henkel/Colgate* and *VW/MAN*, and by the texts of relevant regulations and notices, careful examination of EC practice does not reveal wanton tolerance of cooperation.

1) The Commission interprets its 1968 notice quite restrictively.[48] For example, in *Beecham/Parke, Davis*[49] the parties believed their agreement (to develop jointly a long-term medication for hypertension) met all the conditions of the notice and hence could not be considered a violation of Article 85(1). The Commission decided otherwise, however, arguing that the agreement extended beyond pure research because it required the parties to exchange technological information gathered after marketing of the new drug had commenced. In other words, an agreement to exchange information on improvements is not a research agreement within the meaning of the 1968 notice.

2) The language of Regulation 418/85 effectively prevents its use to exempt the cooperative research of major manufacturers from the prohibitions of Article 85(1). In *Continental/Michelin*,[50] for example, the parties did not even apply for block exemption because their combined market share exceeded the 20 percent maximum specified in Article 3(2) of the regulation.

3) In the few cases to be considered under the opposition procedure of Regulation 418/85, the Commission did not award block exemptions indiscriminately. With respect to notifications under Article 7(1), the Commission actually challenged more agreements than it chose not to oppose.[51] With respect to notifications under Article 7(4), it has also challenged agreements.[52] Thus the Commission has not used its discre-

tion under Regulation 418/85 to dismantle a dike, real or perceived, restraining cooperative research.

4) Although the Commission has granted many individual exemptions to the prohibitions of Article 85(1), it has frequently obliged the parties to remove ancillary restraints before authorizing their agreement. In general, the Commission tends to react unfavorably to ancillary restraints which
   - prohibit all research ties to third parties,
   - commit the parties to long-term exchange of information on improvements made individually to the new technology,[53]
   - prohibit purchase from third parties of components assigned for production to one of the participants,
   - prohibit any party from selling in one country or more of the EC,[54]
   - entail profit-sharing within the EC,[55] or
   - entail cooperation in production or marketing of goods not developed jointly.[56]

   The Commission is prepared to open formal proceedings against an agreement in order to secure its modification. Given its propensity to bargain over the contents of agreements, the Commission's willingness to exempt agreements - as reflected in the number of exemptions granted - cannot be considered proof that the Commission tolerates virtually all forms of agreement in the research area.

5) The Commission is prepared not to renew an exemption when it feels the social benefits no longer exceed the costs to competition. For example, when the *Henkel/Colgate* agreement came up for renewal, the Commission announced a tightening of conditions. Not only did the Commission require that each party be free to sell anywhere in the EC such products as resulted from joint research - a condition the initial agreement had satisfied - but it also required that each party be free to license the results of its research to third parties without the consent of its partner - a condition the initial agreement had not satisfied. Rather than accept this new condition, the parties chose to abandon their cooperation and withdraw their request for individual exemption.[57]

6) Although the Commission usually comes to terms with prospective cooperators, it is prepared to prohibit a research agreement if the parties fail to modify it sufficiently. In November, 1970, for example, two

large (unnamed) producers from different member states but the same (unnamed) industry "showing oligopolistic tendencies" notified an agreement to form a joint venture.[58] The joint venture would reexamine the unsuccessful research conducted independently and previously by the two and attempt to enhance it to the point where it could be used to improve the parties' existing products. The joint venture would also hold any patents to result from the project. Each parent would be entitled for ten years to a royalty-free license for use in its home marketing area. Each parent would also be entitled to a license for use in other geographic areas but only upon payment of a royalty not exceeding two percent of the net sales value of the relevant product. The Commission feared that the asymmetric pattern of royalties would reinforce the natural advantage of each firm in its home area, and hence exacerbate the danger of market division between the parties and use of patent rights to block parallel imports. When the parties proved unwilling to change this feature of their agreement, the Commission refused to grant an individual exemption, explaining that the licensing provisions were not indispensable to the project as a whole. The parties then dissolved the agreement.[59]

Feasibility of a Rule of Reason

The European experience suggests the availability of two very different types of rule of reason for application to cooperative research. The first, embodied for example in Regulation 418/85, creates categories into which particular agreements can be assigned and then attaches to each category a presumption, more or less strong, as to the legality of agreements within it. The second rule of reason, exemplified by the individual exemptions authorized under Regulation 17/62, evaluates each agreement on its merits according to a statutory list of benefits and costs. I shall refer to these respectively as the categorical and the case-by-case rules of reason. What does the European experience reveal about the social desirability of each?

Experience with the opposition feature of Regulation 418/85 supports the skepticism of Ordover and Willig (1985) regarding categorical rules. Ordover and Willig argued that streamlining through categorization is unlikely to work well in this area because it is impossible to devise simple categories which separate desirable from undesirable cooperation.[60] Regulation 418/85 attempted to create two categories of reasonable agreement: one so desirable that its constituents would receive automatic exemption from the prohibitions of Article 85(1), the other sufficiently desirable that its constituents would receive exemption unless the Commission acted within six months of notification. Surely the Commission hoped that the opposition procedure would permit quick and easy exemption of many desirable agreements. And yet, such has not been the case. However beneficial are agreements satisfying the conditions of this category, the category contains virtually no agreements. Apparently, many cooperators find it impossible to renounce all ancillary restraints appearing on the black list. As a result, parties to agreements failing to qualify for automatic exemption under 418/85 have had to opt for case-by-case evaluation under 17/62. In this sense, the categorical rule of reason has not proved useful in Europe.[61]

Experience with individual exemption under Regulation 17/62 suggests two basic problems. In the first place, the individual exemption procedure hardly eliminates the legal uncertainties associated with cooperation. The Commission tends not only to render decisions well after it receives the relevant notifications but also to require modifications before exempting an agreement. Neither the delay nor the modifications can be predicted with certainty. Even if they could, delay itself deflates the value of agreement, especially in high-tech industries where techniques and products evolve rapidly.

In the second place, only rarely does the Commission adduce the empirical evidence needed to make its decisions convincing. This poverty of empirical justification applies to each of the particular assessments required of the Commission by Article 85(3) of the Treaty. For example:

1) Promotion of technical progress. Cooperative research usually consists of coordinating the separate investigations undertaken by each party in its own facilities. Such cooperation is most likely to promote technical progress if it prevents wasteful duplication of effort or permits exploitation of complementarities among the assets (tangible and intangible) of the several parties.
   Unfortunately, "wasteful duplication" is not a redundant term: some duplication is socially productive (Nelson, 1961). And yet, judging from the texts of its decisions, the Commission never attempts to distinguish between productive and unproductive duplication. Is it possible to do so?

2) Improvement of production. Cooperation in research is often accompanied (in Europe) by cooperation in production. The latter type of cooperation usually consists of specialization.[62] According to the Commission, specialization improves production because it permits realization of scale economies in production.

   To be sure, "economies of scale" is a plausible concept a priori, but neither the degree of economy nor the range of scales over which economies are realized is likely to be equally and strongly pronounced in all industries. In other words, quantitative estimates are required before the concept can be applied to a particular industry. And yet, the Commission rarely provides evidence of minimum or maximum efficient scale in the relevant industry; nor does it report frequently the cost-disadvantage of operating at various nonoptimal scales.[63]

3) Amount of competition suppressed. To be considered for antitrust immunity under Regulation 17/62, an agreement must otherwise contravene Article 85(1). In other words, paradoxically, the Commission only grants immunity to those who restrict competition.[64] As a result, the issue to be resolved when granting an individual exemption is how much, not whether, competition is suppressed.

   Evidence on market structure - on market shares and seller-concentration - is certainly relevant and often supplied;[65] but this evidence often points toward oligopoly and market power. Thus, when the Commission plans to grant exemption, it should provide evidence that the relevant market does and would function tolerably competitively despite its level of seller-concentration. Evidence on price-cost margins, or on price-convergence within the EC, would certainly be helpful in this regard; but the Commission presents neither it nor any alternatives.

   Instead, the Commission usually justifies its belief that competition will remain adequate by pointing to the presence in the relevant market of sellers larger than those involved in the agreement. And yet the mere existence of such firms surely does not suffice to establish that a satisfactory level of competition will obtain if the agreement is allowed to stand. Do those larger sellers now coordinate their marketing? Do prospective parties to the cooperation agreement now coordinate their marketing? In concert with the leading sellers? If successful, will the cooperative research confer major or minor advantages on the cooperators? Will cooperation in research impede subsequent competition among cooperators in marketing? These are just some of the questions which must be answered before the expected effects of cooperative research on the state of competition can be quantified. Although they are difficult to answer ex ante, systematic evidence from previous cases could be presented; but it is not.

4) Benefits to consumers. Consumers benefit from cooperation when cooperation increases the volume of consumer surplus. In the Commission's view, consumer surplus will rise as long as innovaters charge reasonable prices; and innovators will charge reasonable prices as long as they face adequate competition in relevant markets. In effect, therefore, when the Commission argues that the presence of larger firms in the market will preserve adequate competition therein, it is also arguing that consumers are assured a fair share of cooperation's benefits. The empirical defects in this argument have already been described.

5) Indispensability of the restraints. The most difficult of the Commission's assessments concerns the indispensability of each restraint in a proposed agreement. The Commission does little more than assert what is necessary and what is unnecessary to deliver the social benefits ascribed to the agreement. The assertions are usually plausible a priori, but they are not based on empirical evidence. Although it is difficult to envisage conclusive empirical evidence on indispensability, reference to actual experience with similar agreements would not be irrelevant.

In conclusion, even before reaching the problem of aggregation, measurement of the costs and benefits of a particular research agreement, for the purpose of evaluating the wisdom of granting antitrust immunity under Article 85(3), requires quantitative as well as qualitative evidence. And yet the Commission usually bases its decisions on qualitative features of the situation: Certain kinds of ancillary restraints tend in practice to be illegal per se while others tend in practice to be legal per se.

Given the difficulty of accumulating solid evidence on particular market structures and performances, even without the temporal constraints imposed by a quasi-judicial proceeding, it is hardly surprising that the Commission does not engage in subtle quantitative analyses of markets touched by cooperative research. Is it realistic to think that a case-by-case rule of reason, administered by antitrust agencies as we know them in the United States, would or could contribute more to the public interest?

6. Conclusion

Technological change is indeed a fundamental element of economic progress. Technological cooperation should not necessarily be treated the same way as price cooperation. Pure technological cooperation is not always more beneficial than cooperation in production or marketing. Given the difficulties theoretical and empirical of determining which agreements serve the public interest - difficulties due in good measure to the incentives held by powerful firms to manipulate strategically the rate and direction of inventive activity, facilitating the exclusion of actual and potential rivals - it is not obvious that governments should opt at the moment for libertine tolerance of cooperative research, whether or not it is accompanied by cooperative production.[66] Presumptive acceptance of cooperation among relatively small firms is not inconsistent with this conclusion; but it is unlikely to affect appreciably the rate of technological change, the direction of technological change, or the position of the national economy in the international division of labor.

Bibliography

Adams, William J. (1970). "Firm size and research activity: France and the United States", *Quarterly journal of economics*, 84 (August), 386-409.

d'Aspremont, Claude and Alexis Jacquemin (1988). "Cooperative and non-cooperative R&D in duopoly with spillovers", *American economic review*, 78 (December), 1133-1137.

Blair, John M. (1972). *Economic concentration: structure, behavior, and public policy*, New York, Harcourt Brace Jovanovic.

Brodley, Joseph F. (1990). "Antitrust law and innovation cooperation", *Journal of economic perspectives*, 4 (Summer), 97-112.

Congressional Budget Office (1990). *Using R&D consortia for commercial innovation: SEMATECH, x-ray lithography, and high-resolution systems*. Washington: Congressional Budget Office (July).

Dasgupta, Partha (1986). "The theory of technological competition", in Stiglitz, Joseph E. and G. Frank Mathewson (eds), *New developments in the analysis of market structure*, Cambridge, MIT Press.

Dasgupta, Partha and Joseph Stiglitz (1980). "Uncertainty, industrial structure, and the speed of R&D", *Bell journal of economics*, 11 (Spring), 1-28.

Gilbert, Richard J. and David M. G. Newbery (1982). "Preemptive patenting and the persistence of monopoly", *American economic review*, 72 (June), 514-526.

Grossman, Gene M. and Carl Shapiro (1986). "Research joint ventures: an antitrust analysis", *Journal of law, economics, and organization*, 2 (Fall), 315-337.

Jorde, Thomas M. and David J. Teece (1990). "Innovation and cooperation: implications for competition and antitrust", *Journal of economic perspectives*, 4 (Summer), 75-96.

Katz, Michael L. (1986). "An analysis of cooperative research and development", *Rand journal of economics*, 17 (Winter), 527-543.

Katz, Michael L. and Janusz A. Ordover (1990). "R&D cooperation and competition", *Brookings papers on economic activity*, (Microeconomics), 137-203.

Levin, Richard, Alvin Klevorick, Richard Nelson and Sidney Winter (1987). "Appropriating the returns from industrial research and development", *Brookings papers on economic activity*, (Winter), 783-820.

Nelson, Richard R. (1961). "Uncertainty, learning, and the economics of parallel research and development efforts", *Review of economics and statistics*, 43 (November), 351-364.

Ordover, Janusz A. and Robert D. Willig (1985). "Antitrust for high-technology industries: assessing research joint ventures and mergers", *Journal of law and economics*, 28 (May), 311-333.

Saxonhouse, Gary R. (1985). "Japanese cooperative R&D ventures: a market evaluation", Discussion paper no. 156, Research seminar in international economics, The University of Michigan (August).

Scott, John T. (1988). "Diversification versus co-operation in R & D investment", *Managerial and decision economics*, 9, 173-186.

Scott, John T. (1989). "Historical and economic perspectives of the National Cooperative Research Act", in Link, Albert N. and Gregory Tassey (eds.), *Cooperative research and development: the industry-university-government relationship*, Boston, Kluwer Academic Publishers.

Shapiro, Carl and Robert D. Willig (1990). "On the antitrust treatment of production joint ventures", *Journal of economic perspectives*, 4 (Summer), 113-129.

White, Lawrence J. (1971). *The automobile industry since 1945*, Cambridge, Harvard University Press.

Notes

1. The spirit of the times, and some formal tests of its conventional wisdom, are described in Adams (1970).
2. As Grossman and Shapiro (1986) point out, "the (Department of Justice) has never challenged a pure (research joint venture) without ancillary restraints..." The only major proceeding in this area, discussed in note 43 and accompanying text, is *United States v. Automobile Manufacturers Ass'n*, 307 F.Supp. 617 (1969).
3. I shall limit my discussion here to the approach of the European Communities. On the perception of its counterpart in Japan, see Jorde and Teece (1990).

4. I.e., unaccompanied by cooperation in production, in distribution, and in the dissemination of intellectual property.
5. "II. The Commission takes the view that the following agreements do not restrict competition. ... 3. Agreements having as their sole object: (a) The joint implementation of research and development projects, (b) The joint placing of research and development contracts, (c) The sharing out of research and development projects among participating enterprises." Notice Concerning Agreements, Decisions and Concerted Practices in the Field of Cooperation between Enterprises, JO C75/3, 29.7.1968, as corrected. See also Article 4(2)(3) of Council Regulation (EEC) No. 17/62, JO No. 13, 22.2.1962, p. 204/62, as amended, which exempts agreements having joint research and development as their sole object from the notification requirement of Article 4(1). Note that "research" includes development "up to the stage of industrial application."
6. Commission Notice of 19 December 1977 Concerning Agreements of Minor Importance which Do Not Fall under Article 85(1) of the Treaty Establishing the European Economic Community, OJ C313/3, 29.12.1977, replacing a notice bearing the same title, JO C64/1, 2.6.1970. The 1970 notice had established a threshold for combined annual sales of 15 or 20 million units of account, depending on whether the relevant enterprises were engaged primarily in production or in distribution activities. The threshold for combined market share was the same as that in the 1977 notice. Unlike the 1977 notice, the 1970 notice allowed violation of either threshold as long as the violation amounted to less than 10 percent and lasted no more than two consecutive years.
7. Commission Regulation (EEC) No. 418/85 of 19 December 1984 on the Application of Article 85(3) of the Treaty to Categories of Research and Development Cooperation Agreements, OJ L53/5, 22.2.1985.
8. These are contained in Article 2 of Regulation 418/85. For example, the cooperation must have a specific objective, and all parties to the agreement must have access to the results of the cooperative effort. If the agreement does not provide for cooperative application of the results, then each party must be free without the approval of the rest to exploit those results as it sees fit.
9. See Article 7(1) of Regulation 418/85.
10. Under Article 8 of Regulation 17/62, exemptions to the prohibitions of Article 85(1) must be finite in length. In principle, the Commission tries to tailor an exemption's length to its appraisal for the relevant industry of the amounts of time needed for research to bear fruit and for bugs to be removed from new products. Upon expiry of the initial exemption, or alteration of the circumstances which prompted it, the Commission is allowed to renew or reconsider. The Commission has made use of this authority. See, for example, *Sopelem/Vickers*, Commission Decision No. 78/251/EEC, OJ L70/47,

13.3.1978; and *Sopelem/Vickers*, Commission Decision No. 81/1066/ EEC, OJ L391/1, 31.12.1981.

11. Public Law 98-462, 98 Stat. 1815, 15 USC 4301.
12. Note, however, that duplication of effort and result do not imply total waste. Duplication may develop in each explorer the capacity to absorb knowledge created by others and/or the capacity to participate in future rounds of exploratory activity.
13. The asymmetry in information available to the two groups of rivals can be justified in terms of the asymmetry in historical contact with the inventor.
14. I assume that the social cost of the research exceeds the social benefit. Note that without cooperation the potential explorer has no incentive to undertake the cost-reducing research.
15. This point is recognized by Katz (1986. p. 528), when he cites Dasgupta and Stiglitz (1980) to the effect that firms might have incentives to engage in socially excessive research.
16. Gilbert and Newbery (1982) discuss this syndrome under the heading of sleeping patents. Often, but not always, sleeping technologies and products are socially inferior to others already in use. To the extent that cooperators can preempt rivals credibly without actually engaging in research on sleeping technologies and products, preemption reduces the likelihood of undesirable investment in research.
17. I say "probably" because I can imagine two circumstances in which such research might prove socially desirable. First, to the extent that participation in research helps the explorer to absorb knowledge created by others and to participate in future rounds of exploratory activy, it may serve a public purpose even if the nominal results of the project lack value. Second, in a world of uncertainty, products and processes explored ex ante for the purpose of shelving might ex post become privately and socially desirable to introduce.
18. David Encaoua and I are currently developing models of strategic research on technologies with inefficiently large scales.
19. Gilbert and Newbery (1982) discuss the potential complementarity of these two types of strategic behavior.
20. For example, Ordover and Willig (1985) may underestimate the danger of preemption when they claim (p. 332) that "significant R&D competition from other firms removes incentives for R&D-repressing co-optation".
21. As Schmalensee put it, in comments following Katz and Ordover (1990), "this topic is such that the more careful and the more detailed the models, the more opposed noncomparable effects one comes up with. It is, of course, at this point where one turns to the empirical work" (p. 196).
22. Witness the elaborate, cumbersome, and unenlightening definitions of cooperative research contained in recent American and European legislation (respectively, Section 2(a)(6) of the National Cooperative Research Act of 1984 and Articles 1(2) and 1(3) of Commission Regulation (EEC) No. 418/85).

23. The following passage exemplifies a complete description of purpose as published in the *Federal Register*: "Bellcore and NEC entered into an agreement effective November 9, 1987, to collaborate in research on broadband technology and the establishment of standards for interfacing and cross-connecting signals in particular formats, such as the emerging SONET format". Antitrust Division, Notice Pursuant to the National Cooperative Research Act of 1984; Bell Communications Research, Inc., 53 *FR* 5059, February 19, 1988.
24. In the words of Katz and Ordover (1990, p. 146), "Case studies are particularly valuable in this area because the details of organizational structure may be important determinants of the effects of R&D cooperation, and to date little work has been done analyzing these issues from a theoretical perspective".
25. Examples of leading Commission decisions on cooperative research are: *Eurogypsum*, JO L57/9, 5.3.1968, (1968) CMLR D1; *ACEC/Berliet*, JO L201/7, 12.8.1968, (1968) CMLR D35; *Henkel/Colgate*, JO L14/14, 18.1.1972; *MAN/SAVIEM*, JO L31/29, 4.2.1972, (1974) 2 CMLR D123; *Rank/SOPELEM*, OJ L29/20, 3.2.1975; *Vacuum Interruptors*, OJ L48/2, 19.2.1977; *Beecham/Parke, Davis*, OJ L70/11, 21.3.1979; *Vacuum Interrupters*, OJ L383/1, 31.12.1980; *VW/MAN*, OJ L376/1, 31.12.1983; *Carbon Gas Technologie*, OJ L376/17, 31.12.1983; *BP/Kellogg*, OJ L369/6, 31.12.1985; *BBC Brown Boveri*, OJ L301/68, 4.11.1988; *Continental/Michelin*, OJ L305/33, 10.11.1988.
26. Saxonhouse also examined the effects of each Japanese agreement on the securities-market values of rival American companies. Despite the absence of impact on the market values of their participants, nine of the twenty Japanese agreements affected negatively the market values of their American rivals.
27. At least one piece of evidence from the EC corroborates this finding. In renewing a cooperative research agreement between Sopelem and Vickers, the Commmission noted that the combined market share of the parties had not increased during the life of the initial exemption. *Sopelem/Vickers*, Commission Decision No. 81/1066/EEC, OJ L391/1, 31.12.1981.
28. See note 9 and accompanying text.
29. Commission of the European Communities, *Seventeenth Report on Competition Policy*, pp. 37-38; Commission of the European Communities, *Eighteenth Report on Competition Policy*, p. 41. Note that Article 7(4) of Regulation 418/85 permits parties who had notified agreements prior to March 1, 1985, in connection with requests for *individual* exemptions (under Council Regulation 17/62), to request application of the opposition procedure. One apparent example of such a request is reported in *BP International/Kellogg*, Commission Decision No. 85/560/EEC, OJ L369/6, 31.12.1985, discussed below. As a result, the opposition procedure has been used in more cases than the text might lead one to believe. Unfortunately, the Commission's annual report on competition policy does not reveal

the number of requests for application of the opposition procedure to agreements notified before March 1, 1985. Presumably, this number should now be declining rapidly over time.

30. Commission of the European Communities, *Eighteenth Report on Competition Policy*, p. 41. Note the dovetail with the American experience as summarized by Katz and Ordover (1990, p. 170): "It is fair to say that U.S. firms have not rushed into registering under the NCRA to obtain its limited protections".
31. *Sopelem/Vickers*, Commission Decision No. 78/251/EEC, OJ L70/47, 13.3.1978. The initial exemption decision could refer to research results because the agreement had been notified (February 26, 1976) and implemented (April 17, 1975) well before the Commission got around to making its decision December 21, 1977).
32. *Sopelem/Vickers*, Commission Decision No. 81/1066/EEC, OJ L391/1, 31.12.1981.
33. The absence of true joint venture seems to occur in the United States as well. According to the Congressional Budget Office (1990, pp. 112-113), "While consortia by their nature agree on a research agenda, little evidence exists of more centralization than this". In Japan, "the interfirm cooperation which does take place is quite secondary to the research and development which each firm conducts independently of cooperative efforts" (Saxonhouse, 1985, p. 19).
34. In *Carbon Gas Technologie*, Commission Decision No. 83/669/EEC, OJ L376/17, 31.12.1983, for example, before making the case for an individual exemption, the Commission went so far as to say (p. 20), "True, each of the groups to which the parties belong would be able on its own to achieve the object of the cooperation..."
35. Scott's measure of appropriability is that of Levin et al. (1987).
36. A current examination of this information, which appeared too recently to receive adequate attention here - appears in Katz and Ordover (1990).
37. See note 39. The European evidence confirms the prevalence of absolutely and relatively large companies among the list of cooperators: Henkel and Colgate, Michelin and Continental, were all among the leading sellers in large, tight-knit oligopolies at the times they agreed to cooperate. Note, however, that this finding accords well with the theoretical prediction, emphasized by Katz and Ordover (1990, p. 168), that cooperation is especially likely to increase research where product-market competition is restrained.
38. Seller-concentration is measured as the four-firm concentration ratio adjusted for a variety of factors including competition from imports.
39. For example: "consider the Software Productivity Consortium which is developing complex computer software. ...the venture includes all of the largest (by sales or R&D) eight firms listed in *Business Week*'s aerospace category. Other important firms in aerospace are also included in the venture, but do not appear in *Business Week*'s category because of their diversified sales" (1988, p. 184). Note that Saxonhouse (1985, p. 20) finds the opposite membership pattern in

Japan: Fearing an obligation to share their existing stock of knowledge, leading sellers with established technological advantages do not like to join governmentally sponsored research consortia.

40. Incidentally, Brodley (1990) points out correctly that as difficult as it might be to measure concentration and rivalry in product markets, it is harder still to measure them in research. Exercises in defining the latter border on unadulterated speculation.
41. *Video Cassette Recorders*, Commission Decision No. 78/156/EEC, OJ L47/42, 18.2.1978. Note that this case does not involve cooperative research.
42. I.e., television sets conforming to the PAL or SECAM standard. Several other manufacturers, Japanese and European, were in the process of developing recorders suited to the purpose.
43. *United States v. Automobile Manufacturers Ass'n*, 307 F.Supp. 617 (1969); see also *United States v. Motor Vehicle Manufacturers Ass'n*, 1982-83 Trade Cas. (CCH) Para. 65,175, October 28, 1982.
44. On the sources of scale economies in the automotive industry, compare White (1971, chs. 3-4, esp. pp. 24, 51-52) with Blair (1972, pp. 133-144).
45. *Henkel/Colgate*, Commission Decision No. 72/41/EEC, JO L14/14, 18.1.1972.
46. *Continental/Michelin*, Commission Decision No. 88/555/EEC, OJ L305/33, 10.11.1988. Worldwide, the ten largest manufacturers accounted for 84 percent of relevant production; Michelin and Continental ranked second and fourth, respectively, with 22 percent between them of the business.
47. *VW/MAN*, Commission Decision No. 83/668/EEC, OJ L376/1, 31.12.1983.
48. See note 5 and accompanying text. In the notice itself, the Commission qualifies its encouragement of cooperative research by pointing out that it might consider competition to be restricted if: (1) in the absence of joint research activity, the parties agree to refrain from individual research; (2) the parties agree to limit their individual research in areas outside the agreed scope of the joint research; (3) the parties agree to specialize in research agendas without agreeing to share the results of their research; (4) the parties agree to exclude, to a degree inexplicable in terms of their proportionate research efforts, certain among them from exploiting the fruits of cooperative research; (5) the parties agree that under no circumstances will they license third parties; (6) the parties agree also on "the practical exploitation of the results of research and development work carried out jointly, particularly if the participating enterprises undertake or agree to manufacture only the products or types of product developed jointly or to share out future production among themselves".
49. *Beecham/Parke, Davis*, Commission Decision No. 79/298/EEC, OJ L70/11, 21.3.1979.
50. *Continental/Michelin*, Commission Decision No. 88/555/EEC, OJ L305/33, 11.11.1988.

51. As reported in the text accompanying note 29 above, the Commission has received just five notifications under Article 7(1) of Regulation 418/85. In one case, the Commission decided that the agreement qualified automatically for exemption (because all of its ancillary restraints appeared on the regulation's white list). In a second case, the Commission decided not to oppose block exemption. In two other cases, the Commission decided to deny block exemption (despite the absence of black restraints) but consider the agreement for individual exemption. Regarding the last case, the Commission revealed neither the identities of the parties nor the status of their agreement (*Seventeenth Report on Competition Policy*, Comp.Rep.EC 1987, pp. 37-38). I suspect, however, that the case in question was *BBC Brown Boveri*, Commission Decision No. 88/154/EEC, OJ L301/68, 4.11.1988. This case involved an agreement notified on June 17, 1987, and regarding which the Commission denied block exemption but granted individual exemption on October 11, 1988.
52. Article 7(4) is explained above in note 29. A case in point is *BP International/Kellogg*, Commission Decision No. 85/560/EEC, OJ L369/6, 31.12.1985. As part of the research it conducted on catalysts, undertaken with petroleum refining in mind, BP had discovered a catalyst suitable for use on plants designed to produce ammonia. It agreed with Kellogg, a leading designer and builder of such plants, to develop jointly an ammoania plant suitable for exploitation of the new catalyst. The Commission refused to grant a block exemption because the research leading to the new catalyst had been conducted prior to the agreement between the two companies. Hence the cooperation in question was considered to involve less the pursuit of new knowledge than its commercial exploitation. The Commission did, however, grant an individual exemption to the agreement.
53. *Beecham/Parke, Davis*, Commission Decision No. 79/298/EEC, OJ L70/11, 21.3.1979.
54. The Commission evaluates geographic divisions of the EC market along two dimensions: duration of the restraint, and degree of the restraint. With respect to the latter, it distinguishes between so-called active and passive sales. By "active" the Commission means that a seller solicits business; by "passive", the Commission means that a seller merely responds to orders placed by a buyer. The Commission is especially unsympathetic to long-term bans on passive as well as active sales. See *BBC Brown Boveri*, Commission Decision No. 88/154/EEC, OJ L301/68.
55. *Beecham/Parke, Davis*, Commission Decision No. 79/298/EEC, OJ L70/11, 21.3.1979
56. *VW/MAN*, Commission Decision No. 83/668/EEC, OJ L376/1, 31.12.1983.
57. Commission of the European Communities, *Eighth Report on Competition Policy*, pp. 77-78. The Commission justified this added condition in the following terms: "But the Commission could not be entirely confident that the results of the research could be used freely

so long as one of the parties was obliged to obtain the consent of the other before issuing a licence to a third party. ... The relevant market ... is, after all, very much an oligopolistic market surrounded by high barriers to entry..." (*Ibid*, p. 78). Interestingly, the Commission gives the impression of being surprised as well as disappointed that Henkel and Colgate chose to coordinate separate research instead of conducting joint research: "In its Decision of 23 December 1971 authorizing the cooperation between the two undertakings, the Commission was under the impression that the joint research would be carried out by a joint venture set up by the parties. Later, however, the parties opted to carry out the research individually and exchange results" (*Ibid*, p. 77). Could the Commission have come to believe that it had erred in exempting initially this agreement between two of four major players in an important industry? If so, perhaps the Commission's new demand was calculated to be unacceptable to the parties.

58. Notice IV/148/71-E of 15.3.1971; *Bulletin of the European Communities*, 5-1971, p. 40; (197.1) CMLR D31.
59. After receipt of the Commission's statement of objections but before the Commission issued a formal decision. To my knowledge, this and the renewal in *Henkel/Colgate* are the only recorded cases of complete abandonment of cooperative research in response to actual or threatened action by the Commission.
60. In the words of Ordover and Willig (1985, p. 313), "We are aware of no suitably mechanistic formula for characterizing those (research joint ventures) that should come within the scope of a 'safe harbor' protection clause".
61. This is not to say, of course, that the automatic exemption provision of 418/85 has not been useful. Since agreements qualifying for automatic exemption need not be notified, there is no good information on how many such agreements exist.
62. Each party is allowed to produce certain components for, or models of, the new product. It then purchases its requirements of other components or models from fellow cooperators.
63. On occasion, the Commission seems to argue that the existence of larger producers in the industry demonstrates the desirability of concentrating the group's output in a single party. On that logic, however, the existence of smaller producers would demonstrate the lack of need for cooperative specialization.
64. Most research agreements that result in a Commission decision under Regulation 17/62 are found to restrict competition because they aim to prevent each cooperator from gaining technological advantage over the rest. (This is considered anticompetitive even if each cooperator is no more ex ante than a potential competitor in the relevant market.) Secondarily, the Commission points to the combined market share of the cooperators and to seller-concentration in the relevant market.
65. The Commission does not often consider other structural evidence, such as the existence of durable interlocks with or between enter-

prises outside the agreement. For example, in *VW/MAN*, it nowhere mentions that MAN had already concluded a similar agreement with SAVIEM covering trucks in the next larger weight range.

66. In his comments on Katz and Ordover (1990), Fisher puts it this way: "I take a very skeptical view of a policy of allowing cooperation where one is unsure that it is a good idea" (p. 194).

12 COMPETITION AND COMBINATION IN THE EUROPEAN MARKET ECONOMY

HENK W. DE JONG

"La multitude qui ne se réduit pas à l'unité est confusion"

PASCAL

1. Introduction: Capitalism and the Market Economy - a Dichotomy?

So general a theme as I have chosen befits a valedictory address. It is loaded with a plenitude of current events and covers the past as well as the future. It encompasses the widening European market, but also the motives, moves, strategies, and results of various types of enterprises. Nor are Governments - primarily those of the European Economic Community - absent as players influencing the scene, while, last but not least, Europe is not an isolated entity, but is intertwined with the other powers in the world economy.

In such a broad context change is pervasive. Since Schumpeter wrote down these words in *Capitalism, Socialism and Democracy*, it is a platitude to say that "capitalism is change"; still, the expression contains a whole research programme concerning the why's, how's, whereabout's, and what for's. The heart of the matter, it seems to me, is in those terms used in the title: the market economy, competition and combination, so let me elucidate and define how I understand them.

The French economic historian Fernand Braudel, in a masterly survey summarizing his voluminous works, took up an old line of thinking by differentiating the market economy both from material life as a largely autarchic substrate and from capitalism as a dominating, hierarchical, superimposed and superior system.[1] In the market economy, exchange and competition prevail, linking production and consumption according to the scheme devised by Aristoteles[2] and adopted by Marx, in which goods are exchanged for money, which in its turn is being exchanged for goods. On the other hand, capitalism is supposed to break this chain, by substituting the money-goods-money circulation for a market economy's exchange process, because the intermediating economic agent - be it a large merchant, an industrial entrepreneur, or a financier - knows both ends of the exchange. He is informed about the conditions of production as well as about those of consumption; consequently, he is able to calculate and amass the profits, to dispose of capital, to eliminate or control competition, and to command the surplus which the market economy generates.[3] This triad division of the total economy is likened to a pyramid with three layers, of which the highest - capitalism - lives on, benefits from the lower ones, and shifts its position through time.

This type of reasoning, which Braudel exposed with all the forces of his brilliant command of facts, circumstances, and language, is shared by many others. For example, the Catholic moral philosopher Von Nell-Breuning (who was also a prominent economist) makes use of the distinction, though he takes out the sting of Braudel's scheme by stating, first, that the profit making of the capitalists can also occur in pre-capitalist regimes, and, more importantly, that "the great successes of the capitalist economy can, altogether, only have been achieved by means of productive services".[4]

For another example, two US economists, discussing mergers and acquisitions in the age of Wall Street, state that the great restructuring movement in the US economy - the contest for corporate control - features elements of both greed and lust. The arena is Wall Street, where America's business elite is playing a game for profit without production: "The game is played not to enhance manufacturing efficiency and productivity, not for research, development and technological innovation, not to expand jobs for workers and raise the national standard of living, but in order to make profits for the players." That is "... profit without the burden of producing durable, tangible, real economic wealth".[5]

Even Schumpeter came close to these views by stating that by "... our economic system, we mean an economic system characterized by private property (private initiative), by production for a market and by the phenomenon of credit, this phenomenon being the *differentia specifica* distinguishing the "capitalist system" from other species..."[6] Consequently, Schumpeter was once induced to write that, in capitalism, production is only a by-product of the achievement of profits.

2. A Dubious Division

Notwithstanding the high authorities thus separating capitalism from the market economy, I do not follow this procedure, because it is utterly unconvincing. Quite apart from the arguments advanced by the moral philosophers who hold that only people, but not a system (unless unjustly personalized) can misbehave, there are two main question marks.

First, the schemes advanced and contrasted, viz. goods-money-goods, and money-goods-money, are both finite, circular presentations of on-going processes. In reality, the market economy is not only an endless process, an infinite series of affairs in and between markets, which may expand or contract, but has a structure (together producing results) as well. Structure and process are mutually linked, in an endless sequence and nothing is said about the structures, how they arise and adapt.

It is a serious error in economic thinking to artificially and schematically give causal precedence to the one over the other, and so, as in the Braudel scheme, to superimpose a capitalist structure upon a market economic process. Is it really true, as Braudel says, that the successive centres of "capitalism" have done nothing but copy their predecessors? "Les pays du Nord n'ont fait que prendre la place occupée longtemps et brillamment avant eux par les vieux centres capitalistes de la Méditerranée. Ils n'ont rien inventé, ni dans la technique, ni dans le maniement des affaires. Amsterdam a copié Venise, comme Londres copiera Amsterdam, comme New York copiera Londres".[7]

Withholding any innovative influence of structures like the East India Companies or the Bank of Amsterdam, or of the Bank of England upon the enfolding process of the market economies, such a view closes itself off from an investigation into the mutually productive causation of structure and process.

That brings me to the second point. It can hardly be shown that markets of a so-called market economy work differently from those of the so-called "capitalism". As Dempsey has rightly remarked, the latter term is superfluous: "... there is no such thing as capitalism. The word is incapable of scientific definition".[8] An economy with Schumpeterian entrepreneurs, but using savings only, instead of credit creation, is capable of working as well as the so-called capitalism, probably even less hectic and fluctuating. Do not the W. German and Japanese economies, with their high rates of savings, demonstrate the truth of this proposition? The credit lever predominantly used in the Anglo-Saxon economies is a powerful, but often destabilizing substitute for an insufficient rate of spontaneous savings. Moreover, capital markets and their institutions like banks show similar development processes as industries producing goods.[9]

3. The Dialectics of Competition and Combination

This second argument leads me to the other terms: competition and combination. All types of markets, whether of goods, of services, or of such "capitalist" signature as finance or company control, are subjected to the forces of competition and combination. That is, as long as they are not artificially closed or regulated by the authoritative hand of state or local authorities, they will show, sooner or later, the dialectical movements of intensifying competition leading up to combination, and, in reverse, of combination being undermined by increasing competition. Competition is understood here to comprise not only horizontal rivalry between sellers *or* buyers, but also the vertical rivalry between sellers *and* buyers for the best price or conditions.[10] It is driven by the expansionary mood of the human race, striving for surplus value to be achieved through the conversion of lower into higher values. Alongside this creative dimension, competition also has a distributional aspect: imitation and emulation erase the gains for the innovator and allocate them to households and production factors. In addition, the demand side - primarily the large trading buyers - is of major importance, especially in setting the upper price limit in a market.

What was said before expresses the idea of the competitive cycle, in which entrepreneurial moves based on innovations, superior organizational efficiency, or an efficacious copying with uncertainty, lead up to profits (being a net-economic surplus of income over costs). Such profits are subsequently undermined and eroded by the imitating and emulating actions of rivals or by the countervailing actions of the players on the demand side of the market, who ultimately threaten to bring the industry into a state of profitlessness. The market players then have resort to the various forms of combination - be it cartels, collusions, alliances, mergers or take-overs. Still, this is usualy not the final stage. If dominant positions are established by means of such combinations, they will be contested, unless barriers are created against new entry by either the state or the combinations themselves (in either horizontal or vertical linkages, or both). Even if barriers exist or are instituted, they can often be circumvented by producers or sellers coming up with innovations or differentiated supplies carving up markets. The computer industry offers a prominent example amongst others: the mainframe market, for long dominated by IBM, is contested by the Japanese, and is succeeded by mini-computers, PC's, and, recently, the laptop machines. Moreover, the software market increasingly subjects the hardware section to its standards (see The Financial Times of 20-4-1990).

In other words, the relationship between supply and demand is all-important: if, because of, say, an innovation, demand growth exceeds supplies, there will be a sellers' market, with initial price increases, until more supplies (e.g. based on larger scale output or more numerous sellers) reduces these, mostly to lower levels. In a buyers' market, which may come when market growth stabilizes, or a cyclical downturn occurs, the reverse takes place: sellers try to stem the price declines by means of combination, capacity reduction, or withdrawal. Such processes are more real and more general than most academic economists would admit or consider in their models. In other words, equilibrium in a market is an exception rather than the rule, and market cycles or fluctuations with their varying degrees of regularity, amplitude, and periodicity, occur in nearly all branches of economic activity.[11]

4. Waves of Combinations...

Now, my hypothesis is that combination movements - but primarily mergers and take-overs - occur when competition intensifies because of a shift in the demand-supply relationship towards a buyers' market.[12] This is a necessary condition and is expressed by the saying that "the urge to merge is fed by the need to compete". However, there is also a sufficient condition to be satisfied, for a merger or take-over requires an uncertain investment, whether it is financed by cash, equity or debt. And so "the will to merge derives from the spur of gains". This double condition, in which intensified competition acts as the stick and the prospect of gains (or the avoidance of losses) provides the carrot, has been the mechanism, I think, of the four major merger waves of the past hundred years.

Those waves of combinations are one of the most striking phenomena of the western market economies, for, notwithstanding their varying forms and types in the several countries, they did occur more or less at the same time in the economically developed continents of the world. There was the turn of the century boom, with huge consolidations taking place in the United States and Britain, cartel formation and banking mergers in Germany and other continental countries, and the formation of the Zaibatsu in Japan.[13]

In the twenties, likewise, combinations like Unilever, Daimler-Benz, IG Farben, Vereinigte Stahlwerke, the four Britisch railway systems, ICI, United Steel, et cetera, arose parallel to the US consolidations such as Bethlehem Steel and National Dairy Products, the latter one alone absorbing

360 other firms during that decade. And in Japan, the Zaibatsus first, and the cartels later in the period, extended their market positions.

The European merger wave of the sixties can be used to illustrate the central thesis. Several conditions converged to provide the competitive stick: the formation of the EEC in 1958 - which accelerated the tariff reductions anticipated for 12 years into a period of 10 years, abolished quotas, and provided freedom of establishment; the currency convertibility of 1959, the OECD trade liberation, and the penetration of US multinationals onto European shores increased competition.

When one looks at the flat or declining export manufacturing prices of the six continental countries that integrated their economies, and at the same time sees the fast rise of foreign penetration of the respective domestic markets, the spur of mutual competition becomes understandable. At the same time, the growth of economic output was more than satisfactory, inflation rates were low, energy prices were declining, thus creating the necessary conditions for investments - whether internal or external.[14] Consequently, the merger boom developed, the more so as cartel agreements were undermined by foreign competition and became suspect under the newly instituted EEC rules.[15] Detailed figures of the mergers and take-overs in the leading continental economies of Germany, France, and the Benelux countries are available. They show a three to fourfold jump in the number of operations, a two and a half to threefold increase in the number of firms being absorbed, and a fifty percent rise in the number of mergers and take-overs per firm per annum between the fifties and the sixties. As usual, a limited number of already large firms carried out a disproportionately large share of these operations, and the distribution over the industrial sectors was equally lopsided.[16]

What about the outsider - the United Kingdom? In that country, cut off from EC integration by its own insular policy and General de Gaulle's veto on entry later on, the merger boom had started earlier and was probably more broadly based than on the continent. Moreover, hostile take-overs made their appearance. But the two main causes were not fundamentally different: several forces - among them enlarged scale, wider markets, the policies against restrictive business practices - made for more competition; others, such as Government promotion of merger (e.g. the IRC), but mainly the real or presumed advantages in a promising economic environment of growth and stability, provided the lure.[17]

The fourth merger wave of the eighties, starting in 1983 on the Continent and - again - somewhat earlier in the UK, can be explained in a similar way. Fiercer competition was provided by the surplus capacities generated during the severe 1979-1983 recession, the technologically based innovations displacing older products and systems, rising Japanese competition, and the liberalizing policies of most European governments. However, as from 1983 hopes were entertained of renewed economic growth. They were soon fulfilled when profits, trade, and real GNP began to rise. That is why profits, merger activity, and - somewhat lagged - investments in fixed capital assets rose together:[18] process and structure are correlated and mutually influence one another.

5. ... and their Petering out

The mechanism outlined thus requires the fulfilment of both a necessary and a sufficient condition, and the absence of one or both of them explains the decades when combination movements were absent or on a relatively low level.[19] Thus, in the fifties - a period of good prospects and profits in business, but with closed markets - there was a paucity of mergers. During the thirties and seventies (since 1973/4), to the contrary, there was much competition - if only resulting from the overcapacities - but economic prospects were such that mergers and take-overs took place at a much reduced level - if at all. (Only W. Germany and the Netherlands, two countries with a relatively stable and modest growth, had a rising tide during the second half of the latter decade.)

The answer to the question why merger booms end can now also be given: either because the competitive intensity is reduced again to a level acceptable to the main firms in their markets - that is: they will have gained sufficient control of them - or because the advantages to be gained by further combinations become so small or their prospects so uncertain, that they are not worthwhile. (Rising prices for the firms to be taken over obviously play their role.) Both conditions were fulfilled at the end of the twenties, when markets such as steel, chemicals, margarines, soaps, matches, oil products, artificial fibres, coal, et cetera, were sufficiently consolidated, and, moreover, after 1929, economic prospects were severely dimmed. Similarly, the merger wave of the sixties was arrested after market concentration had risen appreciably,[20] and stagflation dampened the economic outlook. Finally, it is noteworthy that merger waves have occurred in a context of positive economic growth, low or declining inflation rates, and a far quicker rise of international trade and investment than of output.[21]

6. Other Theories: Sufficiently General?

What alternative explanations do we have? First, combinations are said to be managerially inspired. To run a bigger group boosts prestige, income, and power, and so the quest for size is said to be inspired by greed, prestige, and power. However, either the economist has to assume that such psychic motivations are *always* entertained by managers, in which case the merger *waves* cannot be explained; or, such motivations would tend to fluctuate heavily through time, in which case the instability in human behaviour would follow from external events. But then, it is precisely those events which have to be made clear.

Do merger waves reflect the replacement of bad managers by good ones? Or, stated otherwise: do the bidders have superior information justifying a take-over?

Again, a number of questions crop up: Why is the combination movement so lopsided, both in time and in sectors of activity? Superior information must be assumed to be always present in every market and in every period of time. Some players always know more than a host of others, and this argument therefore seems to be at odds with the irregular evidence. Moreover, empirical research has not uncovered a systematically better performance for the merger intensive firms, once one looks beyond the one week or the one month ex-ante and ex-post merger events so dear to the hearts of financial economists. Such very short periods are virtually useless in judging merger performances, because superior management needs more time to achieve results. Even for those longer terms, industrial organization economists have not been able to establish a better performance for the firms or industries which were merger intensive.

7. Mergers and Efficiency

What about the efficiency hypothesis, or, as it was formerly called, the synergy explanation? (In the eighties, the word was "critical mass", meaning a size to reap all the available benefits.)

It is a well-known finding from research, undertaken in all countries for which evidence is available, that the merger intensity rises with the size of the firm. The larger the firm, the more mergers and take-overs it effectuates on average per annum. In reverse, the decline is continuous if irregular, the more the size of firm class is reduced. Merger activity of those firms comprising the fourth group of 25 or the tenth group of 25, respectively, is only one-fifth or one-tenth the merger intensity of the top 25 firms.[22] Given this heavy merger and take-over activity of the very largest firms in the world, one should expect their profitability to be better than that of smaller firms undertaking less combinations.

Now, figuring out the respective profitability of the 50 largest firms in Europe and in the world, and comparing this with that of the 50 firms with a rank order of 250 to 300 (in 1973), or 450 to 500 (in 1989), it turns out that the average profitability of the 50 largest firms in Europe was 3.7%, as against 4.9% for the group numbered 250 to 300. Similarly, in 1989, after the world-wide merger wave of the eighties, the fifty largest companies in the world achieved a rate of profit on sales as well as on assets of 4.3% as against rates of 4.5% to 5.0% for the firms with a ranking from 450 to 500. The picture is substantially the same if one compares the Rate on Capital Employed of the 500 largest European firms, which includes gross profits and interest paid, divided by total capital employed.[23]

Thus, I have been unable to find a better profitability for the largest firms when compared with the smallest ones in those lists of the 500 most important companies, both in general and in the various sectors to which they belong. However, it might be that the sectoral composition of the largest firms differs from the sectoral composition of the companies down the lists. And sectoral profitability is known to differ appreciably. For example, pharmaceutical firms earn on average 9.7% profit on sales, against only 2.3% on average for motor vehicle companies. So, if the largest companies were indeed more than proportionally represented in the low profit sectors, this might depress their results without justifying a conclusion about inefficiency.

To correct for this influence, I have constructed a normative profit rate based on the sectoral composition of the 25 largest European firms and the median profit rate earned in those sectors by the 500 companies in general.[24] It turns out that those large companies did achieve better results than the normative rate.

Does this outcome - a factual rate of profits on sales of 5.13% as against a normative rate of 4.41% - speak in favour of the efficiency argument of size?

The answer is: not yet. If similar groups of 25 firms, also in the very smallest size classes, would be able to achieve better factual than normative profit rates too, then the deviation might be attributable to something different than the size-efficiency relationship. This is indeed the case. For the group of the 25 smallest firms there was also a higher rate of factual profits than of normatively calculated profits, and the deviation was even stronger: 6.19% against 5.06%.

8. The Quest for Stability

Further inspection of those deviations, also among other groups of companies than the largest and the smallest ones, reveals that they are strongly influenced by the presence in those groups of both highly profitable firms and loss-making companies. And, it would appear that the variation in profit performance is stronger among smaller firms than among the largest corporations.[25] This vindicates what we concluded earlier, namely that "The reward of being a large firm appears to be not higher profitability, but greater security, as expressed by profit stability".[26]

Still, mergers and take-overs take their toll also among the 100 largest, mainly, it appears, to the benefit of the top firms. In 1977, A. Jacquemin and I published a survival rate of the 100 largest European firms for the period 1962-1971. I have calculated similar survival rates for the 1973-1981 and the 1981-1989 periods. The findings show that, for the 25 largest European firms, the rate went up from 67% in the earlier period to over 80% during the eighties, whereas for the 50 and 100 largest firms the rate has declined.[27] Obviously, life for the lower half of the 100 largest has become less secure: about half of the disappearances from the group of the 100 largest European firms is to be attributed to mergers and take-overs, the other half fell back to a lower ranking.

9. Overall Concentration and Small Firms

The greater stability in the profit rate and the better survival rates of the largest companies do not imply that their part in the total economy has been conserved. This is a matter of separate investigation. In the fifties and sixties, until the mid seventies, the share of the 100 largest European firms in the GDP rose continually, even apart from the oil price explosion. Since 1982/1983, this tendency seems to have been reversed: the decline was continuous throughout the eighties, though confined to a few percentage points.[28] In the United States economy, the relative decline of the group of the leading firms was established somewhat earlier, again of a modest dimension, but nevertheless persistent.[29]

Given the paucity and limited value of the European data, we have to be cautious in supposing parallel developments; but there is little ground for assuming that the fourth merger wave did contribute as much to the growth of overall concentation in Europe as did the third wave.[30] On the contrary, there is a slight tendency for overall concentration to recede in terms of sales, but still more in terms of employment. The reflected image of this should be a rise in the share of small and medium-sized businesses, nowadays generally defined as those companies with a labour force of up to 500.[31]

In the eighties, this has indeed been the case, though in different dimensions in the various European countries, and hardly commensurate with the growth of small companies in the United States. This trend towards small and medium-sized enterprises is a reversal of the tendency which prevailed during the whole of the twentieth century and has become notable in Europe since the end of the seventies. The evidence we have for the four major countries of the EEC plus the Netherlands points towards an increased share in employment, and in some countries - but not generally - in sales, in profits, in investments, and even in exports. In most European countries, moveover, the stock of SME firms rises, indicating a net surplus of creations over reductions throughout the last decade, contrary to earlier times.[32]

The reasons for this revitalization are pluralistic. There is said to be a renewal of the individual and creative spirit, a dislike of giantism, coupled with a preference for working in smaller scale organizations. This change in mentality is supported, or made possible, by decentralizing techniques, vertical specialization of work, the pressures of unemployment, and, probably, also by the restructuring of big businesses, where the necessity to fall back on a flat and flexible organisation has cut into staff and supervisory personnel. And, finally, the various government-provided incentives may have stimulated people to put on an entrepreneurial mantle. Interpretation of the data, such as are coming forward, remains difficult, however, and there are several restraints which may gain in importance when the economic circumstances become less bright than they have been.

First, the survival rate of small and medium-sized enterprises is rather lower than for large firms. At least, that is what the data say for countries such as France, the UK, Italy, and the Netherlands. Economic recessions, in particular, may take a heavy toll and reduce the profitability of small businesses relatively more.[33]

Second, the spread of subcontracting may not generally have increased the dependency of small and medium-sized enterprises vis à vis large firms, especially if they provide technologically advanced goods or specific services, but the dependency situation is nevertheless heterogeneous and in several sectors far from secure.[34]

Third, it would seem that the equity basis of small business, and its financing in a general sense, is much weaker.[35] The finance for growth is often problematic and is frequently mentioned as a reason why a sell-out of privately owned small firms takes place.[36]

Still, the renewed growth of small business in Europe during the eighties, after a long period of stagnation, spurs on competition, and governments would be well advised to take further measures (in taxation, deregulation, finance, et cetera) in support. Although governments may not be able to reverse fundamental trends, such as the development of a dual economy model in the services sector,[37] they can prevent excesses, promote open entry, and influence concentration tendencies.

10. Sectoral Tendencies

If one looks at the sectoral shifts which have occurred among the one hundred largest corporations in the three major economies of the world during the past decades,[38] one notes similarities as well as divergences. In the US, Japan and the EEC, the maturing sectors (such as steel, shipbuilding, paper, textiles, foods, tyres, oil, and energy), and the older parts of the chemical industry are invariably losing their representation among the one hundred largest per country. This shows that the industry growth cycles are still at work. In reverse, such newer sectors as electronics, computers, pharmaceuticals, media, and publishing, are gaining in importance, although the Europeans are relatively weak in electronics and computers. In contrast, European firms have a comparatively strong presence in chemicals, pharmaceuticals, steel, and building materials. Americans dominate the aircraft industry, computers, and telecommunications. The Japanese dominate the electronics and (small) motorcars industries. And, in summary, it would seem that the time-honoured specialization fundamentals still make themselves felt.[39] Traditionally, materials have been scarce in Europe, space in Japan, and distance (time) presented itself as an American problem, so major efforts were directed in each area towards overcoming these handicaps. With the progress of internationalization, such differences may disappear in the future, though this is not yet visible.

It is noteworthy that the group of companies which grew most strongly between 1973 and 1989 (to repeat: both years of high economic activity and situated after a merger boom) in the EEC were the strongly diversified or conglomerate firms among the 100 largest. The much talked about back-to-the-core of the business tendency of the eighties is certainly not a general one among the top European firms. Most of such diversifying giants, like Daimler-Benz, Hanson Trust, BAT-Industries, Ferruzi, Péchiney, BTR, and Grand Metropolitan, apparently undertake these sectoral diversifications because they experience or fear increasing competition in their main business and try to benefit from alternative opportunities.

In the services sector, like insurance, banking, and travelling, the liberalization of markets spurs on the restructuring moves.[40] And in not a few sectors, from cement and steel to electrical equipment, the race is towards geographical diversifications.[41] As of old, conglomerization depends very much on the presence of expansion-minded entrepreneurs at the top of those firms, and, likewise, the ultimate outcome is not sure. But for the moment at least these firms belong to the top profit makers and to the fast growers in the European context.[42]

Summing up, research based on an investigation of the tendencies among the 100 largest European firms shows that there are varying forces at work: growth and decline, specialization and diversification, concentration and internationalization. These tendencies are best explained by means of industrial growth cycles, the theory which links process and structure in a circular way.[43] But it is true that it is not a mechanical theory, for individual entrepreneurship and the grasping of (international) opportunities largely determine the wherewithals of individual companies. One may lose its leading position in an expansionary sector, and one may rise from a base in a maturing or declining industry, though, admittedly, these are exceptions.

11. Co-operative Agreements

Short of mergers/take-overs (and dominant control), there are other combinations, which we may term co-operation. They have always existed, but have acquired a new dimension in recent times. In former times, cartel agreements were important, but successively the major countries have practically outlawed them. Many small countries take a more tolerant attitude, not always to their advantage.[44] Such collusive agreements or practices certainly have not disappeared from the economic scene, as many actions by the EC authorities testify. But their existence is precarious, because complaints by those hurt are taken seriously in competition policy.[45]

Alternatively, the three forms of co-operation between firms which have recently pressed forward, are:

a) agreements or contracts, whether horizontal or vertical, of which especially the research and development agreements, licence and franchise agreements form a substantial part. A still more loose form of co-operation is the so-called informal know-how trading;
b) joint enterprises or joint-ventures, and the consortia (also called contractual joint-ventures); and
c) minority participations in other firms, or in closely circumscribed activities.

Such co-operative agreements share with cartels the quality that the participating firms retain their independence and are able to withdraw their co-operation. This is the principal feature distinguishing them from "concentrations".

It is remarkable that co-operative agreements (at least those which have been statistically registered) have grown, on average, as fast as mergers and take-overs: joint-ventures somewhat less, but minority participations the more so.[46] Also, they show the same lopsided distribution over the various sectors as mergers/acquisitions do, with industries like chemicals, foods, mechanical industry, and electronics, and service sectors like banks, insurance, and trading, figuring prominently in all three categories distinguished. Indeed, five leading sectors (of the 15 distinguished in the European Competition Policy Reports) have between 56.3% and 64.1% of the registered activities of the 1,000 largest European firms, which formed the base of the 1984-1988 registration.

Such findings suggest that those three forms of combinations could be regarded by business as partial alternatives, the more so because it is again the largest companies that show themselves to be the most combination intensive (cf. Appendix).

In common with mergers/take-overs, co-operative agreements can serve to bridle what is considered to be excessive competition, and/or to capture an attractive victim. The joint actions against Irish Distillers Group by three leading beverages groups in May 1988 and against Plessey by General Electric (UK) and Siemens may serve as examples, even though the first was forbidden, while the second was not.

Like mergers/take-overs, co-operative agreements can also be concluded to achieve minimum sufficient size, where the tasks to be executed are too large, too varied, or too many-sided for individual firms. Joint-ventures and consortia score good in these respects. Airbus, the Channel Tunnel, and Dutch Delta works may serve as some prominent examples. And, similarly, co-operative ventures may be used to rationalize and restructure an industry which is in distress because of overcapacities or a declining demand. For example, both in response to receding demand for heavy electrical equipment and to the giant merger of Asea and Brown-Boveri in 1986, General Electric (UK) and Alsthom (France) pooled their resources in a joint-venture.

Apart from serving similar goals - and thus being an alternative -, co-operative agreements may be complementary: they may be a prelude to a later merger or take-over, or bind a competitor, or consolidate a trading relationship and at the same time ward off an unwanted intruder. Indeed, the variety of goals to be served by co-operative agreements (including the "strategic alliances" in the current jargon) is immense, and their overriding advantage is the flexibility and independence retained by the partners. Also, in most cases, they are less costly than a merger or a take-over.

However, the big disadvantage of any co-operative activity is the paradoxical or double-sided nature. Co-operating partners both keep their independence and (partially) lose it; they also contribute to the results and have to share them in proportions which can be fixed ex-ante, but may turn out differently ex-post. Consequently, the lapse of time, the uncertainty resulting from technical change or market development, induce caution, and it seems indeed that the rule prevails that the more technological change occurs, the less firms will be inclined to commit themselves to important investments in large mergers/take-overs, and the more they will choose looser co-operative agreements. In technologically advanced sectors, such as chemicals, electronics, and informatics, simple, loose, and adaptable contractual agreements are relatively preponderant, whereas in traditional sectors mergers and acquisitions prevail.[47] In the latter industries, the usual goals of market consolidation and enlargement of market share require control. In contrast, small high-tech firms or those with differentiated products are favoured objects of a take-over by the very large companies.

It is more difficult to make valid statements with respect to the performance or success of co-operative agreements. For one thing, their starts and dissolutions are less easily traced, and, moreover, their decomposition does not automatically imply failure. For another, the link between effort and result is less close and stretches over a longer time period.

Nevertheless, economists who have studied the phenomenon do not estimate that the failure rate of co-operations deviates much from that of mergers and take-overs. Most investigations of the successes or failures of mergers arrive at the conclusion that the division is some 40-40-20%, that is an about equal rate of successes and failures, with about one fifth of the total not having been worthwhile, without being an outright failure. Many of these studies, it is true, were made in the Anglo-Saxon countries, where the take-over market functions differently. Yet, research undertaken for W. Germany, the Netherland, and France points to a similar outcome.[48]

Co-operative agreements are not much better. Of joint-ventures it is said that "quite a number of studies indicate that 30 to 40% of all joint ventures fail...", a conclusion supported by other research.[49]

As to minority participations, one of the few studies devoted to the subject[50] suggests that information asymmetries, based on those participations, result in abnormal benefits to the acquirer. That sounds plausible, but whether this finding applies equally to continental minority holdings is not certain: lesser disclosure requirements and the absence of frequent take-over bids may well diminish the advantage. Even a substantial minority, gained against the will of the established management, may sometimes be more of a hindrance to the promotion of further objectives, than a facilitating instrument.[51]

12. Concluding Remarks: the Need for an Institutional Framework

From the above analysis it follows that the market economy is a largely autonomous complex of the forces which make up the processes and the structures, mutually influencing one another. It shows regularities, which, however, are hardly predictable, because they are influenced by entrepreneurial behaviour and sectoral tendencies which do not necessarily coincide.

Does this mean that the market economy is best left to itself, because the outcomes would then guarantee the best of all possible worlds (though maybe even not an optimal one)?

When I said earlier that even combination movements within the market economy which lead up to dominant positions are being contested by actual or potential competitors, that statement was meant to express a general tendency, reflecting the pervasiveness of competition. In economics, however, it is important to recognize the tendencies, as well as the qualifications accompanying them. Whereas competition may be comprehensive, it manifestly is not always so, nor does it invariably work sufficiently fast. To paraphrase Keynes: in the long run, all power positions may be dead; but such a long run may be too long. Moreover, institutional rules, relating, for example, to taxes, regulations, corporate law, quality standards, et cetera, have a habit of being conserved, even though no longer being adequate. For these reasons, the market economy needs a framework, laid down in a constitutional charter and warranted by the (state) authorities. It is a dangerous illusion to think that such a framework is superfluous and that the market economy is a self-equilibrating system, producing optimal results.

In the European Community, such a constitution is provided by the Treaty, and the Commission, the Court of Justice, and the national states have an obligation to enforce its principles and the articles expressing these. Amongst others, these principles comprise stable money, free competition, non-discrimination, and judicial access for all concerned, be they states, companies, or individuals.[52] Within our field, that entails the need for a competition policy, to curb the excesses of national or corporate power and to keep market entrance open. It also means the establishment of a regulatory network of rules meant to enforce the basic principles. It has gradually evolved within the EC during the past thirty years, but more remains to be done. There is no room to go into these tasks, but let me finally single out three main ones:

First, the merger regulation of December 1989 should be made to work, alongside the policies developed vis à vis cartels and dominant positions.[53] The leading principle here should be to secure as much as possible the development of a competition for productive purposes (a "Leistungswettbewerb", as the Germans say), and to counter power games.

Second, there is a heavy distortion between member states in the take-over conditions and these need to be brought into line under the same rules, creating an orderly market for mergers and take-overs, restricting at the same time speculative deals.[54]

Third, a consistent effort has to be made to create as much as possible equal conditions for competition by small and medium-sized companies, which up till now are often unnecessarily handicapped and restricted. Such a programme is surely an uphill task to fulfill in coming years, and requires the best of economic analysis, of legal council, and of policy judgements. Still it can be done, and the price to be gained is very large: a free and equitable European society.

Notes

1. F. Braudel, La dynamique du capitalisme, Editions Arthaud, Paris, 1985. It might be thought that Braudel, as an economic historian, restricts his conceptual apparatus to the period he mainly discusses, viz. 1400-1800. But his concluding observations (see pp. 114-120) can leave no one in doubt.
2. The scheme is fundamentally Aristotelian, including the capitalistic monopoly positions and the burden of interest. The germs of the three-stage schema are already contained in the philosopher's presentation. See *Politics* in the Jowett translation, The Modern Library, New York, 1943, pp. 63-74.
3. Braudel, o.c., p. 62. Capitalism is not the driving force, but only the beneficiary of the progress achieved in the two lower stages (pp. 72-73).
4. Why this author retains the distinction is not clear. O. von Nell-Breuning, Kapitalismus - Kritisch betrachtet, Herder Bücherei, No.497. Freiburg im Breisgau, 1974, pp. 50-51, 59-60, and 82.
5. W. Adams & G.W. Brock, Dangerous Pursuits. Mergers and Acquisitions in the Age of Wall Street, Pantheon Books, New York, 1989, p. 10. These authors contrast "creative capitalism" and "the casino society" and, obviously, condemn the latter.
6. J.A. Schumpeter, The Instability of Capitalism. In: Economic Journal, Vol. 38, No.151 (September) 1928. Also reprinted in his Essays, edited by R.V. Clemence, Addison-Wesley Press, Inc., Cambridge (Mass.), in particular pp. 67-72. Schumpeter contrasts for the first time "competitive capitalism" and "trustified capitalism", defended the latter, and held that this type "softened" the waves of capitalism and "automatized" progress. Both predictions were clearly belied in the following decades.
7. Braudel, o.c., pp. 69-70. The Bank of Amsterdam was an exchange and clearing bank, the novel contribition of which was its own

monetary unit - the florin banco -; the Bank of England carried this process one important step further by creating bank notes (adopted, it is true, from the goldsmith bankers of the 1660's, but nevertheless, a decisive step because of the Bank's great capital). The East India Companies had as a novelty the joint stock form, of which A. Smith indeed had no high opinion, but in which he clearly erred. It was an "institutional innovation", as Steengaard said. See N. Steengaard, The Dutch East India Company as an institutional innovation, in M. Aymard (ed.), Dutch Capitalism and World Capitalism, Cambridge University Press, Cambridge, 1982.

8. Von Nell-Breuning, o.c., pp. 58-59. B.W. Dempsey, The functional Economy. The basis of economic organization, Prentice-Hall, Inc., Englewood Cliffs, N.J., 1958, Chapter 8, p. 162.
9. The total of current accounts, the number of depositors, and the stock of metal in the Amsterdam Exchange Bank, for example, developed according to a growth cycle - with intermediate ups and downs - throughout its two hundred years' existence. The US investment banking industry has had a traditional "apex" structure, which, however, seems to mask competition in the various segments of the securities industry, also generated by the demand side of the market: the in-house competence in corporate finance among US business firms. See S.L. Hayes, A.M. Spence & D. Van Praag Marks, Competition in the Investment Banking Industry, Harvard University Press, Cambridge (Mass.), 1985. During the eighties the ups and downs continued, profits dwindled since 1986, and in 1989/90 "... the securities industry is staring depression in the face" (The Economist, 21-7-1990, Capital markets Survey II). So, what is the difference between these "capitalist industries" and the rest?
10. Vertical rivalry - including as a limited case the bargaining or haggling in the concrete market - has not been neglected by economists, but has surely not been given its due place. Exceptionally, writers have explicitly given it *the* outstanding role, as the Webbs did when they wrote that bargaining power always lays with the buyer as against the seller, from the production of raw materials to the sale by retailers of finished goods. This is a paradoxical theory, as Macgregor pointed out, because it would give us the conclusion: "... that the persons whose bargaining strength is normally greatest are those who do not bargain at all. ... They are the least capable of organisation and it would be surprising if their advantage lay with the policy of passivity" (D.H. MacGregor, Industrial combinations, Bell, London, 1906, pp. 67 ff.). Implicitly, Neo-Classical theory with its postulate of consumer sovereignty is in the same line. Galbraith (American Capitalism, The New Industrial State) takes the opposite view by proclaiming the preponderance of the "technostructure" and of the "revised sequence". It is one of the advances of market theory that such dogmatic positions have been replaced by investigative programmes. See e.g. the writings of H. Arndt a.o., Leistungswettbewerb, Dunckler u. Humblot, Berlin, 1986.

11. This type of analysis, based on a long-standing European tradition (see De Jong & Shepherd, Mainstreams of Industrial Organization, Kluwer Academic Publishers, Dordrecht/Boston, 1986), has led to the erroneous conclusion that competition policy is largely superfluous. This point will be taken up in the final part of this essay.
12. One should, of course, be more precise than can be the case here. What in particular determines price in a market? Adam Smith held that "the market price of every particular commodity is regulated by the proportion between the quantity which is actually brought to market, and the demand of those who are willing to pay the natural price of the commodity, or the whole value of the rent, labour and profit, which must be paid to bring it thither" (Wealth of Nations, Oxford Edition, 1976, p. 73). This natural price varies with the natural rate of each of its component parts according to the particular society's circumstances (p. 80). Only monopolies form an exception. Alongside competition, J.S. Mill gave custom an equivalent place (Political Economy, Book II, Ch. IV); Böhm-Bawerk stressed frictions, of which there are in practice "countless" examples (Kapital und Kapitalzins, II, pp. 247 ff.); Schmoller underlined the role of power (based on unequal market knowledge, finance, and the urge to do business; see his Grundrisz der Allgemeinen Volkswirtschaftslehre, Leipzig 1900-1904, Vol. 2, pp. 112 ff.), and the marginalists focussed upon scarcity and the roles of the marginal suppliers and consumers. My view is that in most markets price is determined by the policy of the leading or centroid seller(s) or buyer(s), taking into account his/their strategic aims. The other players necessarily have to adapt themselves, either by copying or by restricting their differences (plus or minus) with the leader's price. Needless to say that the "leader" may be an individual firm or a combination, that he is not always the largest or traditionally established player, and that what counts is not nominal price, but effective price (e.g. the price-quality or variety relationships).

    In a sellers' market, demand outruns supply at given prices and price declines generate disproportionate sales increases, such as is typical of expansionary market developments; buyers' markets show the reverse tendencies. If the buyers' market tendencies are (or are expected to be) durable, instead of incidental, competition intensifies, as is visible from increased market fluidity, price declines, overcapacity, et cetera.
13. E. Hadley, Antitrust in Japan, Princeton University Press, Princeton, N.J., 1970, pp. 21-22 and 33-37; K. Imai, Evolution of Japan's corporate and industrial networks, in B. Carlsson (ed.), Industrial Dynamics, Studies in Industrial Organization, Vol. 10. Kluwer Academic Publishers, Boston/Dordrecht, 1989, pp. 127-133. Especially on pages 129-130 Imai advances a view which is close to the one I have developed; see H.W. de Jong, On Market Theory, in B. Dankbaar, J. Groenewegen & H. Schenk (eds.), Perspectives on Industrial Economics, Studies in Industrial Organization, Vol. 13, Kluwer Academic Publishers, Boston/Dordrecht, 1990, pp. 29-40.

14. On this background, see e.g. M.M. Postan, An Economic History of Western Europe 1945-1964. Methuen, London, 1967, Chapters 4 and 5; C.S. Kindleberger, Europe's Post War Growth,. Harvard University Press, Cambridge (Mass.), 1967, Chapter 6. Between 1958 and 1973, intra-Community exports as a share of GDP doubled. Developments during the first combination movement are recorded by A. Marshall, Industry and Trade, Macmillan, London, 1919, Book III; J.H. Clapham, The Economic Development of France and Germany 1815-1914, Cambridge University Press, Cambridge, 1966, pp. 303-314; and the works of such authors as H. Levy, D. MacGregor, and Macrosty, as cited by Marshall, o.c., p. 577.
15. Regulation No.17 came into force as of March 1962.
16. See my survey on mergers in Jacquemin & De Jong (eds), Markets, Corporate Behaviour, and the State, Martinus Nijhoff, The Hague, 1976, pp. 95-108. In addition to the literature cited there, see F. Jenny & A.P. Weber, Concentration et Politique des Structures Industrielles, La Documentation Française, Paris, 1974, pp. 16-45.
17. L. Hannah, The Rise of the Corporate Economy. 2nd Edition. Methuen, London/New York, 1983, Chapter 10, especially pp. 148-150; D.C. Elliott & J.D. Gribbin, Cartels and structural change in the U.K., in Jacquemin & De Jong, Welfare Aspects of Industrial Markets, Martinus Nijhoff, Leyden, 1977, pp. 346-366; D. Hague & G. Wilkinson, The IRC, An experiment in industrial intervention, Allen and Unwin, London, 1983, pp. 6-8 and 235-239.
18. In the EEC, the curves develop in a parallel way: see my Free versus controlled competition, in B. Carlsson, Industrial Dynamics, o.c., figures 2 and 3, pp. 281-282. On the increase in France, a relative latecomer, see B. Prot & M. de Rosen (eds), Le Retour du Capital. Les fusions-acquisitions en France et dans le monde, Editions Jacob, Paris, 1990, pp. 187-196. A historical survey of the four European merger movements was given in my article De concentratiebeweging in de economie, in Economisch-Statistische Berichten, March 2, 1988, pp. 224-229.
19. The explanation harks back to older European analyses, as based on the Mengerian process. H.W. de Jong, European industrial organization: entrepreneurial economics in an organizational setting, in De Jong & Shepherd, Mainstreams, o.c., pp. 69-80.
20. In the absence of sufficiently detailed statistics on the EC level, that is the deduction from the tables as provided in the EC Competition Policy Report. See my Market structures in the European Economic Community, in H.W. de Jong (ed.), The Structure of European Industry, Kluwer Academic Publishers, Dordrecht, 1988, tables 4 and 5.
21. Since 1983, international trade growth has consistently been above output growth, according to GATT figures (Financial Times, 22-4-1990), inflation has declined, and foreign penetrations have increased. Mergers and acquisitions in the world are said to have risen from

$ 430 billion in 1986 to about $ 900 billion in 1989 (Prot & De Rosen, Le retour du Capital, o.c., p. 22).

22. This declining merger intensity related to size (the same seems to apply to alliances and joint-ventures) is a finding for all the countries for which evidence exists.

23. The first mentioned calculations were made on the basis of the Fortune lists for 1973 and 1989. The latter one was done on the basis of the Financial Times list of the 500 largest European firms and avoids a possible (but non-existent) net-profits distortion. See my The take-over market in Europe, Proceedings of the Conference on Mergers, Oligopoly and International Trade, Aix-en-Provence, June 1990.

Profitability rates
for the largest and smallest recorded companies

	50 largest	50 smallest
1973 Europe	(1-50)	(250-300)
(net profits on sales)	3.68%	4.88%
1989 World	(1-50)	(450-500)
(net profits on sales)	4.34%	5.02%
(net profits on assets)	4.32%	4.46%

24. *Apparent and normative profit rates*
European firms

	25 largest		25 smallest	
	apparent rate	normative rate	apparent rate	normative rate
Net profits on sales	5.12	4.41	6.19	5.06
Net profits on assets	5.13	4.07	6.04	4.91

Source: The Fortune 500, 1989.

25. Similar findings were discovered earlier for the Netherlands (1964-1968); see H.W. de Jong, Ondernemingsconcentratie, Stenfert Kroese, Leiden, 1971, table 6, pp. 154-157; for 1977: Paradoxale Economie, Stenfert Kroese, Leiden, 1979, pp. 34-37. For European studies, see Jacquemin & De Jong, European Industrial Organization, o.c., pp. 144-151 and the research cited there. For US studies, see W.G. Shepherd, The Economics of Industrial Organization, Prentice-Hall, Englewood Cliffs, N.J., 1979, pp. 122-133.

26. Jacquemin & De Jong, European Industrial Organization, o.c., p. 151.

27. Survival rates of the 100 largest European firms:

Size class	PERIODS 1962-1971	1973-1981	1981-1989
1 - 12	0.66	0.75	0.83
1 - 25	0.68	0.67	0.80
1 - 50	0,80	0.82	0.73
1 - 100	0.74	0.84	0.71

Note: Calculations based on sales, as recorded in the Fortune 500 list. Survival rate is the share of the companies belonging to the class in the earlier year which still were part of that class in the later year. The comparable US survival rates for the top 100 corporations, during the periods 1966-1977 and 1977-1985, were 0.75 and 0.71, respectively (see G.H. Stine, The Corporate Survivors, 1986, table 10-2).

28. Share of the 100 largest European firms in the EEC Gross Domestic Product: 1962: 21.2%; 1972: 24.3%; 1977: 29.0%; 1989: 28%. Share of the 50 largest manufacturing firms: 1962: 14.7%; 1972: 17.1%; 1977: 19.2%; 1989: 18.0%. Also see the discussion in The Structure of European Industry, o.c., p. 3-5.
29. L. White, Mergers and aggregate concentration, in Keenan and White (eds), Mergers and Acquisitions, Lexington (Mass.), 1982, pp. 97 ff.; K.M. Davidson, Megamergers, Cambridge (Mass.), 1985, Chapter 14.
30. See K.D. George and T.S. Ward, The Structure of Industry in the EEC, Cambridge University Press, Cambridge, 1975, Chapter 4.
31. See the definitions used in Institut d'Etudes Bancaires et Financières, Les Petites et Moyennes Entreprises. Caractéristiques et financement des PME en France et en Europe et dans les autres pays industrialisés, Berger-Levrault, Paris, 1989.
32. See the various contributions to the following books: P. Burns and J. Dewhurst (eds), Small Business in Europe. Macmillan Education Ltd., London, 1986; Institut d'Etudes, les Petites et Moyennes Entreprises, o.c., 1989; Z.J. Abs and D.B. Audretsch, The Economics of Small Firms. A European challenge, Kluwer Academic Publishers, Dordrecht, 1990. For the stagnation which prevailed for much of the period 1960-1980, see my Free versus controlled competition, in B. Carlsson (ed.), Industrial Dynamics, o.c., pp. 271-298.
33. Institut d'Etudes, o.c., p. 30; Burns and Dewhurst, o.c., pp. 68/69; on profitability, pp. 69-72. In the Netherlands, Professor Wever has done much work: E. Wever, Nieuwe Bedrijven in Nederland, Van Gorcum, Assen, 1984. The French survival rate is 66% after 5 years, the Dutch rate is some 50% after 6 years, and the British rate (in the seventies) is 43% after 8 years, which are much below the rates for the large firms quoted above.

34. Institut d'Etudes, o.a., p. 31: "D'une part, la situation est hétérogène ... D'autre part, la sous-traitance n'est pas un epiphénomène entre les seules grandes et les seules petites entreprises".
35. See the figures given in the paper by K. Notzel on W. Germany (p. 138) in Institut d'Etudes, o.c., pp. 137-142.
36. Dutch data in CBS, Maandschrift voor het Financiewezen, December 1971-1974; on W. Germany, see W.P. Möller, Der Erfolg von Unternehmenszusammenschlüssen, München, 1983.
37. See J. Howells, Economic, Technological and Locational Trends in European Services, Gower Publishing Company, Aldershot, 1988, pp. 80-83.
38. This follows easily from the industry divisions as given by Fortune in its list of the 500 largest. Of those large corporations, Japan had the largest share in motorcars, electronics, and textiles, Europe in chemicals and pharmaceuticals, industrial equipment, steel, metal products, and building materials, while the US came out first in aerospace, computers, the oil industry, and scientific equipment. Since 1973, these relative specializations seem, if anything, to have become more pronounced.
39. These specialization bases were already outlined by Prof. Hollander in the ENSIE (the First Dutch Systematic Encyclopedia) in 1946, and were later taken up by R. Vernon in the so-called Harvard Multinationals Project. See a.o. L. Franko, The European Multinationals, Harper and Row, London, 1976.
40. See Howells, o.c., pp. 70-76. As to an evaluation of European strength in services, see the contrasting chapters 3 and 5 of this book.
41. Partially spurred by fast growing South European markets, partly by cost advantages (a.o. cement and pflaster board, which underly the moves of such companies as Ciments Lafarge, BPB, and Redland).
42. In the Competition Policy Report for 1989, the EC Commission has voiced objections with respect to the mutual behaviour of such conglomerates in concentrated markets.
43. See my article On market theory, in Dankbaar, Groenewegen and Schenk, o.c., Section 2.
44. H.W. de Jong, Competition policy in Europe, in K. Groeneveld, J. Maks and J. Muysken (eds), Economic Policy and the Market Process, North-Holland, Amsterdam, 1990, pp. 114-117.
45. This is what in the Brussels jargon is commonly called the "peep system".
46. The respective multiplication factors were (1,000 largest European firms):

Joint-ventures	2.7	
Mergers and take-overs	4.0	} See Appendix, Table 1.
Minority participations	5.1	

47. Base chemicals, foods, trading, and banks accounted for about 50% of the acquisitions in the period 1984-1988. See the Appendix.

48. W. Möller, Der Erfolg von Unternehmenszusammenschlüssen, München, 1983; R. Smeehuyzen and J.H. Kets, Van concernstrategie tot concurrentievoordeel, Universiteit Twente, 1989, who found a divestment rate of 41% for the acquisitions undertaken in 1970-1980 by 17 leading Dutch corporations (excluding the five MNO's Shell, Unilever, Philips, Akzo and DSM).
49. See J.P. Killing, Strategies for joint venture success. London/Canberra, 1983, p. 12; and J.M. Hoekman, The role of the joint venture in the strategy of corporations, Diss. University of Amsterdam, 1984, pp. 125-128 and 177-179.
50. S. Meadowcroft and D. Thompson, Minority Share Acquisition: the impact upon competition, Report No. 84, Commission of the European Communities, Brussels, 1986.
51. S. Meadowcroft & D. Thompson. o.c., 1986, Part 4.
52. To have stressed the need for such principles as well as to have worked them out has been the invaluable contribution of the Social Market Economy School, represented by W. Eucken, F. Hayek, W. Röpke, H.O. Lenel, and others. See e.g. W. Eucken, Grundsätze der Wirtschaftspolitik, Third Edition. J.C.B. Mohr (P. Siebeck), Tübingen, 1980; and F. Hayek, The Constitution of Liberty, London and Chicago, 1960.
53. For a broader view of EC competition policy, see my Competition policy in Europe, o.c., pp. 125-138.
54. Compare the six proposals advanced by Adams and Brock in Dangerous Pursuits, o.c., Ch. 15: Choosing the right game.

Statistical Appendix

Table 1 *Total number of mergers, majority acquisitions, minority participations, and joint ventures, by the 1,000 largest EC companies; 1982/83 - 1988/89*

Year	Mergers and acquisitions	Minority participations	Joint ventures
1982/83*	168	53	69
1983/84*	186	72	86
1984/85	275	105	100
1985/86	297	163	102
1986/87	415	172	121
1987/88	558	303	164
1988/89	666	273	183

* The figures for 1982/83 were given by the EC Commission on a 10-months basis; they have been put here on an annual basis. Figures for 1982/83 and 1983/84 have been estimated - because the Commission did not include services for those years - by adding 20% for mergers and acquisitions, 25% for joint ventures, and 33% for minority participations - these being the services combination's shares for the neighbouring years. As a result, the totals for Table 1 add up to somewhat higher sums than those given in Table 2.

Source: EC Commission Policy Reports, various years.

Table 2. *Share of national, community, and international operations in business combinations of the 1,000 largest firms in the EC, 1982/83 - 1988/89 (Manufacturing, mining, construction, and services).*

Total operations by the 1,000 largest companies, 1982-1989		of which: National	Community	International
Number	4,371	2,533	1,067	771
Per cent	100	58.0	24.4	17.6
OF WHICH				
- mergers & majority participations	2,483	60.7	26.3	13.0
- minority participations	1,103	60.3	21.0	18.7
- joint ventures	785	46.1	23.3	30.6

Note: Services cover the period 1984-1989; 1982/83 on a 10-months basis.

Source: EC Competition Policy Reports, Part 4; various years.

Table 3 Shares of the leading sectors in all mergers, acquisitions, minority participations, and joint ventures, 1984/85 - 1988/89.

Place	Mergers and Acquisitions		Minority participations		Joint ventures	
1.	Chemical ind.	16.9	Banking	21.5	Banking	16.0
2.	Banking	10.8	Foods	10.0	Electro.ind.	15.2
3.	Foods	10.6	Chem.ind.	9.2	Chem.ind.	15.1
4.	Trade & distribution	10.4	Paper & printing	7.7	Mech.ind.	9.0
5.	Mechan.ind., machine tools	8.3	Electro-ind.	7.1	Metallurgy	7.2
6.	Paper & printing	7.5	Trade & distribution	7.0	Trade & distribution	5.2
7.	Electro-ind.	7.3	Insurance	6.7	Insurance	5.2
8.	Metallurgy	5.8	Mechan.ind.	6.7	Paper	5.1
9.	Insurance	5.8	Metallurgy	6.7	Foods	4.5
10.	Construction	5.4	Construction	4.9	Transport equipment	4.0
Numbers all sectors		2,211		1,015		670
3 leading sectors		38.3		40.7		46.3
5 leading sectors		57.0		55.5		62.5
8 leading sectors		77.6		76.3		78.0

Note: 15 sectors of manufacturing industry, mining and construction, and services were distinguished.

Source: EC Competition Policy Report, various years.

Table 4 Share of large mergers and acquisitions (combined sales of more than 1 billion ECU)

	'84/'85	'85/'86	'86/'87	'87/'88	'88/'89	'84/'89
Large mergers						
Industry (nrs.)	92	108	171	268	373	1,012
Services (nrs.)	40	34	53	74	76	277
Total L.M.	132	142	224	342	449	1,289
Total mergers						
Industry (nrs.)	208	227	303	383	492	1,613
Services (nrs)	67	70	112	175	174	598
Total mergers	275	297	415	558	666	2,211
Share of L.M.	%	%	%	%	%	%
In Industry	44.2	47.6	56.4	70.0	75.8	62.7
In Services	59.7	48.6	47.3	42.3	43.7	46.3
In total mergers	48.0	47.8	54.0	61.3	67.4	58.3

Source: EC Competition Reports; various years.

Figure 1 Mergers and acquisitions in manufacturing, mining, construction and services in the EC, by the 1000 largest companies: 1973-1989. See note table 1

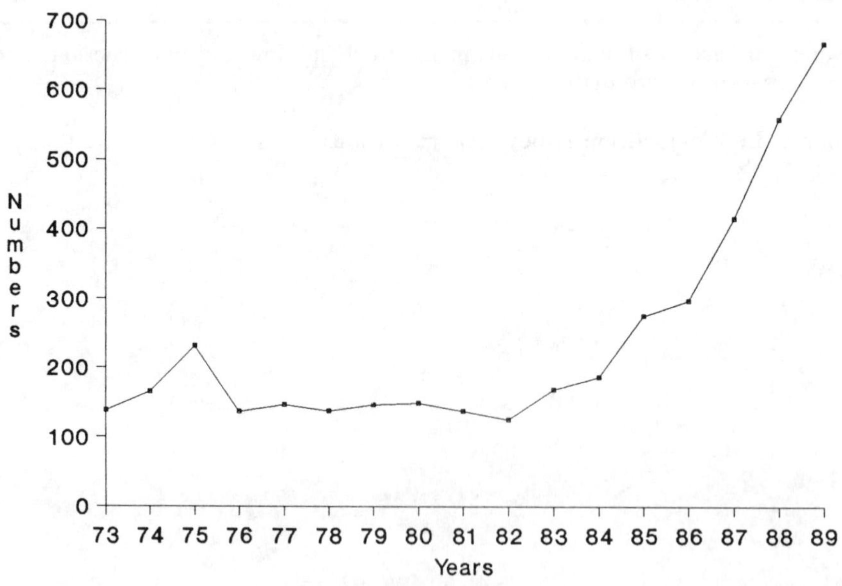

CONTRIBUTORS

William James Adams, Professor of Economics and Law, the University of Michigan, Ann Arbor, Michigan, USA

Richard E. Caves, Professor of Economics and Business Administration, Harvard University, Cambridge, Massachusetts, USA.

Gunnar Eliasson, The Industrial Institute for Economic and Social Research (IUI), Stockholm, Sweden.

Ken George, Professor of Economics, University College of Swansea, Swansea, United Kingdom.

Denys Gribbin, The Monopolies Commission, London, United Kingdom.

Alexis Jacquemin, Professor of Economics, University of Louvain, Belgium; Advisor of the Commission of the European Communities, Brussels, Belgium.

Henk W. de Jong, Professor of Economics, University of Amsterdam, President European Association for Research in Industrial Economics, 1990/1991.

Henk W. Lambers, Emeritus Professor of Economics, Erasmus University Rotterdam, The Netherlands.

Remo Linda, Economist, former Advisor of the Commission of the European Communities, Brussels, Belgium.

Pieter W. Moerland, Professor of Economics, University of Brabant, Tilburg, The Netherlands.

Peter Oberender, Professor of Economics, University of Bayreuth, West Germany.

William G. Shepherd, Professor of Economics, University of Massachusetts, Amherst, USA.

Studies in Industrial Organization

Volume 14

Studies in Industrial Organization

Series Editors:
H. W. de Jong, *University of Amsterdam, The Netherlands*
W. G. Shepherd, *University of Massachusetts, Amherst, U.S.A.*

Publications:

1. H. W. de Jong (ed.): *The Structure of European Industry.* Revised edition, 1988: see below under Volume 8
2. M. Fennema: *International Networks of Banks and Industry* (1970–1976). 1982 ISBN 90-247-2620-4
3. P. Bianchi: *Public and Private Control in Mass Product Industry.* The Cement Industry Cases. 1982 ISBN 90-247-2603-4
4. W. Kingston: *The Political Economy of Innovation.* (1984) 1989 2nd printing ISBN 90-247-2621-2
5. J. Pelkmans: *Market Integration in the European Community.* 1984 ISBN Hb: 90-247-2978-5; Pb: 90-247-2988-2
6. H. W. de Jong and W. G. Shepherd (eds.): *Mainstreams in Industrial Organization.* 1986
   Book I: *Theory and International Aspects.* ISBN 90-247-3461-4
   Book II: *Policies: Antitrust, Deregulation and Industrial.* ISBN 90-247-3462-2
   Set ISBN Book I + II: 90-247-3363-4
7. S. Faltas: *Arms Markets and Armament Policy.* The Changing Structure of Naval Industries in Western Europe. 1986 ISBN 90-247-3406-1
8. H. W. de Jong (ed.): *The Structure of European Industry.* 2nd revised ed. (of Volume 1). 1988 ISBN Hb: 90-247-3689-7; Pb: ISBN 90-247-3690-0
9. I. L. O. Schmidt and J. B. Rittaler: *A Critical Evaluation of the Chicago School of Antitrust Analysis.* 1989 ISBN 90-247-3792-3
10. B. Carlsson (ed.): *Industrial Dynamics.* Technological, Organizational, and Structural Changes in Industries and Firms. 1989 ISBN 0-7923-9044-X
11. Z. J. Acs and D. B. Audretsch (eds.): *The Economics of Small Firms.* A European Challenge. 1990 ISBN 0-7923-0484-5
12. W. Kingston: *Innovation, Creativity and Law.* 1990 ISBN 0-7923-0348-2
13. B. Dankbaar, J. Groenewegen and H. Schenk (eds.): *Perspectives in Industrial Organization.* 1990 ISBN 0-7923-0814-X
14. P. de Wolf (ed.): *Competition in Europe.* Essays in Honour of Henk W. de Jong. 1991 ISBN 0-7923-1050-0

Kluwer Academic Publishers – Dordrecht / Boston / London